THE TELEOLOGICAL
GRAMMAR OF THE
MORAL ACT

■ ■ ■

INTRODUCTIONS TO CATHOLIC DOCTRINE

This series provides readable scholarly introductions to key themes in Catholic doctrine, written by preeminent scholars from around the world. The volumes of the series are suitable for college, university, and seminary courses, as well as for educated readers of all ages who seek to grow in their understanding of the Catholic faith.

■ ■ ■

PUBLISHED VOLUMES

Avery Cardinal Dulles, S.J., *Magisterium, Teacher and Guardian of the Faith*

Daniel A. Keating, *Deification and Grace*

Steven A. Long, *The Teleological Grammar of the Moral Act*

Charles Morerod, O.P., *The Church and the Human Quest for Truth*

Kenneth D. Whitehead, *The Renewed Church, the Second Vatican Council's Enduring Teaching about the Church*

THE TELEOLOGICAL GRAMMAR OF THE MORAL ACT

SECOND EDITION

STEVEN A. LONG

Sapientia Press
of Ave Maria University

Sapientia Press
of Ave Maria University
5050 Ave Maria Blvd.
Ave Maria, FL 34142

Cover Image:
Traini, Francesco (14th century)
The Triumph of St. Thomas Aquinas
S. Caterina, Pisa, Italy
Photo: Scala/Art Resource, NY

Cover Design: Eloise Anagnost

Library of Congress Control Number: 2015952751

ISBN-13: 978-1-932589-73-3

Contents

Acknowledgments

I SHOULD LIKE to thank those who have helped me with this project. In particular, I am indebted to my wife, Anna Maria, without whose understanding, patience, counsel, and support this book would not exist. Likewise, my five children—Christopher Ambrose, Penelope Rose Marie, Catherine Mary-Therese, Augustine Bruno, and Monica Gabrielle—have shown various gradations of response, from mystification to sage comprehension, as to why their father couldn't go swimming, or watch that film, or go to the karate class: all the while realizing that *some kind of work* was going on in that study. Even the most acidulous critic of the following work, who—considering the familial sacrifice—is tempted to think that "never have so many sacrificed so much for so *little*," must honor such exemplary familial devotion.

Before going further, I should like to take this occasion to thank His Eminence Avery Cardinal Dulles for the decisive encouragement that he has given to my work and teaching.

This project was not initially my own idea, and it took time for me to realize that I should pursue it. It was first suggested by a variety of philosophers and theologians whom I greatly respect and admire. Ralph McInerny, Fr. Romanus Cessario, O.P., Russell Hittinger, Matthew Levering, and Matthews Grant are among those who have recommended this work to me—over a period of years—before finally I undertook it. May this book be such that these scholars and friends need not hesitate unduly before recommending another project! I am deeply indebted to them for the inspiration of this book and for much else.

The editor—Matthew Levering—has been unremittingly supportive, critically bracing, and insightful. Likewise to be thanked are Fr. Matthew Lamb, the Chair of the Graduate Theology School of Ave Maria University, who by word and deed has encouraged this work, and whose patience, wisdom, and kindness are the constant recourse of the author and his family; Fr. Joseph Fessio, S.J. whose friendship, encouragement, and support are indispensable, and whose generosity is a continuing joy and inspiration; and Dean Michael Dauphinais, whose friendship, intelligent criticism, and remarkable practical acuity are constant encouragements. I would also like to thank President Nicholas Healy of Ave Maria University for welcoming me to join the graduate faculty of a university that esteems the Catholic theological and philosophic tradition in deed and not merely in name, supporting research such as that reflected in this book.

Every publishing project has readers. In addition to those already mentioned, I should like to thank Matthews Grant, John Goyette, and Mark Discher for the benefit of their intelligent commentary and suggestions. All of the readers contributed to the strengthening of the book. Many suggestions were implemented, and others—often no less perspicacious—were put to one side solely for the sake of bringing this analysis to readers sooner than might otherwise have been possible. I am particularly thankful to Matthews Grant, whose thoroughness and philosophic acuity have been of special aid in preparing this manuscript.

I should also like to take this occasion to thank John Boyle for his encouragement and outstanding example of fidelity to truth; Janet Smith, for the many occasions when she insightfully argued through difficult questions with me; and Christopher Thompson for his magisterial appreciation, encouragement, friendship, and critical eye. Nor would it be just to fail to thank either Fr. Serge-Thomas Bonino, O.P., whose profound insight into the teaching of St. Thomas, and whose understanding of my work, has been a great and constant encouragement, or Fr. Lawrence Dewan, O.P., for the benefit of his friendship, example, and instruction. Friends and savants, all. Of course I should also thank Diane Eriksen for her editorial acumen and patience, and Matthew R. McWhorter for indefatigable proofreading.

Yet while anything of value in this book reflects many created intelligences—chief of all, that of St. Thomas Aquinas—it should be noted that any failures or mistakes are exclusively the fault of the author.

As the last note indicates, I wish most of all to evince thankfulness for the opportunity to contemplate and share the teaching of St. Thomas Aquinas, which is constantly a source of theological and philosophic contemplation, wisdom, and joy. This indeed gives one a certain real participation in what is signified by the great words of J. Maritain: *"Vae mihi, si non thomistizavero"*—"Woe to me, if I do not Thomisticize."

Introduction to the Second Edition

THE THESIS of this book regarding the moral analysis of St. Thomas Aquinas is one whose essential implications I had only begun fully to fathom at the time of its composition.[1] Accordingly, this introduction seeks (1) to correct certain modes of expression in the book, and to add certain formal points that clarify or augment the analysis. More importantly,

---

[1] In fact, it also calls for a wider consideration of authors whose work is largely congruent with the analysis given here, although not developed in the same way and degree, among whom I would now list the work of Fr. Servais Pinckaers, O.P. While this is not the right forum in which to engage his precise set of considerations, they have done much to encourage my basic sense of the twin pillars of this book: (1) assertion that the act itself, its integral nature, and *per se* effects always are included in the object of the external act; and (2) realization that when an initially adequate and specific rather than overgeneric knowledge of the object of the external act is reached, this may indicate that the object is *per se* ordained to what the agent intends, such that the object-species is contained within the end-species as an essential determination of the latter. For the instigation to reconsider the analysis of Pinckaers, I am indebted to the as yet unpublished work of a young scholar, Matthew Kuhner: "Reading *Veritatis Spendor* #78 with Servais Pinckaers, O.P.: Thomistic Action Theory and 'The Perspective of the Acting Person'." While observing what, to this present author's mind, is the misunderstanding of Billuart by Pinckaers, Kuhner draws attention to the final anti-intentionalist judgments of Pinckaers. These judgments seem in critical respects to vindicate Billuart and even to signify a strong middle term with the rejection of casuistic intentionalist minimalism, even despite the earlier erroneous criticisms made by Pinckaers of Billuart. However, the present task here remains simply the straightforward speculative presentation, rather than the insertion of this analysis within the adequately contextualized exegesis of several historically pivotal figures who address this question in the twentieth and twenty-first centuries.

(2) this introduction attempts to articulate essential aspects of the strategic framework of St. Thomas's teaching that are important for understanding the thesis of the book—aspects either only implicit in the work or not clearly articulated in the work, as well as certain crucial judgments that are not forwarded in the book. The object, of course, is to render the thesis of the book clearer and more conspicuous. Lastly, (3) I here respond to a few of the repeated criticisms of this work's analysis so as to make clearer the nature of the thesis and also, once again, to clarify the framework of the analysis as derived from the teaching of St. Thomas Aquinas.

Because the criticisms to which I seek to respond are penetrating and pertain to the very strategic framework of Thomas's teaching, and also for the purpose of avoiding unnecessary repetition, the treatment both of points pertaining to the framework of St. Thomas's analysis and principal responses to criticisms are conjoined in one section below. Yet, even in the first section, advertence is made to certain criticisms for the sake of making the analysis clear by way of contradistinction. The remarks below are divided between a first subdivided section of "Comparatively Simpler Observations" and a second similar section addressing "The Strategic Framework of St. Thomas's Teaching and Responses to Objections," followed by a brief conclusion.

The first section, addressing comparatively simple points, is perhaps more ad hoc than are the ensuing two, because it combines simple corrections with a recapitulation of certain more fundamental points, especially in regard to St. Thomas's analysis of self-defense. The exegesis of St. Thomas's teaching on defense is particularly important, because authors turn to Thomas on this question simply assuming what there is no reason to assume: namely, that he cannot have meant the question he addressed to refer to directly morally significant and imputable conduct. Once it is clear what the question is, the answer Thomas gives is conspicuous.[2]

---

[2] With respect to the understanding of *The Teleological Grammar of the Moral Act*, I would strongly encourage the reading of two essays, one of which—my essay "Natural Law, the Moral Object, and *Humanae Vitae*" published in *Ressourcement Thomism: Sacred Doctrine, the Sacraments, and the Moral Life*, ed. Reinhard Hütter and Matthew Levering (Washington, DC: Catholic University of America Press, 2010), 285–311—is quoted at length below in the text. The other is my essay "Engaging Thomist Interloctors," *Nova et Vetera* 9, no. 2 (2011): 267–95. In the latter work I had the honor of responding to the late Fr. Lawrence Dewan regarding St. Thomas's teaching in *Summa theologiae* II–II, q. 64, art. 7, who to my mind

I have more or less let the original text, with all of its limitations, stand (a principal exception being the point regarding *ratio of appetibility* mentioned below). However, in this edition I do add an appendix containing the treatment of two additional difficult cases: the HHS mandate of the Obama administration vis-à-vis the analysis of cooperation with evil (an account which follows the prior analysis of *operation*); and the question whether a married woman who uses a contraceptive to regularize her cycle ought to abstain from marital relations during its use, and whether this is true necessarily and in every case or whether double effect may justify a couple's pursuing relations during the therapy.

It seems fitting here to observe that it may be reasonable for those reading this book for the first time to read this introduction *last* rather than *first*. I gave thought to placing this essay as an appendix for this very reason. But since several of these considerations are very formal, it seems reasonable to accent their importance by placing them here. Thus, those who are familiar with the thesis of the book can revisit it in the context of a more adequate framing of its arguments and responses to major criticisms; whereas those who are not, while they may possibly draw partial profit from this introduction initially, will (I hope) certainly be able to draw more significant profit from it by reading it after consideration of the original argument. So, to repeat the strong suggestion—for readers approaching this text for the first time, the author strongly recommends that you read the book first and *then* return to this introduction.

I. COMPARATIVELY SIMPLER OBSERVATIONS

A. *Regarding the* Ratio of Appetibility

The argument of the book distinguishes the object of the external act—formal with the formality of "essence" that in material things includes form and matter—with form taken as a "part" of the whole. But the book also

---

offered the best defense of the Cajetanian reading that is possible. Were I persuaded that the question Aquinas raises was not a directly morally significant question about imputable conduct, this account would seem to me preferable as providing the strongest reading of Cajetan. Surely it is not unreasonable here also to note that those who seek instruction from the Angelic Doctor have the best of reasons to seek out and profit from Fr. Dewan's remarkable work, and to be grateful for his witness and teaching as a disciple of St. Thomas.

affirms that the "most formal" part of the object concerns the agent's reason for choosing it. On page 12, in note 12, I wrote of this formal part of the object of the external act as simply being the end, and this is an error (although my initial formulation is closer to the truth). Here is what I initially wrote, with the error in bold (and this error *is* corrected in this edition):

> Hence the choiceworthiness of the act to the agent—which is defined in relation to the internal act of the will—may be placed fractionally atop the object of the external act. Each of these is a hylemorphic constituent of the form of the whole act which is the object *simpliciter*. For the act is unitary, and the object of the act *simpliciter* is the *form of the whole* and not merely the form of the part. Thus, the relatively more formal part of the object of the act simply speaking is represented by a relation to the object of the interior act. This is referred to in the text above as the "relation to reason" because it is the external act's relation to this object of the internal act of the will which is the reason for the external act's appetibility and choiceworthiness to the agent. This object of the internal act is placed above the material part of the object which is the object of the external act (as Thomas says—*ST* I–II, q. 18, a. 6, resp.—the object of the internal act of the will is formal with respect to the object of the external act). Both are included in the object as such, which is the form of the whole unitary act, and neither can be excluded.

The object of the internal act is the end, and the end is not the formal part of the object of the external act. But what is said prior to this line is correct: "the relatively more formal part of the object of the act simply speaking is represented by a relation to the object of the interior act." But *what* is this relation, and in what is it founded? I do not say. The correct answer is that the agent must give *consent* to the means—that is, if there is only one way to move toward the end he intends, he must consent to move to the end *in this way* if he is to be willing to consider this means as a proper object of choice. Likewise, if there is more than one means available, he must *prefer* the means he chooses (even if the reason for preference is simply that it is the least objectionable in accidental terms of an array of options none of which is ideal). What founds this *relation* to the object of the interior act of the will, which is the end, is the *ratio of appetibility* for a particular act, or that about the act which makes it to be choiceworthy or preferable to the agent.

It is true that the most formal part of the object of the external act is closely related to the end. But this is not the end itself, but rather the *ratio of appetibility* of an act, *or that about the act which constitutes the reason why it is desired as preferred in relation to other possible options, or—if there is only one option—why this sole available particular means is judged acceptable in the act Thomas refers to as "consent."* In the case where there is only one way to attain the end, we see why it is easy to conflate the *ratio of appetibility* for the action with the end. In the case in which there are not multiple ways of moving toward an end but only one, the *ratio of appetibility* seems to be simply the insistent willing of the end, even though implicitly this suggests that the deliberated action must have been found to be not gravely objectionable but rather generally acceptable, which suggests a wider consideration than *simply* that of the end.

An assassin might be perfectly willing to kill a vicious regent for a child king in order to avoid civil war, but when it is clear that the regent is too well protected, he might blanch at killing the child himself as a device to end the regent's power. The willing of the end *in this way* must be distinguished from the willing of the end *simpliciter*, since the nature of the action through which the end is achieved must be accepted. There must be a judgment that this way of moving to the end is acceptable, and when there are many possible options, there must be some reason of preference howsoever minimal. Thus, even in the case where it seems that the acceptability of the action is no more than continuing to will the end, in fact there is another consideration: the choiceworthiness of the act to be performed. And even if there is but one way to move toward the end, the general moral judgment of this act is not exclusively performed in relation to the particular end sought. This is why a judgment is needed.

Thus, the *ratio of appetibility* is the most formal part of the object—most formal because without it there will be no act, and because it is, as it were, closest to the intention of the end, being constituted by the mode of its relation to the end—whereas the act itself, its integral nature, and *per se* effects are the material part of the object. The fact that the *ratio of appetibility* is formal with respect to the object does not mean that the act itself, its integral nature, and *per se* effects may be considered irrelevant to the object.

The object is something formal with respect to the act, as Thomas constantly says (and indeed in a distinct sense the intended end is of even greater formality, since even in cases of *per accidens* ordering of object and end, it most characterizes the agent, as the one who steals for the sake of adultery is both thief and adulterer while yet *more* adulterer than thief). What concerns us here, however, is that the object is something "formal" with the type of formality that pertains to form as a whole rather than form as a part. This is the type of formality that pertains to the essence of a material thing, which contains both form and matter, and whose proper matter is indeed "essential" to its nature. Thus, in "rational animal" both "rational" and "animal" are included in the nature, and both are essential. It is not true that simply because "rational" is in a sense more formal than "animal" (inasmuch as the former is derived from the rational soul, which is the form, and the latter derived from the matter of the composite as actuated by the soul) that "animal" is not essential to human nature. Likewise, the proper matter of the object of the external act is not inessential to it and cannot rightly be excluded from it. Excluding the integral nature and *per se* effects of the external act from the object leaves us with intentionalism; excluding the *ratio of appetibility* would leave us with a physicalism that would necessarily fail to explain the human act as human, and leave the relation of the choice of the act to the intention of the end hanging in midair, as it were.

B. Regarding "Simple Acts"

Throughout the book, acts are distinguished as "simple" or "complex." If an act is not *per se* ordered toward an end, it is "complex" because of the *disjunct* species of the object of the external act and the end. If the object is *per se* ordered to the end, then it is "simple" because of the unity of species. Just so far, this analysis is correct and corresponds with St. Thomas's teaching in *Summa theologiae* I–II, q. 18, art. 7. However, the sense of "simple" can suggest a sort of atomic simplicity, as though the openness of acts to be ordered to further ends is necessarily complex. But this last is untrue. One act may be *per se* ordained to several distinct ends, such that all the species are formally enclosed in the species derived from the end. So the simplicity involved in *per se* order is not a material simplicity, but a formal simplicity upon the formal comprehensivity of the species derived from the end unifying the objects involved. Many distinct objects may all share the same *per se* order to the end, and there may indeed be a series of ends each of which is with respect to the further ends a means *per se* ordained to it. To make this clear, I do not believe I can fail to avail myself of a long passage (no pun intended!) from my work "Natural Law, the Moral Object, and *Humanae Vitae*" published in *Ressourcement Thomism*:

> Thus it is clear there may be sequences of acts each of whose constituents could under other circumstances be pursued for different reasons, yet where in fact the end is such by its nature as to require one act, and that act is such by its nature as to require another, and so forth, like Chinese boxes each contained within the other, with the most containing moral species being derived from the end. Such sequences are not *per accidens* and disjunct. The understanding that an end of its nature requires a certain act presupposes the understanding of the nature of that act in relation to the end: one must know the purpose of heart surgery and the nature of anesthesia to judge that the end of heart surgery requires anesthetizing the patient. As St. Thomas teaches, the upshot is that where the end is such by its nature as to require the object, the moral species derived from the object is contained in and most formally defined by the moral species derived from the end. The sequence aspect resolves into the most containing species derived from the end, and what is materially manifold (sequence, acts) is in the case of *per se* order formally unitary. Not three distinct moral acts—anesthesia, opening the chest cavity, and repair of the heart—but one, heart surgery, whose moral species is that of medical surgery to repair the heart as defining a material manifold of acts that *might* but yet *do not* exist outside of the order to the end of heart surgery. For example, anesthesia, or opening the chest cavity, could be done to different purpose, but in the case of heart surgery this is not the case.
>
> What renders the "simple" case to be simple is its *per se* order, which permits the greatest material diversification within formal unity. The simple case is simple not with the simplicity of the material atom, but rather with the simplicity of formal unity derivative from *per se* order in respect of the end. This is quite different from *per accidens* complex acts, wherein neither does the object essentially tend toward the end nor does the end essentially require the object; similarly, theft does not tend toward adultery, nor does adultery require theft. Such acts are truly and formally complex because not unified in moral species. So these are the alternatives: *simplicity of formal unity* derivative from *per se* order in

respect of the end with its unifying and containing moral species; or *complexity of formal disjunction and disunity* derivative from lack of *per se* order in respect of the end with consequently distinct moral species. From this vantage point, there is morally speaking one act of performing heart surgery, each of whose component acts is *per se* ordained to its particular proximate end, while itself being essentially part of the *per se* effect sought (e.g., in the medical illustration, if anesthesia does not suppress the pain and perhaps the consciousness of the patient; if opening the rib cage does not reveal the heart; and if surgical repair does not correct the disorder in the heart or palliate its effects, then there can be no achievement of the more global purpose). And the proximate end is conceived precisely along the lines of the powers of lower forms possessed *in virtute* by higher forms: that is, the higher unity of heart surgery possesses of its nature what the lower discrete act of anesthesia possesses, but possesses it in a distinct way as essentially part of heart surgery. The integral nature and *per se* order of the act is always retained, but under the *ratio* of the relation to reason, which is that whereby the act is appetible to the agent: in this case, because the end sought by the agent of its nature requires an act whose proximate end is anesthesia. That is to say, just as the intention to play a piece of music on the piano involves playing all the notes essentially required for the piece, each of which is essentially ordained to the whole, so intending one act that essentially requires other acts involves moving toward component ends that are ordained to the further end. But just as in the human body iron is not "freestanding" but is defined by the formality of the human body, while retaining all that is requisite for the operational definition of "iron," so what might have been but is not a freestanding act of "giving the patient anesthesia" retains its character but as saturated by the moral species derived from the end which is repair of the heart.

A simple act that could be sought independently must be known in relation to its proximate end if one is to be able to judge and identify its further relation/proportion to a further end whose nature is such to require it. Yet when such an act that could be sought independently is sought because the very nature of a further end requires it, then that act and its proximate end are saturated in the most formal species derived from the further end (indeed: the component act would not exist save for the intention of the end). But the proximate end is required, just as the integral nature and *per se* natural ordering of one's action is always materially included within the object of the moral act.

The essential element constituting the intelligibility and simplicity of human action is *per se* order; that is to say, either the object is such by nature that it tends toward the end, or the end is such by nature that it requires the object. This order in *per se* sequences of acts is materially more complex but nonetheless formally simple—for even in the case of a sequence of acts that might have been freestanding, but which are only chosen as essentially required for some further end actively intended by the agent, this material sequence enjoys the simplicity of the unity of form. Such sequences, in moral terms, form components of one act with material parts, and the proximate ends of these parts exist within the given act only owing to the order to the further end which essentially requires them and whose moral species most formally contains and defines them: e.g., heart surgery. Formal simplicity in action derives from *per se* order of object to end, for in this case, the species derived from the end is most formal, definitive, and containing.

Yet it is surely true that both to be, and to be known, all other act structures presuppose prior acquaintance with the case of stand-alone actions wherein object is *per se* ordered to end with no further *per se* ordering: for example, anesthesia *simply* for the sake of pain relief with no reference to any further surgical act, as opposed to anesthesia performed solely owing to the intention of the end of heart surgery. For the performance both of *per accidens*, formally complex acts and of materially more extensive sequences of *per se* action (action that incorporates act components that might have been but in fact are not performed as stand-alone *per se* acts) presupposes prior awareness of simple "stand-alone" *per se* acts. The formally complex case is made up of two or more such acts (e.g., the famed illustration of theft for the sake of adultery); and the materially richer sequences of *per se* acts involve a prior judgment of proportion between the ends of the component acts and that end which by its nature requires them and whose species contains their species.

Hence both in order *to be* and in order *to be known*, all other act structures depend upon these "stand-alone" *per se* acts. If one likes, these "stand-alone" *per se* acts are accurately described as materially and epistemically the simplest of *per se* act structures. Yet all *per se* act structures nonetheless enjoy a certain unity and so simplicity of form owing to the *per se* order toward the end and the containing of all subordinate species in the species derived from the end. Not only these simplest of *per se* act structures, but also materially rich sequences of *per se* action, enjoy the simplicity of unitary form, in which the species derived from the end contain all lesser species (the integral nature and *per se* ordering to the end/effects of action are always included in the object of the act). But the components of such rich sequences are understood as potentially freestanding—as stand-alone *per se* acts—prior to being included in such sequences. And so, while simplicity is a function of *perseity*, the clearest case of *perseity* is not the materially rich *per se* sequence, but the case of act *per se* ordained toward end as sufficing to define action (e.g., deliberately taking possession of what is not one's own as defining theft; administering pain relief for no intended purpose beyond relieving pain; and so on). Nonetheless, despite this material and epistemic greater simplicity of the stand-alone *per se* act structure, it is important to keep in mind that *perseity* always brings along with it the simplicity of formal unity derivative from the unitary containing species derived from the end.

Thus we may amend the earlier proposition, and speak of three alternatives:

1. a stand-alone *per se* act, e.g., theft (just for money) or administering anesthesia (just to relieve pain);

2. a sequence of what could have been such stand-alone *per se* act structures but in fact are not because these act components are willed into existence only owing to the nature of an intended end that (a) naturally requires the act components (e.g., anesthesia and opening the chest cavity for the sake of heart surgery) in question, and (b) whose species contains the species derived from these components;

3. a *per accidens* ordering of two *per se* act structures, where neither of its nature requires or tends toward the other. The first two cases both exhibit *per se* order to the end, and so the most defining, containing species is derived from the end, vouchsafing such acts a simplicity and unity of form (and retaining the *per se* ordering of the act components within that more defining and containing species: the integral nature and *per se* ordering of the act is always materially included in the object of the act). The first case is materially and epistemically simplest. Hence, provided that one realizes that all *per se* act structures enjoy the unity and simplicity of form, it is not unreasonable to refer to this as, *simpliciter*, the "case of the simple, *per se* act." The third case is formally complex and characterized by disjunct and nonunified species, as neither contains the other.[3]

---

[3] Steven A. Long, "Natural Law, the Moral Object, and *Humanae Vitae*," in *Ressourcement Thomism: Sacred Doctrine, the Sacraments, and the Moral Life*, ed. Reinhard

St. Thomas's analysis of human action is hylemorphic, following in many ways the analysis of a substance's possession of formal properties *in virtute*. Just as a substance by its form possesses the properties of lower forms "in its powers"—*in virtute*—so either the action whose intended end by its nature requires an act, or the intended end that an action simply of its nature tends toward, will be such that the species of the end formally contains the species of the object of the external act (or acts). But this requires applying similar terminology to two very different cases. The first use or application of this terminology occurs in the analysis of substance, whereas the second application regards the far different topography of human action. Owing to the different subject matter, certain essential and specifically different features pertain to the second rather than the first. This will be further addressed below, both with respect to the strategic context for understanding St. Thomas's teaching, and in attempting to give a response to certain repeated objections that seem predicated on the confusion of the analysis of substance with the analysis of action.

C. "End"

Throughout the work, the language used is that of "object" and "end." But "end" is meant to signify precisely "intended end" or "end as intended." This is important because manifestly there is a difference between the normative order of ends—which, as normative, is not subject to deprivation—and our intention of ends, which is subject to deprivation, such that certain intended ends are in fact disordered with respect to human flourishing and are defective with respect both to reason and to eternal law.

Of course, the order of object to intended end is in a real secondary sense "normative" in that it provides part of the foundation for our judgment of *the actual moral character of the action*, and in that it is necessary in order finally to judge the act in relation to the "simply" normative order of ends. If we do not know whether the object of the external act is *per se* or *per accidens* ordained to the intended end, then according to St. Thomas we do not know whether the species derived from the object of the external act is contained essentially under the species derived from the

---

Hütter and Matthew Levering (Washington, DC: Catholic University of America Press, 2010), 285–311.

end. And we *must know this* if we are finally to judge the action in relation to the normative order of ends. But it was never the intention of the book to forward the notion that the teleological understanding of the relation of object to end could substitute for the larger normative contemplation of the ordering of ends that constitutes the *ratio boni*. Nor, frankly, can the latter substitute for it in determining the species of an action, since one must determine whether the object-species and end-species are disjunct or whether to the contrary the object-species is contained within the end-species as an essential determination of the latter in order completely to judge the species of an action.

D. Analysis of Defense

The divergence of Vitoria's analysis of *Summa theologiae* II–II, q. 64, art. 7 and the case of defense both from the analysis of Cajetan and from the type of analysis found in New Natural Law Theory derives from a point of great simplicity that the book does not sufficiently engage. This point is the following: Does the question that q. 64, art. 7 addresses concern directly morally significant and imputable action, or does it not? It is the custom since Cajetan for exegetes to dive progressively more wholeheart-edly into the language of intention and what is "*praeter intentionem*" before even so much as taking stock of the nature of the question that the article addresses. St. Thomas makes that question quite clear: "whether it is lawful to kill in self-defense." And to that question he does indeed give an answer: "It is not unlawful." Since in a real subject, negation of nega-tion is something positive—as when one says "you do not *not* have a nose" this means "you have a nose"—this answer converts to "it is lawful."

What is the question to which the article is addressed asking? The next article raises the question "whether one is guilty of murder through slaying someone by chance." Presumably we are to distinguish these two questions, since it hardly makes sense to ask exactly the same question twice. Vitoria rather clearly takes the question of q. 64, art. 7 to pertain to directly morally significant imputable action, which absolutely and mini-mally requires that what is concerned be either intended as end or chosen means or action. Otherwise, the question is not about directly morally sig-nificant and imputable action and is cognate with the query "whether it is lawful to kill in self-defense *by accident*." To the contrary, the sense of the question for anyone who does not approach the article with the preconception that its purpose is that of elaborating a doctrine of double effect is patently that of whether killing in defense can ever be morally lawful. It has somehow eluded many commentators that his answer is given very clearly (and early in the article), and that the answer is yes.

Of course, something neither intended nor chosen is something for which one may be *indirectly* responsible and that is *indirectly* morally significant—as the drunk who becomes violent upon drinking is indirectly responsible for the mayhem he causes. But the direct moral significance and imputable character of what the drunk chooses pertains to the choice to drink, knowing the effects it is likely to bring forth, and knowing that it will lead to his acting destructively once his rational capacity is submerged in alcohol. But the drunken acts are not simply in themselves directly morally significant and imputable, for these acts of the agent are not directly and imputably morally significant since they are nonvoluntary, and they are not imputed to the agent since he is not directly culpable of those destructive acts by reason of being drunk. Rather the agent is only indirectly (but really!) culpable; whereas the agent *is directly and essentially morally culpable for causing himself to lose control of action in a predictable destructive way.*

The question of q. 64, art. 7 is not framed indirectly; it is about directly morally significant imputable action. "Whether it is lawful to kill in self-defense" refers either to intention or to choice. The plain sense of the question is whether it is or ever can be morally permissible or rightful or good to kill in defense. Thomas's answer to the question is yes, but indeed he makes clear that the act of preserving life in defense "may be rendered unlawful, if it be out of proportion to the end" by using "more than necessary violence." This is to say that if the quantum of force deployed is more than is necessary for defense, the question must be addressed, "Why the extra force?" If it is not justified by defense, then it is unlawful. Such force indeed might in some cases be lawful, *if* it is chosen for the sake of defense and actually ordered to it. It hardly matters whether this is so (a) if it isn't *actually* chosen for defense but for something else, or (b) if it is chosen for defense but is disordered (by reason of panic, or rage, etc.) and so is defective as a defensive act (even if inculpably by way of uncontrollable emotional reaction). Thomas is addressing an ordinary moral question (one whose treatment in positive law Thomas would have been acquainted with, since the use of a lethal stroke in defense was known by the courts and—if clearly proportioned by the agent for the sake of just defense—considered morally rightful and lawful), and he is not preoccupied with what has become the obsession of later readings, a putative doctrine of double effect.

Thomas answers the question "whether it is lawful to kill in self-defense" clearly, stating: "It is not unlawful." He then makes clear that the lawfulness is a function of proportion to the end of preserving life from assault. Finally, he makes clear that the private citizen cannot intend killing as an end, in the way that magistrates may do so in defense. This throws people who lack acquaintance with the legal history of the world off the scent of Thomas's analysis. However, before we refer to this, it must be noted that we have here a clear progression:

1. The question asked in the article is manifestly about morally significant and imputable action—it is literally not the question "whether it is lawful to kill in self-defense by accident" (the question about killing by chance is the subject of the very next article!), and it thus must necessarily pertain either to intention of the end or choice of the means.

2. Thomas says such action is lawful ("is not unlawful," which converts in a real subject to the same as "it is lawful").

3. Thomas associates the defensive action with a means that will be justified or not according to its proportion to the end.

4. Thomas says that the private citizen may not intend to kill.

The question is about morally significant and imputable action that accordingly must concern the end intended or the action chosen. *St. Thomas answers that the action is lawful, and we already know that as morally significant and imputable to the agent it must concern intention of the end or choice of the means.* Since the act must be proportioned to the end to be lawful, and since he rules out a private citizen's rightly *intending* to kill in defense, *the only remaining way we can sustain his answer is that the act is a chosen means that is lawful when and as chosen under the ratio of, and in proportion to, the intended end of defense, which is preservation of life from the undue harm of grave assault.* (It must be proportionate to a moderate defense, Thomas argues: "Si vero moderate violentiam repellat, erit licita defensio, nam secundum iura, *vim vi repellere licet cum moderamine inculpatae tutelae.*")

If we were to interpret Thomas, in his denial that the private citizen can "intend" to kill in defense, to mean by "intend" the precise secondary sense of intention *that includes the end through the already determined means* (for this sense is one—although not the most formal or principal one—of the possible significations of "intend"), *then* it would follow that Thomas must be contradicting himself within the span of one article. The act cannot be essentially lawful or good if it can never rightly be intended or chosen, and Thomas concludes that the killing in defense is not unlawful (which in a real subject logically converts to "is lawful"). Thomas argues (a) that the action is lawful and (b) that it cannot be intended. We must either deny the first or understand that Thomas is using "intention" in its *principal sense*, namely, that sense associated with the intention of the end as *ratio* for the means and prior to deliberation and determination of the means. The principal sense of intention, by reason of its causal supremacy, is the intention of the end as *ratio* for the means. It is thus not surprising that St. Thomas rules out the private citizen's intending, as the *ratio* for the whole act, the killing of the assailant—killing in the way that the magistrate may justly undertake it as an essential part both of just penalty and of enforcing the law.

Any other way of reading the article amounts to altering the question to which Thomas is responding in the article, turning it into the question "whether accidental homicide is a mortal sin"—because such a way of reading the article, assuming the less formal and principal sense of "intention," makes it necessary for one to hold that Thomas rules out both intention of lethal outcome as an end *and* also any deliberate choice of lethal means in defense. And in this case Thomas's given answer would then be wrong, because on these terms it is *not* morally lawful to kill in defense, since it can neither be intended nor chosen. From asking whether it is lawful to kill in self-defense—an *obvious* question about directly morally significant and imputable conduct, faced by the defender whose conscience implores an answer as to whether one may choose a lethal means if only it will stop the assailant—we suddenly change the question to "whether it is lawful to kill in self-defense *by accident*." Is it lawful to destroy a whole city—by accident? May one ever *eat* one's mother-in-law—by accident? The juxtaposition of the very serious *particular* and *grave* moral question with stark accidentality is ludicrous. When Thomas wants to inquire about accidental homicide, he puts it in the subject of the question: "whether accidental homicide is a mortal sin." But there is no reason whatsoever to think that Thomas is asking *this* question in article 7, especially since (a) he simply and literally isn't—the words are not to be found—and (b) *this question of killing by chance is the question addressed in the very next article*, and (c) he does *answer* his own literal question (a question that does not concern killing by accident) with the answer that *this act is not unlawful* (whose obvious sense is that one may do it) followed by the insistence that it is not unlawful when proportioned to moderate defense. When we realize that it was the common practice of the courts in St. Thomas's own day to acknowledge the legitimacy of deliberate lethal action when required for (and so proportionate to) the end of defense, it is difficult any longer to justify foisting upon the text of St. Thomas the double effect preoccupations that often are taken to be the objective concern of the text. This is a classic case where the later readings of Thomas, which are of speculative value and have indeed contributed to our understanding, nonetheless do not get Thomas's actual teaching on the matter of defense right.

Summa theologiae II–II, q. 64, art. 7 does not attempt to develop a doctrine of double effect. It attempts to answer the question whether it may be moral for the private citizen to kill in self-defense, and it answers the question yes—for so long as (1) the action is rightly proportioned to the end (which *proves* that Thomas is distinguishing the choice of the means from the intention of the end, since the latter is *proportioned* to the former and the *intention of itself doesn't suffice to justify the action*) and (2) the reason for the lethality is exclusively defensive. This last means both that any added quantum of force beyond what is needed for defense is inherently questionable—it may be a result of panic, but it could be a sign that murder and not defense is what is being done—and that the agent may not simply seek the death of the assailant but rather only the defense of himself or others.

As for magistrates killing intentionally in defense, it has been the case throughout history that legal regimes have given the command to stop marauders either by bringing them in for trial or by slaying them: "dead or alive." In numberless cases one finds a magistrate who seeks to apprehend brigands who are looting, pillaging, and raping over a wide area. The magistrate engages these criminals, but they frequently flee and when cornered fight only to free themselves. At some point he resolves that the next time they try to fight themselves free, they must be slain—the effort to bring them in alive is over—because justice requires that their malefaction be suppressed. This "killing in defense" is formal. It is *not* like that of the private citizen, for the private citizen may only will to kill owing to the need to ward off a grave assault, and he must answer as to the proportionality of the means to *defense*. If the magistrate restrains himself to using only the force needed to ward off such ad hoc assaults as the criminals undertake in order to successfully flee, it may apparently be the case that he will either never stop them or only do so when too much destruction has been wrought. The magistrate's mission[4] is *not* simply to defend himself, *and thus when and as he defends himself, he is also commissioned to act beyond defense: to kill the marauders if necessary to stop them.*

The private citizen, however, can only rightly act to defend against assault and not seek to kill, whether for the sake of justice or out of anger or spite. Where the action is chosen under the *ratio* of defense, and is indeed proportionately ordered to defense, there what is intended as end is simply defense, and the slaying while chosen and willed is not intended with the most primary and formal sense of intention, which is the intention of the end (contrasted by Thomas constantly with "choice").

Of course, a secondary sense of "intention" concerns the end *through* the means; and "intention" may even designate any part of the motion

---

[4] It might be thought that private lethal defense could only be just as a delegation of state power. But it must be observed that the state itself must make a judgment of justice as to whether such delegation is morally permissible. Moreover, on the analysis here presented, there is a just claim of individuals to preserve their lives against wrongful assault (just assault—law enforcement apprehending a criminal and, when he flees, if necessary choosing to slay rather than permit a brigand to remain at large—is another matter), provided that the defense mounted is proportionate to the end. I would still consider the argument in the book criticizing the idea of delegation to be sound: that one assailed still has a duty to protect those entrusted to him, and a just claim to preserve his own life through proportionate means (although if no one depends on him, the option to die rather than risk slaying a man in his sins out of charity for the sake of the felon's salvation is always possible, and some are moved by God to do this).

toward the end whatsoever. But the primary sense of intention regards the end, inasmuch as without intention of the end there will never be either a human act nor any part of the motion of such an act toward the end. As Thomas reminds us (*Summa theologiae* I–II, q. 12, art. 4, ad 3), intention of the end can exist prior to any determination of means whatsoever (because it is the reason why such determination is sought). There is more in cause than in effect, and the end is the noblest cause and the reason for being of the moral act. Intention in this sense has a causal primacy vis-à-vis intention in the sense either of the end through the means, or of any part of the motion to the end.

Were one to consider analysis of intention to mimic substance, then one would take the sense of intention of the end *through* the means as the primary sense, because in so doing one would treat the completed act, just as in the analysis of substance we treat the whole actually existing substance. But the zone of action is different than substance—a fact that causes those who are beguiled by the derivation of the language used from the analysis of substance at times to misprize the distinctive characteristics of the analysis of action. By virtue of its causal primacy and its superior fecundity, what is most formal in action is the intention of the end. *There is indeed a formality of the object which gives species*, but while this species may be completely disjunct from the species derived from the end and so constitute a different moral act-type than the end, it may also be contained in the species derived from the end and so be an essential determination of that species.

These points remain conspicuous because q. 64, art. 7 is the font of the contemporary preoccupation with double effect, an anomaly precisely because Thomas never intended in q. 64, art. 7 to do other than answer the question he asked. Least of all is there reason to suppose he took himself to be propounding a general doctrine of "double effect," because he used the phrase "two effects" to refer to the life preserved and the killing in lethal acts of defense.[5] Suggestions that we should "start elsewhere" in

---

[5] This does not mean that the classical schema derived by Cajetan is of no intelligible value, nor that it is not helpful with respect to a certain array of cases. To the contrary, in some cases it is helpful. But this value presupposes we can place actions in their species as a condition of applying it. The four general conditions of double effect in the common rendering of the teaching derivative from Cajetan all

understanding St. Thomas's account of the object are quite helpful, but comparatively unpursued, since the categories drawn from the fascination with Thomas's article on defense in question 64 of the prima secundae of the *Summa theologiae* are often simply transposed on the rest of the *Summa theologiae*, with the result being that the same dislocation of categories is affirmed. But q. 64, art. 7 addresses a question about directly morally significant and imputable conduct; it answers that question; and the answer Thomas gives is not adequately explained by most contemporary exegeses of Thomas's action theory. Q. 64, art. 7 remains a remarkable *pons asinorum* for contemporary exegesis of St. Thomas's account of human action.

E. "Per Se" *and* "Per Accidens" *Order of Object to End*

Thomas is very clear in teaching that when the object of the external act is *per se* ordained to the end, that the species derived from the intended end is "more formal" and "containing." But this order of "*per accidens*" and "*per se*" refers to actions, not substances. These terms signify *within* an order of human intention, and pertain to the relation of the chosen object of the external act to what the agent intends as end. *Thus, for an act to be* per se *ordained to the end is (a) for it to be chosen under the* ratio *of that end and (b) for it either (1) to be required by the nature of the intended end, or (2) simply of itself to tend toward such an end. It is not enough that something be chosen under the* ratio *of its order to an end for us to hold that it is essentially ordained to that end; nor is it enough that the object of itself tend to some object for us to hold that in the human action at hand the action is* per se *ordained to it (because it may have been chosen under a different* ratio*; thus, someone who deliberately seeks to kill his assailant under conditions that make it defensive— for instance, a corrupt police officer who contrives circumstances in which he*

---

presuppose prior capacity to analyze the action. For example, that there is a *good* action that has two effects, one good and one bad, and that we intend the good and not the bad effect, presumes we can place the act in its species (it is good), which in turn already implies we understand the object and know whether the object is *per se* related to the end, and that we know the species of the end. Similarly, the condition that the good effect not be caused by means of the evil effect presupposes that we can identify the evil effect as something not merely physically but morally evil—that we can distinguish, for example, vomiting to remove a poison for the sake of health from vomiting as a psychological pathology that is destructive of health.

will provoke attack solely for purposes of killing a competitor in the illegal drug market in a way that appears defensive—is not performing a defensive act).

It is perhaps not least by reason of definitional lacuna regarding the *foundation* of the relations *perseity* and *accidentality* between object and end—although the matter also reposes on difficulties that ensue when the analysis of substance is perhaps privileged too greatly in the analysis of action—that Steven Jensen's essay "The Role of Teleology in the Moral Species" might be thought to misprize the import of Thomas's teaching in *Summa theologiae* I–II, q. 18, art. 7. Thus, in his essay, Jensen comments on the analysis of the foundation of these relations given in *The Teleological Grammar of the Moral Act*:

> Long attempts to fill the gap. He explains the per se order in two ways, and Porter in some manner follows him in both. First, he says the per se order is present in necessary means; second, he says it is present in some actions that have a disposition to tend toward some end. Does Long derive these two standards from Aquinas? He gives no indication.[6]

However, that *per se* ordering of one principal element of human action to another—the object of the external act to the intended end—*could* find foundation only with respect to something about one in relation to the other is or should be speculatively manifest. Thomas hardly could intend that the *fundamentum* of a relation be nonexistent. Since it is a relation of two principal elements of human action (object of external act and end), clearly we have to find the foundation of the relation in something about these two. It seems plausible to suggest that Thomas did not spell this out, for the very good reason that it is necessarily implicit in the affirmation of *per se* relation—that is, *either one thing tends through itself to another, or one thing is such that it can only be pursued through another.* What else could constitute the foundation for *per se* relation of object and end? Since we are dealing with but two principal elements, it is hardly terribly complex what "*per se*" can mean. And that which is other than *per se* is *per accidens.* If my claim to originality consists in seeing this in Thomas's work, I fear I must retire empty-handed of any claim to originality.

---

6 Steven Jensen, "The Role of Teleology in the Moral Species," *The Review of Metaphysics* 63 (September 2009): 10.

In the case of *per se* order, the object must by its nature tend toward what the agent intends, and it may even be the case that the very nature of the end intended strongly requires a particular action. In *per se* order of object to end, it is true (a) that the act is chosen *under the* ratio *of its essential order to the end*, while (b) it either (1) of its nature tends to the intended end, or even more strongly (2) is actually required by the nature of the intended end (in which case, of course, it also in some way of its nature essentially conduces or tends to this end—this is simply a stronger instance of *perseity*).

Thus, the *per se* order of act to end is founded either in the essential tendency of the action or in the very nature of the intention of the end as requiring it. For example, the intention of major heart surgery requires gaining contact with the heart by opening the chest cavity, although opening the chest cavity may not be chosen under this *ratio*, and thus to such a case that *ratio* is simply not pertinent. Aztecs performing human sacrifice, and Jack the Ripper mutilating his victims, are not surgeons, because they do not choose the opening of the chest cavity under the *ratio*, of its essential contribution to the surgical repair of the heart, but rather under the *rationes* of torture, mutilation, or murderous sacrifice. And it is indeed the case that opening the chest cavity may be chosen either as ordered *per se* to medical surgery or as ordered *per se* to torture—just as taking the high-dosage pill may be chosen as ordered *per se* toward the regulation of the cycle or as ordered *per se* to contraception.

An object of external action may be essentially orderable to various intended ends. The idea that an act cannot tend essentially to distinct intentions—as using the high doseage pill tends toward regulating the female cycle, and also tends to contracept, and could be chosen under either *ratio*—is simply incompatible with the evidence, while also confusing the physical order with the order of intentions; this idea fails even to see that *perseity* of object to end concerns the relation of the nature of the action chosen to the intention of the agent. The subject of the physics ought not be confused with the subject of human action—subjects that are indeed essentially related but not identical. Of course, what is an end in one respect may in another respect be a means, even a means *per se* ordained to another end.

II. The Strategic Framework of St. Thomas's Teaching and Responses to Objections

A. The Appropriation of Terms Derived from the Analysis of Substance in the Analysis of Human Action

The terminology of Thomas's analysis of action is derived from the analysis of substance. This poses difficulties because certain things that are true of the use of these terms with respect to substance are precisely *not true* of the use of these terms with respect to action. One of the foremost illustrations of this point lies in the analysis of what is most formal in action. For Thomas—even in the case of merely accidental order of object to end—what is most formal in action is the intention of the end. Thus, even in cases of merely accidental order of object to end, the agent is more to be characterized in terms of the intended end than of the chosen object of the external act. For example, the one who commits adultery for the sake of theft is more thief than adulterer (although he is both); whereas the one who commits theft for the sake of adultery is more adulterer than thief (although, again, he is both).

In cases of *per se* order of the object of the external act to the intended end, Thomas expressly articulates a teaching quite contrary to what we would expect if we anticipated that the terminology taken from the analysis of substance would apply to action in a similar way. In substances, and in logic generally, specific difference is always formal with respect to genus. Thus, in man, "rational" is formal with respect to the genus "animal." However, in cases of *per se* order, Thomas tells us in *Summa theologiae* I–II, q. 18, art. 7 that the species derived from the intended end is like a genus, and the species derived from the object of the external act is like a specific difference; *yet, he also insists that the species derived from the intended end is "most formal" and indeed is like the formality of the "genus of formal cause" in relation to the notes included in the definition of a thing.* Thus, Thomas's teaching in the ad 3 to that article follows in this way:

> Difference is compared to genus as form to matter, inasmuch as it actualizes the genus. On the other hand, the genus is considered as more formal than the species, inasmuch as it is something more absolute and less contracted. Wherefore also the parts of a definition are reduced to the genus of formal cause, as is stated in Phys. ii, 3. And in this sense the

genus is the formal cause of the species; and so much the more formal, as it is more universal.[7]

In the sense of being something more absolute and uncontracted, genus is always more formal than species, both in the case of substance and in the case of action. But it is the latter sense taken up in the passage—the sense in which the parts of the definition are reduced to the genus of formal cause—that is most critical here. It is "in this sense" (*"et secundum hoc"*) that the genus is the cause of the species in the case of *per se* order of the object of the external act to the end. It is as the parts of a definition are reduced to the genus of formal cause that the species of the object (or objects) that are *per se* ordained to the end are essentially contained in the species from the end. Like Russian dolls, the species from the objects are contained in the species derived from the ends. And so the species derived from the end is in this case the formal cause of the species of the object (or objects) and contains it (or them). The species derived from the object of the external act in the case of *per se* order is contained within the species derived from the end, and it is an essential determination of that species derived from the end.

The reason this is pertinent at all to action is because in action the intention of the end is the reason for the very existence of the action, and in the case where the object of the external act is *per se* ordained to the end, there the object is most wholly configured to the end and its species is contained in the species from the end. The object always adds a species to the act, but the species that is added in the case of *per se* order is wholly a function of the end—as the key adds something to the lock, but is wholly a function of the nature of the lock; or as the glove adds something to the hand, but is wholly a function of the hand. The species derived from the object adds something in the case of *per se* order, but what it adds is a note contained within the species derived from the end, so it is a further determination of and within the species derived from the end.

---

[7] *Summa theologiae* I–II, q. 18, art. 7, ad 3: "Ad tertium dicendum quod differentia comparatur ad genus ut forma ad materiam, inquantum facit esse genus in actu. Sed etiam genus consideratur ut formalius specie, secundum quod est absolutius, et minus contractum. Unde et partes definitionis reducuntur ad genus causae formalis, ut dicitur in libro Physic. Et secundum hoc, genus est causa formalis speciei, et tanto erit formalius, quanto communius."

In the case of *per se* order, (a) either the object of its nature tends toward the intended end, or the intended end is such by its nature as *per se* to require a particular object; and (b) the object is chosen *precisely under the ratio* of such order (since contrary to some, actions may be such as to tend essentially to different objects of intention—as the high doseage pill might be chosen because of its order to regulating the cycle, but might also be chosen because of its order to contraception, and if one chooses under one of these, the other will not be morally defining. This means that *per se* order refers to the relation of the chosen object of the external act to the agent's intention of an end when the object is chosen, precisely owing to its order to that end and not for another reason. *This is specifically moral order, reducible neither simply to philosophy of nature or physics, nor to logic, although it is, of course, subject to both orders nonetheless.*

Thus, the use of anesthesia in surgery of itself tends to aid the surgery and the purposes of the surgery, by reducing the chance of added injury to the patient and making it easier for the surgeon to work by removing many possible impeding ad hoc motions of the patient during surgery. Anesthesia may be used to help abduct kidnap victims; but the choice to use it under the *ratio* of its aid to the medical act is the choice of something that is *per se* ordained to such an act, because of its very nature anesthesia is such as to aid the motion of the surgical act and thus essentially conduces to its end. (Yet, use of anesthesia might be chosen under a different *ratio*, ordained to an abduction, to which it could be *per se* ordered because of its effect in rendering the patient unconscious.) Likewise is this true of prepping the patient. It is true of the surgical cutting that gains entry to the patient's organs, a cutting which might otherwise be construed as mutilation and torture for the sake of a medical good and viewed as doing evil that good may come. Yet, in surgery this cutting—while materially harmful—is formally surgical, because its species is contained within the species derived from the medical end.

Someone might suppose that such surgical entry is merely the "physical species" of a medical act, but such language can be justified only owing to the order of the act of opening the chest cavity to the intended end of major surgical repair of the heart. Opening the chest cavity is not *simply of itself* heart surgery. One might open chest cavities all day long and never perform heart surgery. It is a distinct action from the action that operates on the heart in major heart surgery. The only reason the opening of the chest cavity in heart surgery is morally justifiable—and can in some sense be viewed as "a physical species of heart surgery" (although more appropriately it is viewed as simply an act *per se* ordained to heart surgery)—is precisely that the nature of the medical act involved in major heart surgery is such as to require and specify such action. *To speak of the object of the external act and the end as* "per se" *ordered is either to say that the object is ordained to the intended end through itself, or that the intended end through itself requires the object.* What else could it possibly mean (granting the significations of "object of the external act" and "intended end," and the equally obvious realization that the first is *for the sake of* the second)? This is hardly complicated, since there are only two related elements; yet, even though Thomas speaks of such *per se* relation, and there are only two such elements, it appears to be the case that there are authors who do not understand what such *perseity* could mean but for whom, lacking a further treatise by St. Thomas on the matter, we must not take it to mean anything much.

The nature of the intended end of medical repair of the heart through major surgery, for the sake of the health of the patient, requires the opening of the chest cavity. In other words, there is within the structure of the action a *per se* order between the intention of major heart repair and the choice of the external object of the act of opening the chest cavity, such that the species of opening the chest cavity is in the case of surgery—where it is chosen under that precise *ratio*—contained within the species of the intended end.

Note again that we are speaking of human action and not of substance; in human action, the end is most formal. Just as what appears to be a circumstance in relation to one consideration may prove not to be a mere circumstance, but may either be the principal condition of the object[8] or even introduce a distinct object; and just as this truth about what appears initially to be circumstance is possible because the determination of the moral species is an essential determination in relation to reason;[9] *so likewise* is it the case that the pertinent natural tendency of the chosen action, or the pertinent nature of the intended end, *in relation to reason* indicates a certain order of object to intended end (because the ordering of object to end

---

8 Cf. *Summa theologiae* I–II, q. 18, art. 19, resp. Note also the ad 2.
9 *Summa theologiae* I–II, q. 18, art. 5, resp.

occurs within reason while embracing the nature of what is chosen, and one rationally chooses either an act that is not through itself ordered toward the end or that is; either one rationally seeks an end that does not by its very nature dictate one sole particular pathway, or one seeks an end that does by its nature dictate one sole particular pathway).[10]

Even where the object of the external act is neither chosen under the *ratio* of its being essentially required by the intention of the end, nor chosen under the *ratio* of its simply tending to the intended end (in other words, when the order is *per accidens*), the species derived from the intended end more characterizes the agent's choice than that derived from the object (although, of course, both characterize the agent's choice).

To return to the confusion of the analysis of action with that of substance, one should see how disparate the application of terminology is to these different subjects. Thus, in the analysis of substance, "rational" is more formal than "animal" (since, as derived from the rational soul, it is a specific difference more defining than is "animal," which designates the genus). Note also that with respect to human substance, "animal" is *for the sake of* "rational"—man's animality is, according to Thomas, for the sake of his knowledge, since he is ordained to draw his knowledge by abstraction from sensible things and so requires bodiliness for the specifically natural perfection of human knowledge.

However, and by contrast, when we come to the analysis of action, the distinctive character of action changes the analysis. The species derived from the intended end is like a genus, whereas the species derived from the object of the external act is like a specific difference. Yet, according to Thomas, the species derived from the object of the external act is contained in the species derived from the intended end, as the parts of a definition belong to the genus of the definition. Thus, "the parts of a definition are reduced to the genus of formal cause," and the species from the object of the external act is reduced to the genus of the species derived from the intended end and is formally contained within it. This species derived from the end is "more formal." Why? It is more universal (but this is always true of the genus vis-à-vis

---

10 Of course this description contrasts the more common form of *perseity*, in which there is a natural tendency of the object to the intended end (although perhaps to the other possible intentions as well) with the stronger form, where the intended end by its nature indicates not several possible means but one.

the species); but even more importantly, it is more formal, because *the object is for the sake of the end, and not the other way around, and in the case of* per se *order, the object is maximally configured to the end.*

One does not say that form is for the matter, but that the matter is for the form. And as the species derived from the end is like a genus, we might think therefore that the end is for the sake of the object. *But this is false; no one intends an end merely for the sake of an object of the external act.* The means is *for the end*, and not the end for the means. So, in human action, the object is *for the sake of the end.* In *per se* order of object to end, accordingly, the object-species is formally contained within the end-species and is most configured *for its sake.* Whereas even in *per accidens* order, the end-species remains more formal, but there the object-species is not contained within the end-species but is *formally disjunct* so that there are two (or howsoever many) differing species of act. In the realm of substance, what is true—that specific difference is always more formal—is not true in the realm of action. It is true that the specific difference constituted by the object-species always adds something to action: either (1) a new species disjunct with that derived from the intended end in the case of *per accidens order*, or else (2) a species that is an essential determination of the species derived from the end in the case of *per se* order. But the species derived from the intended end—which is like a genus—is in fact *more formal* in the case of action. Not to understand this express teaching of St. Thomas will be to miss an important aspect of his moral analysis.

B. Response to a Criticism about the Nature of Per Se Order of Object to End

It may already be sufficiently clear from what has been said, *but* per se *order of object to end is not a unique and exclusive relationship, save within the intentional order of an action.* An action that in the context of one intention is *per se* ordained may later, with respect to a different and even opposed intention, also be *per se* ordained. For example, the same act[11] may be ordained either to the end of regulating the cycle of a woman or to contraception. If the act is chosen under one *ratio*, it does nothing to alter the fact that it might have

---

[11] Of course, here we mean "the same act" in terms of physical species: opening the chest cavity is opening the chest cavity. Yet, sometimes opening of the chest cavity is part of major heart surgery, and sometimes it is torture, etc. In contemplating an action, the reference to physical species is in fact necessary to deliberation. Were an act not more ordered to one thing than to another, reasonable choice would be

been chosen under another. Some have suggested that, for instance, if open-ing the chest cavity is *per se* ordained to heart surgery in major heart repair (because the nature of the intention of major heart repair for the sake of the health of the patient requires opening the chest cavity in this way, lest the operation kill the patient), then all opening of chest cavities should be med-ical. Thus, for example, the Aztecs, or Jack the Ripper, would need to be per-forming salubrious acts. But this is absurd, and so the conclusion is that the analysis given in this book is false. This is a pleasant bit of fallacy that mani-fests the same error that may be found in the following: "Man is *per se* an ani-mal; therefore, man is every animal; therefore, man is not *per se* an animal." But manifestly this is a non sequitur. To say that the intention of major heart repair *per se* requires opening of the chest cavity is not to say that every open-ing of the chest cavity is major heart repair, any more than to say that man is *per se* an animal requires that every animal be a man. But what about the case of *perseity* founded on the order of object to end, rather than the strongest sort of *perseity* founded on the very nature of the intended end? Doesn't say-ing that *x* is through itself ordered to *y* mean that *x* is *always* ordered to *y*? We are speaking here of moral analysis, and so should see that it means only two things: (1) that *x* is always by nature such that it could be chosen for the sake of *y*, and (2) that because the order of object to end embraces the nature of the external act but is within intentional order, the essential tendency of *x* that is morally determining is identified *in part* by the *ratio* under which it is chosen. Thus, for example, the woman who neither intends nor chooses any venereal act but seeks to use the high doseage pill to regulate her cycle per-forms a medical act (but she could intend or choose venereal action, and in relation to such intention and choice, she could decide to use the high doseage contraception pill—in which case, the fact that she *could have* chosen to use the pill under the *ratio* of medical therapy will be irrelevant). Per se *relation is not a unique and exclusive relation, save within the intentional context of the action: which is to say that it pertains to the objective order obtaining between what is chosen and what is intended within an act, and not to say that the* finis operantis *swallows up everything.*

---

impossible. To suggest that this physical causality is something inessential or unimportant for deliberation, consent, choice, and action would be merely to abstract oneself from the actual nature of deliberation, consent, choice, and action. No sane person contemplates getting a haircut with a wet noodle.

One would also ask: What else can justify the opening of the chest cavity? *Materially speaking*, it is indeed mutilation and perhaps even torture; but *formally* it is medical, precisely because it is essentially contained under the medical *ratio* of the end. There is no other justification for the act. We must penetrate to the teleological order of the object chosen to the end intended. Likewise, there are only two ways in which we can find such *per se* order. We are dealing with two principal constituents of human action, the object and the end. Either one is through itself ordered to the other, or one is such that it can be achieved only through another. So, one way such *per se* order obtains is insofar as the object of its nature tends toward the intended end; whereas another way such a *per se* order obtains is insofar as the object is required by the nature of the intended end.

It must be understood that the object of the external act may by its nature potentially tend to more than one potential object of intention—as taking the high dosage pill may tend to regulate the woman's cycle but may also tend toward contraception. Manifestly, since a woman may take the high dosage pill without any intention or choice of a venereal act and may take the pill to regulate the cycle, in such a case, since the pill of its nature tends toward the regulation of the female cycle, when chosen under that *ratio* it is *per se* ordained to that intention and contained within that species. Whereas, to the contrary, when it is chosen under the *ratio* of its essential contraceptive tendency in relation to intercourse, it is *per se* ordained to that intention, and the species of the object is contained under the contraceptive species derived from the intended end.

C. Response to the Major Strategic Difficulty in Action Theory

Thomas speaks of the object of the external act as formal; and he speaks of the intention of the end as formal; and he even says that the object of the interior act of the will (the end) is formal with respect to the object of the external act, which is, as it were, material. There is a tendency to reduce the action either simply to the formality of the end—which reaches its extreme, in the very intelligent (but I believe flawed) analysis of Fr. Martin Rhonheimer,[12] wherein he argues that there indeed is no object of the

---

[12] Fr. Martin Rhonheimer, "The Moral Object of Human Acts and the Role of Reason According to Aquinas: A Restatement and Defense," *Josephinum Journal of Theology* 18 (no. 2): 454–506; note especially p. 472.

external act distinct from the intention of the end—or else to the object of the external act (which Thomas does indeed say gives action its species), and to insist, by way of firewall against intentionalism, that the species derived from the object of the external act is always most formal. In a way, this disparity seems similar to the contrast drawn by Steven Jensen between what he terms "Abelardianism" and "physicalism."[13] Both of these tendencies seem to me to be erroneous.

What is one to make of an act that, as Fr. Rhonheimer has argued, *supposedly* has *two forms* (the formal character associated with the species of the object of the external act, and the formal character associated with intention of the end)? Fr. Martin Rhonheimer argues that this is as impossible as a living body having two souls.[14] But, *sed contra*, it is not impossible

---

13 See Steven Jensen, *Good & Evil Actions: A Journey through St. Thomas Aquinas* (Washington, DC: Catholic University of America Press, 2010). The distinction is made throughout the book. I share with Jensen a concern that the intelligible role of the object of the external act in giving species not be dissolved in any form of intentionalism. Despite the many differences between the approach of the present work and his own, this aspect of Jensen's work seems to me instructive and helpful. I too am concerned that there be an initially adequate judgment regarding the nature of the object of the external act before, and as a condition of, any judgment regarding its order to the intended end. Otherwise, we will be stuck with an over-generic account of the object of the external act, which is morally inadequate.

14 Rhonheimer, "The Moral Object of Human Acts," 472. Of course, with respect to the complete species of the act, there must be the determination of *perseity* or dis-junction, while nonetheless a certain knowledge of the object of the external act is a necessary condition for making this judgment. Fr. Rhonheimer writes the following: "Jensen and others thus conclude that, in reality, there are two moral objects: the object of the interior act of the will (which for me properly is the moral object considered in the fullest sense of the term), and the object of the exterior act, which would be the 'thing' to which this act relates or in which it terminates. This, however, is impossible. Provided the moral object is what primarily and fundamentally gives the moral species to a human act, there cannot be two (or multiple, as at least one of these critics claim) moral objects. This is impossible in the same way as a being cannot have two substantial forms and a living organism cannot have two souls; because substantial forms establish a determinate being's or a determinate organism's species. The same applies to the fundamental specification of human acts: on the level of its primary and fundamental specification it cannot simultaneously belong to two different species." But do either Rhonheimer or Jensen consider *Summa theologiae* I–II, q. 18, art. 7, regarding the crucial role of the order of object to end in determining the complete species of the action, to be important? It seems that each has scant role for it as an important feature of Thomas's analysis. It seems to me—perhaps erroneously—that this is because for Jensen my reading of q. 18,

if we understand the two to be related teleologically, because this is then "formality" in diverse respects, to be understood according to their nature and relation, and in accord with the normative ordering of ends definitive for the *ratio boni*. Properly speaking, the categories with respect to Thomas's action theory are not simply "formal" and "material" but "super-formal," that is, the most formal character of the intention of the end; "formal"—with respect to the object of the external act; and "material"—with respect to pure circumstances that are not, on reflection, discovered either to be principal conditions of the object or to represent new objects, either of which would change the relation of the act to reason.

Why "superformal"? Because even in those cases wherein the object of the external act is only accidentally ordered to the intended end, the intention of the end yet remains the most determinative element with respect to the act, and the absolute causal *sine qua non* for the act. One who commits adultery for the sake of theft is performing acts with different, formally disjunct species, but yet is more thief than adulterer precisely because of this more formal character of the end. Why is the object "formal"? Because the object of the external act determines *what* our act bears upon and gives it its species—a species that may be essentially contained in the species derived from the end (in the case of *per se* order), or that may be wholly disjunct and distinct, *depending on its order to the end*. Why are the circumstances merely material? For so long as they remain pure circumstances, and do not either become principal conditions of the object of the external act nor introduce a new object, they add no species to the act.

Why doesn't this lead to incoherence, as in the impossible case of the body having two substantial forms? The reason is that action is not like substance. The action that is performed bears upon something, and it is specified by what it bears upon and how it bears upon it; but it also is only chosen because it is judged in some particular way to be best ordered, or the sole orderable act, toward the intended end. Without the intention of the end, there *is* no act, and there is no object of the external act. Thus, granted the importance of the object of the external act, we also must judge the nature of what is intended, and then we must gauge whether the

---

art. 7 is too liable to intentionalist deconstruction, whereas for Fr. Rhonheimer my reading is too strongly anchored to the integral nature and *per se* effects of a chosen action as essential to the object of the external act.

relation of the act to the end is *per accidens* or *per se* before we can give a complete assessment of an act.

D. Back to "Per Se" and "Per Accidens"

In this respect, we may identify a problem that some who are centrally concerned with avoiding the evils of intentionalism may think to be inseparable from the analysis of this book. It is a problem with which I have more sympathy than I have with the intentionalist critique, although both must be answered. But this problem derives from intelligent and principled efforts to articulate the importance of the object of the external act for resisting Abelardianism or intentionalism—an effort found, for example, in the work of Steven Jensen, whose work *Good & Evil Actions* is commendable in its gravitas and its thorough consideration of and insistence upon the intelligible centrality of the object of the external act in moral analysis.

In relation to intentionalism, it may seem that the only way to close the door firmly and absolutely is, not only to say that in every case the object of the external act contributes a species, but at least to suggest that in almost every case (if not every case) the species derived from the object of the external act is most formal. If we say this, then we do close the door absolutely on intentionalism. The problem is that we also close the door on many other things: just defense, major heart surgery, vomiting to remove poison when it is impossible to get to a poison control center, and so on. As has been seen, opening the chest cavity is a distinct action but one that is essentially required by the nature of the intended end of major heart surgery for the health of a patient (since any other way of gaining access to the heart for such surgery guts the patient like a fish). If we supposed its species to be most formal rather than precisely subsumed in the species derived from the medical end, we would need to assert that it is mutilation and torture and therefore evil and not to be permitted—one may not do evil that good may come.

The end of major surgical repair of the heart essentially requires the prior act of opening the chest cavity, which thus is *per se* ordained to it, and so its species is contained in the species derived from the end; it is contained, that is, in the species of "major surgical repair of the heart." Morally speaking, we have a clear case of *per se* order of the stronger type in which the very nature of the intended end requires a particular action.

What, then, might a critic of intentionalism think dangerous in this account? First, one might on general principle take oneself to have good reason to be wary of any account stressing intention, since intentionalism is not a straw man but a constant tendency of much moral criticism and even Catholic dissent over the past hundred years (and, indeed, all the way back to Abelard).

But there is a more specific and concrete problem. We have said that there are two criteria for *per se* ordering of object and end: (1) that the act be chosen specifically under the ratio of the end, and (2) that either (a) the object of the external act be such as to tend by its nature to what the agent intends, or (b) the end intended by the agent be such as to require the particular object. If the object is *per se* ordained to the end, then the most formal and containing species is derived from the end, and the species from the object is contained within that species, just as a part of the definition is contained within the formality of the definition. *Secondly and in particular*, then, the specter of the following type of reasoning may seem implied by the analysis given above. Someone might say that the burning of human bodies tends of its nature to produce light and heat; accordingly, the moral species that fundamentally defines burning people alive for the sake of light and heat is that of "lighting up the darkness" and providing heat. This is, of course, absurd; but that is the point. Surely a mode of analysis that permits such absurdities must be resisted.

The very first and obvious response is that the characterization of the act of burning a human being as *per se* ordained to bringing about heat and light when chosen under that *ratio* misses the intelligible density of the object of the external act. *If* a living human person could morally be rightly depicted as merely "stuff" for burning, *then* this depiction of the object could be true. But as it is, it is a perfect illustration of an overgeneric description of an object, a description that leaves out the most decisive content, and which therefore cannot do other than imply error. A human person is not merely "stuff to be burned," and thus to depict the object of the external act in some case as "burning living human beings for the sake of light and heat" would (even if the depiction of the intention of the end, which is mad, were true) indicate that wrongful homicide was being performed. Further, a rational creature—ordered to God both at the level of nature and (in an infinitely elevated sense) at the level of grace—cannot justly be treated as merely combustible matter, because we are dealing with a person, and to kill the person merely for the sake of heat or light is simply wrongful homicide, or murder. The murder of a living person is by its nature evil; the fact that the mode of murder may bring about some physical effect that is desired is then irrelevant. It may be true that setting a man on fire is *per se* ordered to generating light and heat. It is also *per se* ordered gravely to harm, or to kill, the innocent man who is burned. Likewise, the man in line for life-saving therapy, who is so far back in the queue that he will probably never receive it, if he then kills those ahead of him in line, cannot justly describe his action as merely "removing impediments to life-saving therapy." Doubtless it is true that the act does remove impediments to life-saving therapy (as it is true that burning a living human person will generate heat and light), but it is, properly understood, wrongful homicide. Such overgeneric descriptions do not adequately characterize the object of the moral act, which includes the act itself, its integral nature, and its *per se* effects, as well as the *ratio of appetibility* for the act.

One must point out that there is no way of avoiding such reasoning except by achieving adequate analysis of the nature of the object of the external act. It is also true that in order to put the act in its proper species, a judgment must be made as to whether the object correctly understood in its specific character is *per se* ordained to the intended end. This specific judgment will itself reveal whether the species of the object is *disjunct* from the intended end, or whether the species of the object is *contained within* the intended end as an essential determination. Some will say that this is an appeal to intuition. But it is an appeal to evidence.

What is the matter with the absurd illustration is not merely that it is absurd but that it is an *overgeneric* account of the object of the act. It is morally grossly deficient, because it does not properly describe the object of the external act itself as a condition for considering the order of the act to the end so as to determine whether the species of the object is, or is not, contained most formally in the species derived from the end. The mode of analysis proposed by St. Thomas in *Summa theologiae* I–II, q. 18, art. 7 is not defective, merely because there is no magic wand that may be waved to prevent people from rationalizing their actions by taking an overgeneric view of the object of the external act or simply failing to attend to the nature of what is done. Inasmuch as the determination of what is to be done for an end is a function of reason, defects by way of overgeneral or rationalizing depictions of the nature of the object of the external act or by way of simple error will introduce false judgment. The fault lies in the postlapsarian human condition rather than in the realization that some acts are such as to be *per se* ordained to the agent's intended end. We must, then, gain that specific knowledge regarding the actual moral density of the object of the external act to judge correctly whether it is *per se* ordained to the intention of the end by the agent. It is heartening, despite other differences in our understanding of Thomas's teaching, to share with Professor Jensen (whose work on this score is extensive) the judgment of the essential necessity for moral realism of such adequate judgment regarding the object of the external act.

As observed already, the answer to this problem is not one to which the answer is simply "intuition." It is the evidence itself, and attention to it, that provides the answer. We must know what the object of the external act is—we must be able to judge the nature of the action performed and what it bears upon and how—before proceeding to consider the relation of the object-species to the end-species. And adequate knowledge of the object of the external act will then enable us to gauge its relation to what the agent intends, and consequently to determine its *perseity* or accidentality, so as to place it adequately in the light of the normative order of ends.

One may see another illustration of this kind of necessary consideration clearly in the case of craniotomy. In this instance the action bears upon one who is not the patient, and does so in such a way as to cause harm rather than to heal. If we wish to know whether it is a medical act, we have our answer: it directly and principally impacts a living human person in such a way as to do harm and indeed to kill. The fetus is even more harmed than is the mother by its being in the wrong place. The fetus performs no conduct whatsoever, so not only is it free of morally culpable conduct, but it is free of conduct *tout court*, free even of merely "performative" guilt, because it is not performing any operations. It is the classic innocent bystander at the wrong time and place.

The intention of the doctor performing the craniotomy would presumably be to save the life of the mother by removing the child from the birth canal. One could imagine someone saying that the end of saving the life of the mother requires the means of the craniotomy because otherwise the woman will die on the table. But the description of the act as merely narrowing the circumference of the fetus's skull is overgeneric and incorrect. The fetus is a person—as is the mother—and to crush the skull of the fetus is not merely to reduce the size of its skull and conduce to its exiting the birth canal, thus helping to save the mother's life. It also, *per se* and in a causally direct matter, slays an innocent person (innocent in the sense of being guilty of no morally culpable action and no performative guilt of a gravely threatening action, as is found in the case of some who without culpability and owing to hallucinations or psychotic illness might perform action that needs to be stopped). It has been argued[15] that since the life of the fetus cannot be spared, there is no choice available to save its life. But this does not mean there is no choice available wrongly to slay it. Dying soldiers on the battlefield can be wrongly slain by their adversaries. Fetuses, too, even though dying, can be wrongly killed.

Once we see that the act is directly ordered to killing an innocent who is in fact not receiving medical action as a patient but instead is receiving destructive action and being treated, not as a human person, but as a mere obstacle, we are in position to see that this cannot be *per se* ordained as medical aid to a mother. Why? (1) It is not a medical act. (2) It does not help the person it directly impacts; it hurts and kills that person. (3) The

---

15 Cf. Fr. Martin Rhonheimer, *Vital Conflicts* (Washington, DC: Catholic University of America Press, 2009), 82. Here he argues that "it is not even possible" in craniotomy, when the fetus is dying, that it be directly and unjustly killed. This seems to confuse "dying" with "being dead." Even the dying may be unjustly killed. This pertains, also, to the fetus in craniotomy, who is not merely dead tissue to be moved out of the way. It is interesting that in a modern medical textbook to be found online (http://www.meb.uni-bonn.de/dtc/primsurg/docbook/html/x5765.html) craniotomy is described under "destructive operations"; it is noted that the cranium is not reduced until the brain is removed (NNLT proponents, *nota bene*); and the indications are stated as follows: "the baby must be dead." Crushing the skull of a living human being not even performatively guilty of any grave evil, and removing that person's brain, thereby directly killing that person, *is not a medical act*. It seems to be an act of wrongful homicide committed under emotional and medical duress and without sufficient moral realism and clarity on the part of those tempted to perform it. This procedure is different from salpingectomy in that salpingectomy does not directly terminate in the child (although the morality of moving the child to another place where it cannot live and where its prognosis is worse must still be considered). The direct crushing of the skull and slaying of the child in craniotomy is not meaningfully described as a "side effect," since it is the proper, proportionate, and direct effect of the chosen action.

slaying of the innocent, as such—and that is what is being performed—is not *per se* ordained to health. Killing extinguishes—it does not spare—life. *If* there were culpable, gravely wrongful action on the part of the fetus, or even performative guilt on the part of the fetus with respect to gravely harmful action, *then* the *ratio* of defense might arise. But there is no such operation performed by the fetus either culpably or inculpably. It is simply in the wrong place at the wrong time.[16]

Thus, there is no *per se* ordering of the crushing of the skull of the fetus to saving life; nor is an act that helps one's person specifically by means of harming another a medical act. If it were, then the individual in line for life-saving therapy who can't get it in time to save his life because there are too many in the queue in front of him could rightly designate his murder of those in front of him (in order to be able to get the treatment) as merely "removing impediments to life-saving therapy." Murder is not a medical act. But why not? Why is it not even when it might promote someone's health? We must, as a condition of properly considering the *order* of object to tend, understand the nature of the act being chosen. Its species may be essentially contained in the species derived from the end, but we can at least initially determine whether it *can* be subsumed. Murder cannot be a

---

16 How is this different from the removal of a gravid uterus? The hysterectomy removes a diseased organ of the patient's in an act that terminates in that organ itself; it is a specially grave circumstance that this involves moving the fetus from one place where it will not live to another place where it will not live. One still might think efforts should be made to sustain the fetus's life so far as possible. But the action is not directly terminating in the fetus, but it is terminating in an organ that would in any case need to be removed. Here double effect in its Cajetanian formulation seems appropriated: the removal of the organ is not effected by moving the fetus or harming the fetus, and so accordingly the bad effect is not the means for the good effect. The good effect—saving the mother's life—is proportionate to the bad effect, which is the accidental speeding of the death of the fetus. It is a very grave action precisely because of the accidental harm to an innocent. But to compare this with craniotomy is not even to have grasped Cajetan's account of double effect. Of course, I take it as simply the case that it is Cajetan who—in my view incorrectly—most influentially reads *Summa theologiae* II–II, q. 64, art. 7 as propounding a doctrine of double effect, whose account as given by Cajetan is nonetheless in certain matters applicable and helpful. Our actions embrace not merely the *ratio of appetibility* for our actions but the actions themselves in their essential causality. That is why "direct" and "indirect" necessarily refer to physical causality as contained *within* the intentional order.

medical act, because it is of itself opposed to the health and life of the one murdered. Any further effects cannot cancel out that essential datum.

By contrast, consider defense. There is no attempt on the part of Vitoria, for example, to pretend that some defenses are not lethal, or to present them as something else—for example, to say that the chosen lethal stroke in defense was merely a moving of matter and not a lethal act. Its lethality is what poses the lacerating moral challenge to the conscience of the prospective defender. Rather, the issue is simply this: Is the killing of the assailant—who is performatively guilty of assault even when not morally culpable of it, like the man with a brain tumor who inculpably goes on a killing spree—something that can of itself tend to the suppression of assault? But to suppress the assailant is always or for the most part to suppress the assault. To be just, the defense must first be justified (otherwise it is the sin of strife, as, for example, when a criminal resists arrest). Further, the act must be chosen under the *ratio* of defense—if it is chosen for some other reason by the agent, it doesn't matter if it *could* have been chosen defensively, because it was chosen for a different and thus (for the private citizen) morally bad reason. Moreover, objectively, if some other means would have achieved defense with less harm, then the added quantum of force must be justified. But if the force is not justified, this means once again that in such a case the act is not defensive (although it may be inculpably so, as when someone does something unreasoningly forceful in resistance out of terror or panic). Three questions must be answered affirmatively for lethal defense ever to be just: (1) Does killing the assailant always or for the most part suppress the assault? (2) In a truly defensive act (and we are here presupposing a justified defense—there are other kinds), is the act chosen solely for the sake and under the *ratio* of defense, and not for any other reason (to punish out of rage or fear or, alternately, deliberately and cold-bloodedly to murder under the mere appearance of defense)? (3) Finally, is the force that is used truly proportionate to the end of defense?— or put differently (and to be answered negatively), is an effective defense available to the agent that uses less force and is less destructive, but that the agent shuns in preference for something more destructive? It is not enough that this proportionate force is what the agent seeks; the agent needs to make sure of it. If more force is used than necessary, even out of mere involuntary panic, the act will be defective, even if inculpably so. And if the excess of force is deliberate, it will be a wrongful act. Thus, if more force is used than is requisite for and proportionate to the end, then the defense will be excessive and wrongful, but if the force used is proportionate to a moderate defense, the defense will be just.

Adequate consideration of the chosen act prior to and as a condition for the judgment of its *per se* or *per accidens* ordering to the end intended is required in order that the latter consideration be successful. Thus, certain formulations of *The Teleological Grammar of the Moral Act* could be read too one-sidedly (although the affirmation throughout the work that the integral nature and *per se* effects of a chosen action are necessarily included in the object surely should indicate that this is not the way to read the book). That is, while we must know the order of object to end to put the action as such in its species, it must also be understood that a preliminary and accurate understanding of the object of the external act is also required prior to the judgment of *perseity* or accidentality in relation to the end. To repeat, it is for this reason that in *The Teleological Grammar of the Moral Act* it is constantly affirmed that the act itself, its integral nature, and *per se effects* are always included in the object of the external act.

We derive a species from the object of the external act; it may not be disjunct, and it may be an essential part of the species derived from the end. However, we must adequately understand the action itself as a condition for judging whether its species is contained within the species derived from the end. The matter is not in itself complicated. It is not in principle different from seeing that even though killing one's neighbor in order to eat him will bring about nutrition, nonetheless the proper characterization of the action is not merely "eating dinner," because the killing is wrongful homicide. One could call this case "wrongful homicide for the sake of cannibalism," and that would be a more adequate description of the object, since the full and horrible nature of the homicide is cannibalistic. Such prior knowledge, and the evidence from which it is derived, serves as a control upon temptation toward overgeneral and rationalizing accounts of the object of the external act. We must, after all, know something about what our act bears upon and how, in order to judge whether it is ordained *per se* or *per accidens* to the end, and so to judge whether it is disjunct from the species derived from the end or contained within it. That knowledge provides us with the specificity we need to rule out overgeneric and deficient accounts of the object. In fact, it is fallen human nature, and not the need to determine the order of object to end in order to derive the species of the act as a whole, that is responsible for overgeneric and deficient accounts of the object of the external act. And certainly we are in no position to say that we are finished in analyzing action until we have determined the order of object to end, because this alone (presupposing certain knowledge of the object, to be sure) will permit us to determine adequately the complete species of the act and to judge it in relation to the normative hierarchy of ends. But far from excusing overgeneric accounts of the nature of the object, this manifests how essential it is that the object be adequately understood to assure that the judgment of the relation of object and intended end is correct.

D. Response to an Intentionalist Plaint

But isn't action just a matter of intention "all the way down"? One sometimes hears this said. What is in one frame of reference an end becomes a means in another. But this can be taken too far. This is because, in any action, that which stands in the place of the means is chosen only for the sake of the end. For instance, a tired man is asked by his wife to drive to the pharmacy and get medicine for his sick children. And so he rises from his chair, gets his keys, moves to the door, opens the door, shuts the door, walks to the car, opens the door, gets in, and so on. Now, if before he leaves, his wife runs out and says, "I did have the medicine—it was in the other bathroom," he is not taking one more step in the direction of going to the store. The only reason he pursues any of the "mini-ends" is precisely because they are all means with respect to his intended end, and without that end, the whole forest of means, or midway points or mini-ends, vanishes. Within the frame of any given action, means are distinguished from the reason for their being, which is the intended end. The causality of the intended end is accordingly distinctive and central. But not everything is an end, because the means is an act bearing upon something that specifies it and that the act is about in relation to reason, and which is ordered either *per se* or *per accidens* to the intended end.

E. Different Uses of "Per Se"

In his instructive and helpful review of *The Teleological Grammar of the Moral Act*, Fr. Kevin Flannery, SJ, notes the following:

Question 72, article 1 of the *Prima Secundae* is even more difficult to reconcile with Long's reading. There Thomas is also concerned with the species of acts—but of individual acts. He asks whether a sin receives its species from the sinner's object rather than from his intention (and "no one intends to do evil," notes Thomas, quoting pseudo-Dionysius). "It is manifest," says Thomas, "that anything receives its species from that which it is *per se* and not from what it is *per accidens*." A sin is *per se* the voluntary act of a sinner "who intends to perform *such* a voluntary act in *such* material"; and "voluntary acts are distinguished in species according to their objects." So his answer is, yes, "sins are properly distinguished by species according to their objects." This conclusion flies in the face of Long's analysis of question 64, article 7 of the *Secunda Secundae* according to which Thomas is saying that an action's object is *praeter intentionem*; it also confirms the idea just proposed that, when at the beginning of that article Thomas speaks of an act's receiving its species from what is intended and not what is *per accidens*, he is concerned with the way we determine the species of types of acts and not directly with the analysis of individual acts.[17]

What is it that receives species? Acts. And acts are individual although they may be judged by type. Two points seem pertinent here. (1) It is true that sins are defined by the species of objects, but to place the object *in* its species requires a judgment as to its relation to the end. (2) Further, it seems also that the sense of "object" in q. 72, art. 1 embraces both the object of the external act and the object of the interior act of the will.

As for the first point, every individual act *per se* receives species from its object (here taken in the sense of the species derived from the object of the external act). But in some cases, the object-species is merely part of, an essential determination of, the species derived from the end, which is the fundamental species. To say that "voluntary acts are distinguished in species according to their objects" is true, but it does not determine whether the object of the external act is in some case an essential determination of the end such that its species is simply part of, contained within, an essential determination of, a more fundamental species. Because the act chosen always bears a relation and proportion to the end,[18] in the case of *per se*

---

[17] Fr. Kevin Flannery, SJ, "Review of *The Teleological Grammar of the Moral Act*," *The Thomist* 72 (April 2008): 322–25.

[18] *Summa theologiae* I–II, q. 18, art. 4, ad 2: "*Ad secundum dicendum quod, quamvis finis sit causa extrinseca, tamen debita proportio ad finem et relatio in ipsum, inhaeret*"

order of object to end, it is simultaneously true (a) that the object gives species and (b) that the species given by the object is merely an essential determination or part of a more comprehensive species that is derived from the end, such that in this case the fundamental species of the act is derived from the end, the object-species being merely a further determination of that species and contained within it. And thus (c) it will also be true in the instance of *per se* order of object to end that in the very specific and precise sense of providing the *fundamental* species (for example, is this torture and mutilation, or surgical opening of the chest cavity?), the object in this sense *does not* give species. But something that is a sin will be defined by the nature of the terminus of the action both (a) in the sense of end and (b) in the sense of object, since each is distinctly a terminus of the action.

This leads to the second point, that sins are properly distinguished by their objects in such a manner as to extend both to the object of the external act and to the object of the interior act of the will (the end). Thomas seems to confirm this in q. 72, art. 1, ad 1: "The *ratio* of good is found chiefly in the end: and therefore the end stands in the relation of object to the act of the will which is at the root of every sin. Consequently it amounts to the same whether sins differ by their objects or by their ends."[19] The use of "object" here seems not to be confined simply to "object of the external act of the will." This is to say that a "sinful object" may neither be intended as an end nor chosen as a means.

The "putting aside" of intention in this article as accidental seems merely to say that what constitutes sin cannot be an accidental ordering, but rather the nature of the wrongful deed as such. However, intention of the end is taken as "accidental" in this article precisely because it is *sinful action* that is being defined, and were some act *per se* ordained to a good end, *it would be a good action; but one does not define sin as a good action, and thus the case of per se order of object to good end is immaterial to the subject defined.* By the very nature of the case, where sin is involved, *per se* order to a good end cannot be the case (because per hypothesis we know

---

actioni." "To the second it should be said that while the end is an extrinsic cause, still due proportion to the end and relation to it are inherent to the action."

[19] *Summa theologiae* I–II, q. 72, art. 1, ad 1: "Ad primum ergo dicendum quod finis principaliter habet rationem boni, et ideo comparatur ad actum voluntatis, qui est primordialis in omni peccato, sicut obiectum. Unde in idem redit quod peccata differant secundum obiecta, vel secundum fines."

that *qua* sin, its species is evil). Put differently, to *define* sin is not the same as to explain what must be done in order to know that the act in question is evil. This is to say that a voluntary act specified by a wrongful object defines it in relation to the normative order of ends; however, to know that an act *is* inordinate in this way will require that we have determined its species. But determining the species of the voluntary act cannot adequately be achieved without knowing the truth about its object, namely, whether its object is *per se* ordained to the intended end, and, of course, if so, what the species of this end may be.

Thus, the article does not address—nor does it seem intended to address—the question whether we can adequately place the object of the external act in its species prior to judging its relation to the intended end. If an act is evil, it will be a function of its object. But the chosen act of vomiting that is contrary to one's obligation to care for the gift of one's life is not morally the same as the chosen act of vomiting that is undertaken precisely to care for the gift of one's life by removing a poison that will otherwise cause grave illness or death. One may not intend sinful action as an end, nor ought one choose sinful action for the sake of something else that might be good (one may not do evil that good may come). A sinful act is defined by its *per se* order to a defective object, but determining this involves ruling out any *per se* order to a good end.

Our definition of evil can leave intention aside precisely because, *qua* evil, we know the act cannot be *per se* ordained to a good act. In determining the morality of a particular action, we thus need to make judgment positively or negatively as to whether the relation of the object of the external act to the intended end is *per se* or *per accidens*. An adequate understanding of the nature of the act chosen is essential to this process, and as noted above, it is capable of being warped by overgeneric and deficient descriptions of the action. But if we refer to an act identified in its species as evil as what simply defines it, then of course further intention is accidental; the sinful voluntary act is specified by its object. Thus, the object always gives species, but it does not always give the most formal and containing species, and in this latter case, the object gives species equivocally, in that this species is only part of a whole whose fundamental species derives from the end. Thus, it will be true to say: (a) the object of the external act always gives species; (b) the species from the object of the external act is not always most formal, but at times a part of the most formal species is derived from the end; and even that (c), in the sense of being the most formal fundamental species—the species of the act *tout court*—when the object is *per se* ordained to the intended end, the object of the external act does not give species. For example, morally speaking, opening the chest cavity in major heart surgery is simply *part of* major heart surgery, since in this act, morally speaking, "its" species "belongs" to heart surgery and is part of such surgery and so does not provide anything different *even though* it provides something. These different ways of speaking, which seem opposed, are reconcilable inasmuch as the species from the object may itself be part of a more formal and containing species—part of a whole that is the species derived from the end.

F. An Epistemic Point

In relation to what has been said above (E), it might be argued that the insistence that the object of the external act include the act itself, its integral nature, and *per se* effects—the insistence on including the act itself—unduly confuses the difference between the individual act and the type of the act. It seems to me that this is a function of nature abstracted as a whole, which can either be considered abstractly, for example, "man" (here intended as *homo*, not *vir*), or predicated individually, as in, "Socrates is a man." When considering "the act itself," one is looking to the object of the external act as a whole. This includes both the relatively more formal *ratio of appetibility* on the one side, and the act itself and its integral nature and *per se* effects on the other, within the type of formality that nature as a whole possesses. If one were to shorten this to refer simply to the integral nature and *per se* effects of the action, this would for most purposes be sufficient—because anything other, apart from *the ratio of appetibility*, will be a circumstance. Yet, a circumstance may be the principal condition of the object, and therefore bear upon the object itself rather than being a "pure" circumstance. For this reason, it seems still intelligible to me to include within the material part of the object of the external act "the act itself." And on this point, I seem to find myself in surprised and happy partial agreement with Fr. Martin Rhonheimer, athwart all our other differences.[20]

---

[20] Rhonheimer, "The Moral Object of Human Acts," 461. The agreement is "partial" because, while I believe that the act itself must be included in the object, it also

CONCLUSION

The thought of Aquinas, realistic and rigorous from start to finish, is demanding. It is also rewarding. The Magisterium of the Church has rightly always embraced the judgment that we must exert the greatest care in judging the nature of action in determining the object of the external act and moving toward judging its species and whether this species is contained in the species derived from the intended end. May those who labor through the many limitations and defects of this current work be moved by it to turn to St. Thomas's writing, whose speculative light and universality render it to be the most centrally crucial, perennially valid, and comprehensive work of *sacra doctrina* ever written.

---

seems to me that the integral nature and *per se* effects of the act are included materially in the object of the external act, the formal part of the object being the *ratio of appetibility* for the act.

Introduction

THE ENSUING ACCOUNT seeks to fill a very specific need: the need for a primer to articulate the doctrine of St. Thomas Aquinas regarding the intention, choice, object, end, and species of the moral act. It seeks to do so by summarizing, and by providing illustrative applications of, the teaching of St. Thomas Aquinas. This is a highly controverted area of study. The diverse reading of cases by contemporary authors proceeding from nearly identical principles regarding the moral object seems to *exceed* the quotient of disagreement that any application of principle may occasion: and it is this which to my mind invites and requires a project more fundamental than criticism. The very datum that even those who hold roughly the same principles do not achieve consensus on certain prominent cases seems to indicate that intuition is playing a larger role than the principles themselves.[1] And whereas

---

[1] For example, it seems that Germain Grisez, Fr. Martin Rhonheimer, and William May share a similar view of the object of the moral act as simply that which the agent proposes to himself, rather than as ineluctably and materially including the act itself and its integral nature. Yet they disagree amongst themselves regarding whether married couples with AIDS may rightly have as their "proposal for action" the use of a condom to prevent transmission of disease (Rhonheimer thinks this is licit; Grisez and May disagree). They also disagree whether craniotomy (the crushing of the skull of a child to remove it from the birth canal) can ever be a reasonable act (Grisez believes this can be licit; May disagrees). These differences appear to be a function, not of the account of the nature of the object of the moral act, but of the relative degrees of possession of what one might call "good moral intuition." Yet it should be a desideratum of theory to enable one to reach correct generic accounts of moral acts. An account of the moral object which leaves so much to repose upon intuition runs the risk of using the language of Thomas Aquinas while more closely

this will always, to some degree, be true of *prudence*, it ought not—or so it seems to this author—be true of the generic consideration of the object (as, e.g., in the case of craniotomy, or of use of condoms by married couples). Hence a different and more systematic consideration of the elements in play is required. And so this book is not chiefly a critical work ordered to dialectical engagement with contemporary theory of moral action.[2]

Misinterpretations of the nature of the object of the moral act call for an historico-doctrinal rectification and refutation in relation to St. Thomas's

---

approximating the thought of G. E. Moore. For their various views of the object see John F°innis, Germain Grisez, and Joseph Boyle, " 'Direct' and 'Indirect': A Reply to Critics of Our Action Theory," *The Thomist* 65 (2001): 1–44; Fr. Martin Rhonheimer, *The Tablet,* July 10, 2004, and his *Natural Law and Practical Reason: A Thomist View of Moral Autonomy,* trans. Gerald Malsbary (New York: Fordham University Press, 2000); and William May, in his essay to be found at www.christendom-awake.org/pages/may/veritas.htm titled "Pope John Paul II's Encyclical *Veritatis Splendor*".

2 Among such works, I should say that Fr. Stephen Brock's *Action and Conduct* (Edinburgh: T&T Clark, 1998) and the work of Fr. Kevin Flannery, S.J., *Acts Amid Precepts* (Washington, DC: Catholic University of America Press, 2001) stand out as clearly superior. Yet neither of these fine works, with all their strengths, seem to me to carry the analysis of the teleological grammar that governs the constitution of the object and species of the moral act to its systematic completion, although each is laudably cognizant of the crucial role of teleology. One notes that Fr. Brock's analysis of private lethal defense presupposes a univocal sense of "intention" and does not identify the *per se* case of the human act most formally referred to by St. Thomas when he writes in *Summa theologiae (ST)* II–II, q. 64, a. 7 that what is *praeter intentionem* is accidental to the species derived from what is intended. On the other hand Fr. Brock's implicit judgment that the integral nature of the act is to be included within the moral object, and his analysis of craniotomy, are outstanding. Fr. Flannery's account of private defense, and of craniotomy, seem to me brilliantly correct, while nonetheless needing firmer clarification not alone in terms of the *acts and practices constitutive of given disciplines, but of natural teleology as such.* The marked advance in analysis which Fr. Flannery achieves by bringing in natural teleology under the *ratio* of *practices of a discipline* is a genuine contribution. But there remains a need to articulate a systematic account showing how unified natural teleology founds and diversifies the disciplines and their practices. For why is it that properly speaking craniotomy is not a medical act, other than that its motion directly terminates in harm to a being rather than health to a being? And why is this case different than that of defense, save that the teleology of defense, and that of medicine, are distinct? The *purpose,* the very *natural teleology,* of the medical art, is not defense but health, and there is no proper issue of defense against a human person who is not performing conduct (one may seek to *avert* natural menace—short of directly harming or killing an innocent—but this is not properly speaking defense).

actual teaching. Elsewhere I have attempted to offer a model for the shape of such a refutation,[3] and am persuaded that it can be sustained against the most rigorous textual criticisms. Indeed there is need for a thorough textual re-reading of Thomas's teaching on the object and species of the moral act in relation to a renewed appreciation of his defense of unified teleology and the central illustration of his teaching regarding private defense in *Summa theologiae (ST)* II–II, q. 64, a. 7. Such a complete study would attempt to bring into detailed focus both the profound unity of these elements with one another and right reason, and the fashion in which the commentatorial lucidity of Vitoria and other Thomists reasoning independently of Cajetan's nuanced but arguably subtly disequilibrating account can augment and aid in the development of St. Thomas's teaching.

Yet, nonetheless, this is not *that* book. It is not either of the types of book mentioned above, and this for several prominent reasons.

WHY A SPECULATIVE PRIMER IS NECESSARY

This book is not the rich reworking of all Thomas's texts which, paradigmatically speaking, could suffice to persuade an open mind of the need to read Thomas's account more coherently and holistically. Rather, it is a speculative account of the nature and implications of certain crucial principles of St. Thomas regarding the object and species of the moral act. Nor is this book designed to be a thorough engagement with and criticism of contemporary theory regarding the object and species of the moral act, but rather to unfold the positive analysis upon which such criticism necessarily depends. The exigency for such a book is great. Here I will simply list a few of the reasons prompting the writing of such a book.

1. Although I am persuaded that the right way to read St. Thomas is eminently defensible with respect to his text, there is more involved here than merely St. Thomas's text. The issues concerned touch the moral analysis of the most prominent issues of the day, issues on which frankly many moral theologians seem frequently on the verge—or past

---

[3] Cf. my essay "A Brief Disquisition Regarding the Nature of the Object of the Moral Act According to St. Thomas Aquinas," *The Thomist* 67 (2003): 45–71; "Regarding the Nature of the Moral Object and Intention: A Response to Steven Jensen," *Nova et Vetera* 3 (2005): 101–8.

it—of speaking nonsense. So, for the sake of the truth of the matter, a more direct and speculative consideration is required deriving from the text of Thomas as *fons et origo*, but whose principal objective is briefly, yet at the appropriate theoretical level, to articulate the truth of the matter. One need only think of recent controverted issues—the use of condoms by spouses who suffer with AIDS, or what some wish to call the "rescue" or "adoption" of frozen embryonic human beings by placing them in the wombs of surrogate mothers. These and other kindred issues will continue to surface, and their solution requires a cogent understanding of intention, choice, object, end, and moral species.

2. Works that articulate what has come to be known as the "new natural law theory" associated with Germain Grisez, John Finnis, and Joseph Boyle—an account which defends even the licity of the direct crushing of fetal skulls in craniotomy—abound. Yet there is a lacuna with respect to the articulation of Thomas's own account of human action theory.[4] Clearly the traditional account of St. Thomas deserves a hearing, and it has as yet not received one in most academic centers and seminaries in the first world. In this respect, I have that most delightful and noblest of motives to send me into action: my friends have requested that I write such a book. In fact, I have received several requests from various academic sources seeking a work which would lay out the speculative basics of St. Thomas's account of the object and species of the moral act. Because understanding the teleological grammar governing the constitution of the object and species of the moral act is essential to sound moral analysis, it is critical to set forth Thomas's account of the same.

3. With respect to the philosophic and scholarly defense of this account as an *interpretation* of the work of Aquinas, scholars will realize that there is no end to the turning over of texts. In two earlier essays,[5] I have set forth the requisite interpretative judgments. However, it is well known

---

[4] To reiterate, Fr. Flannery is to be applauded for moving in the direction of a more thoroughly teleological account, while such a theoretical effort, to be both comprehensive and coherent, seems further to demand being put on a thorough footing of natural teleology rather than merely of the practices of disciplines (which of course exhibit teleological structure).

[5] Cf. note 3 above.

that once one begins to read texts in a certain way, it can become diffi-cult to break out of the *gestalt* of one's own reading.

If, on the other hand, one holds that Thomas's teaching provides real-ist principles sufficient for the moral analysis of human action, then another way of testing one's reading is to see whether one may generate from it any conclusion which is palpably absurd either in relation to St. Thomas's texts or from the point of view of moral intelligence generally. Hence it becomes critical to sail one's account into the open waters of moral analysis. This latter test has the added benefit of directly contribut-ing to the soundness of general moral reason—either by providing ample occasion for the refutation of one's errors, or by the vindication of the analysis one's account provides. It is this path, therefore, that I follow, happy to indicate the sources for my judgments, along the way, as to what does and does not constitute a genuinely Thomistic engagement with the questions at hand. Allow me to say again, that the failure to pursue these issues by way of dialectical engagement with the work of others implies no derogation of such engagement or of the importance of contemporaneous treatment of these issues. But contemporary authors would be correct were they, in possession of a different work criticizing their positions, to say: "Very well: how, then, do you account for all the varied elements that must enter into this consideration?" Indeed, providing the answer to that question provides the basis for further dialectical engagement. Accord-ingly, this is the path here chosen.

THE STRUCTURE OF THE PRESENT WORK

The present work will proceed in much the way in which I begin with interested students who have become aware that the nature of the object and species of the moral act is now a disputed question, or who have dis-covered those schools of interpretation which treat the object of the moral act exclusively as a proposal enjoying logical existence in the mind and deprived of natural foundation.

First, certain preliminary issues such as the definition of choice and intention, means and end, and more fundamentally the nature of the *ratio boni* and of the natural hierarchy of ends prior to choice are summarily treated. This provides the background for a systematically unified teleology as decisive for moral reflection. Then subsequent attention focuses upon the nature and relations obtaining among the object of the moral act, the end or telos of action, and the moral species of action. This analysis presupposes a certain general level of knowledge, and does not consider all the questions which, *simpliciter*, it might be desirable to take up. For the purpose is to move to the high ground of interpretation regarding the nature of the moral object and its relation to the end sought by action and the moral species of the act chosen and performed. It is maximal theoretic leverage with respect to these considerations, and not all the other matters with which such considerations may be aligned, that forms the target.

In particular, this latter part of the first chapter of the book will exhibit the natural teleological grammar for the constitution of the moral species and the moral object, and show that these elements of St. Thomas's moral analysis are thoroughly saturated with natural teleology in such a manner that they cannot properly be understood without it.

In the second chapter of the book, I apply the teaching of the first part to the strategic proving ground of the analysis of private defense—for it is in regard to the explicit teaching of Thomas on private defense that misreadings of St. Thomas's account of the moral object predictably yield the most thorough distortion. After showing that Thomas's actual account of object, end, and species yields a reasonable reading of *ST* II–II, q. 64, a. 7, I also revisit the effort to retain and vindicate erroneous action theory in relation to the question of just private defense by means of the theory that such defense is deputized by state authority. This theory of deputization provides an excellent illustration of a theory coined wholly for the purpose of avoiding the oddities which ensue when one conjoins erroneous action theory with St. Thomas's express teaching about private defense.

The third chapter takes up the question of the need for some general principle or distinctive schema of "double effect" apart from St. Thomas's basic account of the moral act. It argues that many cases which are thought to require such treatment in fact do not, and that even those cases which meet the standard conditions for double effect reasoning will not be properly understood apart from the St. Thomas's foundational teleological analysis of the moral act. Accordingly, that foundational teleological analysis is prior. Whereas the standard conditions for double effect reasoning may be derived from applying St. Thomas's general analysis to the restricted category of cases requiring such treatment, these standard conditions are doomed to be misunderstood when considered apart from that general analysis. Hence this chapter addresses the quite limited role and usefulness of a doctrine of double effect. It fittingly follows the chapter on private defense, because most accounts of double effect set out from the article of St. Thomas's *Summa theologiae* are devoted to this issue.

In an appendix to the text I address a variety of more or less difficult particular applications of St. Thomas's basic theory of moral action. The aim here is to showcase the eminent applicability and indeed viability of St. Thomas's teleological account to contemporaneous complicated moral issues. Whereas oftentimes such difficult cases are treated in a freestanding manner—apart both from foundational consideration of the basic teleology of the moral act—here the intention is otherwise. Further, such cases are often treated as though they constituted the most critical test for moral action theory. Yet they are in fact a minute percentage of actual cases and their correct treatment is epistemically derivative from the basic teleological account of human action. Nonetheless, it is important to treat such cases both for their own sakes and for the sake of exemplifying the traction which sound analysis provides even in the most difficult instances. However, there should be no doubt as to which is the dog, and which is the tail: I would request that readers of this work bestow their principal attention to the foundational analysis given within the body of the text, and attend to the analysis of difficult cases in the appendix with the awareness that these are merely attempts to apply that prior account to a category of penumbral cases which will always involve a measure of perplexity.

AGAIN: THE PURPOSE OF THIS BOOK

The aim of this book is to show the essential unity, suppleness, and teleological realism of St. Thomas's moral teaching and its principled adequacy with respect to contemporary moral questions. *In particular, it seeks to vindicate the speculative intelligibility and coherence of St. Thomas's account of the teleological grammar governing the constitution of the object and species of the moral act.* It is not the aim of this book to engage with the contemporary discussions that swirl about all these questions, nor is it to provide a thorough and completely detailed historico-doctrinal account—although each of these is a worthwhile endeavor.

Hence this work sets out to articulate one coherent analysis, which never requires anything like a special schema of "double effect" but which simply pertains to a particular category of acts in a distinctive fashion. Even in those cases wherein the standard conditions of what is called the "principle of double effect" apply, it nonetheless remains the case that the intelligibility of these standard conditions *is wholly a function of St. Thomas's one teleological schema for understanding the object and moral species of acts.*

This writing of this book has been catalyzed by the judgment that it is the loss of natural teleology within action theory that has caused this theory to become eviscerated of nature and distorted, and likewise that it is for this reason that the teaching of St. Thomas has come to be seen by some as lacking inner coherence and structure. Yet, once the requisite distinctions have been made, the hall of mirrors of an over-idealizing or logicist contemporary action theory—which has developed in default of a more profound insight into the role of nature and natural teleology—largely dissipates, revealing the essential role of nature and of natural teleology in the understanding of human action. In short, without understanding St. Thomas's account of the teleological grammar governing the constitution of object and species of the moral act, one is lost.

Thus, steering between the contemporary difficulties, on the one hand, and deeper and more thorough historico-doctrinal examination, on the other, I here set forth a principled account of St. Thomas's teaching regarding the object and species of the moral act. It adverts to Thomas's text where textual plausibility is at stake, and for the sake of sheer reference and intellectual justice. But chiefly it seeks to explain and to defend—with the distinctions requisite to *scientia*—the truth and adequacy of St. Thomas's account of the object and species of the moral act.

It should be clear, then, that this is not a work which serves as a complete account of the moral life—any more than the sections in the *Summa theologiae* concerning the object and species of the moral act, and all that is presupposed to understand these sections, would enable one to do without the fuller treatment of law, grace, and virtue that ensue in the remainder of the *prima secundae* and *secunda secundae*. Among the considerations that strategically advance St. Thomas's teleological moral teaching are:

- The correct account of the relation of speculative and practical knowledge;

- the teleology of nature, inclusive of the unified hierarchy of ends, as divinely constituting the passive participation in the eternal law upon which our active, rational, perceptive participation is based;

- synderesis;

- naturally acquired, and theologically infused, virtue;

- the theocentricity of the natural law;

- the inferiority of natural law to the nobler participation of the eternal law known as *gratia*; and,

- the natural centrality of prudence, and the overarching role of charity as the form of every good.

Yet in this present work these are considered either not at all, or only to the degree to which they shed light upon, or prepare for the shedding of light upon, the object and species of the moral act. For example, even essentially unified natural teleology prior to choice is considered only because it is necessary to indicate the natural context defining all moral discourse and inasmuch as St. Thomas's teaching presupposes and formally implies a prior speculative defense of unified teleology.

Thus, although it is crucial for the later unfolding of our contemplation of law, grace, and virtue that we properly understand the object and species of the moral act—for errors regarding *what* is lawful, regarding *with what sorts of acts* the life of grace is *compatible*, and regarding *what is, and what is not, virtuous*, all flow from errors regarding the object and species of the moral act—*nonetheless,* these wider considerations of law, grace, and virtue stand closer to the end sought in the contemplation of the nature of the good life.[6] Yet these considerations are all radically inexplicable without

---

6 Over the past 15 years several important works have appeared contributing to the recovery of a sapiential moral theology and philosophy. Hence we find such masterful achievements as *The Sources of Christian Ethics*, trans. Mary Thomas Noble, O.P. (Washington, DC: Catholic University of America Press, 1995) and *Morality: The Catholic View*, trans. Fr. Michael Sherwin, O.P. (South Bend, IN: St. Augustine's Press, 2003), both by Fr. Servais Pinckaers, O.P.; the scripturally profound *Living the Truth in Love* (New York: Alba House, 1996) by Fr. Benedict Ashley, O.P.;

prior consideration of natural teleology and its normative role in the constitution of the object and species of the moral act. Hence the more or less straightforward casuistry involved in handling difficult cases is—when it serves the purpose of articulating the teleological structure of the moral act—*per se* ordered toward contemplation of *habitus, lex,* and *gratia.* Further, it presupposes virtue—as the *per accidens* presupposes the *per se*—because the principles pertinent to the hard cases are developed and first understood with respect to the ordinary life of virtue.[7] There is a certain reciprocal causality—a natural recognition of *per se* teleological order as pertinent to morality unfolding in daily life, leading to the express garnering of the character of this order and its importance for the object and species of the moral act. The latter, then, comes to be reflectively appropriated and further applied to vexing moral questions.

If anything should be clear by the end of this book it should be the case for the vindication of the teleological grammar governing the constitution of the object and species of the moral act. The idea that nature and natural order can largely be exorcized from moral action theory is gravely erroneous—not only with reference to the teaching of St. Thomas Aquinas, but even more vitally and profoundly, as regards the truth of the matter. To this effort of disclosure the following pages are dedicated.

Ralph McInerny's pellucid *Ethica Thomistica* (Washington, DC: Catholic University of America Press, 1997); Russell Hittinger's incisively penetrating *The First Grace: Rediscovering the Natural Law in the Post-Christian World* (Wilmington, DE: ISI Books, 2003); and of course the rich works of Fr. Romanus Cessario, O.P., *The Moral Virtues and Theological Ethics* (Notre Dame, IN: University of Notre Dame Press, 1992) and *Introduction to Moral Theology* (Washington, DC: Catholic University of America Press, 2001). More recently, and unfolding along these lines, we have the fine work of Fr. Michael Sherwin, O.P., *By Knowledge and By Love: Charity and Knowledge in the Moral Theology of St. Thomas Aquinas* (Washington, DC: Catholic University of America Press, 2005). My book seeks to address one formal part of the teaching of St. Thomas Aquinas that is crucial for harvesting the benefit of the aforementioned works, and for properly understanding the profound teachings of the papal encyclical *Veritatis Splendor.*

7 Ordinary perception of teleological order is actually implicit in the recognition of efficient causality, and particularly with respect to human action. This is one reason why accounts of natural law, virtue, and teleology perpetually recrudesce. Of course, teleological knowledge is presupposed by the ordinary life of virtue. But it is at root natural, and meditations on it of a philosophic sort presuppose this natural knowledge at the root of ordinary virtue.

CHAPTER ONE

■■■

The Teleological Constitution of Object and Moral Species

Preliminary remarks on choice and intention, the means and the end; on the essential hierarchy of human ends prior to choice, happiness, and the good life

ST. THOMAS, as is well-known, makes the distinction between human acts and what have come to be known as "acts of man." A human act is an act performed consequent on choice following from knowledge—an act proceeding from intellect and will—whereas an "act of man" is an act performed by a human being that does not proceed from intellect and will. Choice is the termination of deliberation or consideration of the contingent means to some particular desired end, and is while formally an act of the intellect as directing one to the act, nonetheless substantively an act of the will. After a choice has been made about a more remote matter, a subsequent command of the intellect, *imperium,* may direct us to carry out the choice: for example, one chooses to leave work at 5 P.M., and then, at 5 P.M., the intellect directs the will to execute the decision previously made (if circumstances are not judged to have changed decisively, and of course presuming that the will remains constant). Choice concerns variable means to the end sought.

As St. Thomas constantly insists, intention is an act of will presupposing knowledge and is chiefly of the end. By contrast, choice is materially of the will, but formally of the reason, and is substantially of the will because choice involves a movement toward the good that is chosen. As for intention being of the end, a sign of this is that we may intend the end prior to the allocation of any means whatsoever.[1] I may intend to go to school before I identify a way to fund my schooling; to marry a woman before I know how and where I will "pop the question." Intention is of the end, and choice is of the variable means to the end.

It is a fundamental truth of ethics, and one which modern thought globally ignores, that choice is *not* of the end *qua* end. The reason for this is clear: choice is of the variable means to the end. If no end is given naturally, then of course it follows that naturally speaking no issue with respect to the possible means can arise.

Or, to put it differently, let us undertake the thought experiment of conceiving what would be involved in creating an end. It may seem, superficially viewed, as though we perform this activity all the time. For example, before Steve Jobs and his hearty crew at Apple, Inc., designed my 17″ laptop, I didn't want one. Indeed, in the old days no one had yet thought of placing the hinge all the way at the bottom of the screen and making the screen wider, so that one could open a 17″ laptop *on an airplane*. After Jobs & Co. provided the laptop, *I wanted one*. Did not S. Jobs & Co. then *create an end*? After all, I wanted the laptop only after they made it. Similarly, this might seem true of penicillin, and of many other good things we may come to want. If the avian flu becomes pandemic amongst human beings, we will all want whatever immunization shot can be designed. Why isn't this precisely "creating an end"?

The reason is that, strictly speaking, we want something else first, in terms of which the laptop, or the penicillin, or the immunization shot, are desirable as means. To take the last point first, we desire health as the reason for the immunization shot. Were we not to desire health first, the immunization shot would not be desirable. Ditto for penicillin. Or, we desire to do our work well, even elegantly well, and so we prefer good operating systems to lame ones—and so on. At the font of every contingent choice, we will see there is not alone the proximate end, but a further and natural end which accounts for our desire for the proximate end. Further, we will see, if we consider the matter carefully, that these natural ends are not just a dis- or non-ordered plenum, for they exhibit an intelligible order. For example: life is desirable in itself; but it is also and chiefly desirable as

---

[1] *Summa theologiae ST* I–II, q. 12, a. 4, ad 3; see also *ST* I–II, q. 12, a. 1; *ST* I–II, q. 12, a. 3.

existing for the sake of further ends, such as the achievement of wisdom, virtue, holiness, happiness. All genuine ends of human striving participate in the ordered whole of a good life, and have their place within this ordered whole. Prior to choice, it is clear that the end of friendship is nobler than the end of nutrition, even though nutrition is necessary if we are to live and have friends. But friendship is nobler because it is more proximate to the *finis ultimus*, the final end, of the ordered whole of a good life. We would be more disposed to think a man noble who was willing to go without food for the sake of his friend, than to think a man noble who was willing to go without friends for the sake of food. Yet food and friends are both goods which participate in the ordered whole of a good life.

Aristotle and St. Thomas Aquinas locate the ultimate end of the good life in "happiness," but this term is much misunderstood. It is not merely subjective fulfillment, but the achievement of the good. Hence, Aristotle said that children cannot be "happy"—because happiness means here not joy or exuberance (although it may contain these), but rather the achievement of those ends that define a good life, and this is the work of a lifetime, a work requiring both practical and speculative virtue as authentically *perfective* of the person. Hence the hierarchy of natural ends, prior to any human choice, orients the compass of human persons with respect to the definition of the good life. This hierarchy cannot, by itself, lead to correct choice, because also needed is the speculative and practical virtue of prudence whereby we both judge rightly of our particular circumstances and possess the dominion over ourselves to command the right actions. But without knowledge of the hierarchy of ends—some of which is given naturally and immediately, and some of which requires reflection and inference—human action lacks the compass necessary to discern the objective. Even if we need for a time prudentially to tack against the wind, or to take a detour that mandates that we go west in order, finally, to turn east, the wise will orient themselves in terms of the hierarchy of natural ends as a condition of knowing whether they are moving closer toward, or further from, the ends of a good life.

In any case: without a natural end, either we could never begin to act—because there would, naturally speaking, be nothing to desire, and nothing to fear (because fear is rooted in the awareness of dangers to our possession of the good)—or, if, *per miraculem,* we could begin to act, we could never end (because our acts would lack any natural point of termination). Hence it is not simply that action without natural ends would be "bad"—that is not in the least what is at stake. Rather, it is that action without natural ends is strictly and absolutely *impossible*. We cannot even define what we mean by an efficient cause—a cause that *brings about* its effect or what is sometimes called either a productive cause, or a cause of motion—without referring to the end to which it is ordered. Try, for example to define the act of "snow shoveling" without any mention that the purpose of the act is to move snow by means of some shovel-like implement.

Some authors have denied that any essential hierarchy of ends exists prior to choice, claiming that "basic" ends or goods are "incommensurable," that is, literally incomparable. The idea is that there is no way to *quantify* such ends, and that therefore they exhibit no natural normative order pertinent to ethics prior to a supervening choice. But this idea of incommensurability is predicated upon an incorrect inference. For while ends are not quantifiable, that in no way militates against natural hierarchy. That one eats not solely for nutrition, but in order to pursue the higher ends to which nutrition and bodily health are ordered—such as friendship, wisdom, and the like—does not establish any quantitative relation whatsoever. Indeed, the idea of incommensurable goods exhibits a fallacy similar to the idea that we could absolutely speaking and in the absence of natural ends, *create* our own ends. How is it similar? If no one of the basic goods is objectively ordered to the rest, then there is never any sufficient reason for anyone to seek such a good, because such a good is wholly separate from the basic end of the ordered whole of a good life: there is no reason to call it "good." That is to say, no incommensurable good leads to the final end of a good life (because it is not comparable to any other good). If these incommensurable goods are not objectively ordered to the final end of human striving, to the ordered whole of a good life, *why then do we call them "goods"*?

Further still, there would never be reason to move from the pursuit of one such good to the pursuit of any other, for these basic goods as *incomparable* would simply not exist in any fundamental *order vis-à-vis* one another *as goods*. Hence, prior to choice, these goods do not define the ordered whole of the good life, and any shift from the pursuit of one to the pursuit of another is by the nature of the case wholly and entirely subjective. *But this is merely the apotheosis of subjectivity versus natural teleology with which we have already dealt above.* Nor is it consistent with human experience: we see, for example, that the good of practical reasonableness is more fundamental in a good life than the good of play, even though no one will wish to deny that playfulness is involved in a good life. And when it is time to determine whether to persist in play, this determination is made with respect to practical reasonableness, which thus clearly has a superordinate status relative to play.

Nor is teleological order confined to human matters. It is efficient causality absolutely speaking that cannot be explicated without final causality (i.e., the ordering to the end for the sake of which things exist and act). For example, some may see in evolution the denial of teleology. But the fact remains that when we modify the genes associated with the eyes of flies, we get flies with funky eyes; when we modify the genes associated with the wings of flies, we get flies with no wings, or too many wings, or oddly mutated wings. This is far from randomness. To the contrary, if evolutionary theory involved absolute randomness, then when we altered the gene associated with the eyes of flies, we would occasionally get, say, Barbara Streisand or an ocean liner. To the contrary, all the way down to the genetic level—and further—efficient causality requires finality for its intelligibility.

Of course, that some mammal wanders too close to a radioactive source and so has its genes altered in either a favorable or unfavorable way, is a matter of "chance"—of the novel coming together of causes whose results we may not at first be able to predict. But the obscurity of this "chance" is purely epistemic, purely a matter of our failure adequately to fathom the distinct causal intelligibilities in play, and indeed such chance presupposes intelligible causal order: that is, the novel coming together of causes that brings about a certain effect. It is no part of the vindication of a teleological universe to affirm that causal sequences never intersect in a novel way. But for the theory of evolution even possibly to work, there must indeed be a means whereby genetic alterations are intelligibly passed on to future members of the species, without which evolution would explain nothing: and yet, this biological means whereby mutative changes are passed along to future members of the species is a classic instance of efficient causality ordered toward certain ends.

Only if someone is willing to deny the wealth of genetic research is the denial of finality an intelligible denial, because evolutionary theory asserts, strongly asserts, efficiency, and efficiency implies finality (else we cannot so much as define efficiency). Likewise, whenever contemporary physicists speak of a multiverse, or parallel universes, it should be asked how it is possible to know of the existence of such universes unless there is intersecting causality: and if there is intersecting causality, there is one causal order, that is, a *cosmos*, a *universe*, an *ordered whole*. In both cases we see that the basis on which unified teleology is denied, when adequately considered, instead implies and requires unified teleology.

Some critics, of course, get the sequence of inferences wrong: they assert that teleological order exists *because* it is true that God exists. But the natural order of discovery is the opposite of this: our minds move from unified efficiency and finality (teleology) in the universe to the judgment that God—first efficient and ultimate final cause—exists. That this requires realism with respect to the account of knowledge, and a strong metaphysical vindication of causality, if of course true. Implicitly one might think that these should be understood as a condition of entering into ethical philosophy proper, because the order of the universe, and the relation obtaining among *being* and *good* and *true*, are presupposed to ethical wisdom. For present purposes however, it is sufficient to indicate that ethical wisdom presupposes realism, presupposes that the mind knows the real extending from the reality of human nature and its teleological dynamisms to the truth of the proposition that there is a First Cause that is alike Final End of all created being.

Of course, much more might be said about realism, and natural teleology. But we have said enough to indicate the horizon of human action—naturally ordered toward ends, which are pursued by means. And the end is chiefly a function of *intention*, whereas choice is chiefly *of the means*.

This natural teleology is the very foundation of ethics, for were human nature not objectively ordered toward ends which define the good life, there would be no natural reason for acting nor natural standard for acting virtuously or viciously. Of course some contemporary ethicists, laboring under the influence of the teaching of David Hume, remain inclined to the judgment that "one cannot get an ought from an is." It is true that one cannot get an "ought" from any type of "is" whatsoever; for instance, the fact that people eat one another is not a sign that they should. But it is deeply muddled thinking to suppose that therefore the "ought" is no kind of "is" whatsoever, for we rightly wonder: what kind of thing *is* an ought? That the ought is an entailment regarding the perfection achieved through acting in a way rightly ordered to the ends defining a good life, is the classical answer of Aristotle and of Aquinas as well. To deny universal teleology merely to conciliate modern and postmodern critics exacts a high cost in intelligibility which there is absolutely no objective reason for anyone to pay: or rather, if this toll is to be paid, then the cost is the abolition of causal reasoning as such, since to be an efficient cause is to be ordered toward a natural terminus for the sake of which and in terms of which the action is understood. That some may have drawn inappropriate particular inferences from the reality of natural teleology no more invalidates natural teleology, than errors in physical theory invalidates the pertinence of mathematics and experiment to theoretical physics.

One should also observe that the abstraction from natural teleology for particular cognitive purposes proves precisely nothing regarding the non-existence of teleology or its putative non-fundamentality for moral truth. That one may *abstract* from X hardly is sufficient to demonstrate that X does not exist, or that X is not normative for moral knowledge.

It might be supposed by some that truths regarding natural teleology are merely speculative, and that because truths regarding agency are practical that these accordingly are not derivative from speculative truths. But it will not do to say that truths about natural teleology are speculative and therefore do not contain reasons for action: for precisely what defines the teleology of human nature is that it constitutes *reasons for action. Prior to any practical agency of the human subject, one must know the end which one then ensuingly comes to desire.* Now this knowledge which precedes desire as the condition of desire is *speculative*. Yet while it is accidental to the thing known that it spark desire, it is not accidental to the nature of the agent that the agent be ordered to certain things as ends. And so, this originatively speculative knowledge becomes objectively practical when, inciting desire, the agent is now ordered to this end as something to be achieved by transitive activity, as opposed to intransitive or contemplative activity. *The good known and desired by the agent, taken precisely as defining a field of operation, is essentially a practical object; and yet, even this essentially practical object (a given field of operation in relation to an end) may then be contemplated speculatively, that is, not with a view to action* hic et nunc, *but simply for the sake of contemplating the essential structure of the good life, the* ratio bonitatis.

Thus, St. Thomas in the following two quotations from the same article of the *Summa theologiae* articulates, with precision, both the nature of, and the distinction between, the speculative and the practical:

> Now, to a thing apprehended by the intellect, it is accidental whether it be directed to operation or not, and according to this the speculative and practical intellects differ. For it is the speculative intellect which directs what it apprehends, not to operation, but solely to the consideration of truth; while the practical intellect is that which directs what it apprehends to operation.[2]
>
> The object of the practical intellect is good directed to operation, and under the aspect of truth. For the practical intellect knows truth, just as the speculative, but it directs the known truth to operation.[3]

While the speculative intellect is ordered simply to the consideration of truth, *practical* knowledge adds a *further ordination toward operation*. Inasmuch as the practical intellect knows truth "just as the speculative" but is distinct from the speculative only in "directing the known truth to operation," it would appear that the notion of a truth with no speculative content whatsoever is alien to the thought of Aquinas: a contradiction in terms.[4]

---

[2] *ST* I, q. 79, a. 11: "Accidit autem alicui apprehenso per intellectum, quod ordinetur ad opus, vel non ordinetur. Secundum hoc autem differunt intellectus speculativus et practicus. Nam intellectus speculativus est, qui quod apprehendit, non ordinat ad opus, sed ad solam veritatis considerationem: practicus vero intellectus dicitur, qui hoc quod apprehendit, ordinat ad opus."

[3] Ibid., ad 2: "ita obiectum intellectus practici est bonum ordinabile ad opus, sub ratione veri. Intellectus enim practicus veritatem cognoscit sicut speculativus; sed veritatem cognitam ordinat ad opus."

[4] One notes on this score—ensconced in a treatment of art—Thomas's cognate observation in *De veritate* q. 2, a. 8, resp.: "Sed sciendum, quod artifex de operabili habet duplicem cognitionem: scilicet speculativam et practicam. Speculativam quidem, sive theoricam cognitionem habet, cum rationes operis cognoscit sine hoc quod ad operandum per intentionem applicet; sed tunc proprie habet practicam cognitionem quando extendit per intentionem rationes operis ad operationis finem; et secundum hoc medicina dividitur in theoricam et practicam, ut Avicenna dicit. Ex quo patet quod cognitio artificis practica sequitur cognitionem eius speculativam, cum practica efficiatur per extensionem speculativae ad opus. Remoto autem posteriori remanet prius."—"But the knowledge that an artist has about something that can be made is of two kinds: speculative and practical. He has speculative or theoretical knowledge when he knows the intimate nature of a work but does not have the intention of applying the principles to the production of the work. His knowledge is practical,

Moreover, it is exclusively the rational intent to direct the known truth to operation that causes the accident (*vis-à-vis truth* as such) of some knowledge being practical. Yet, as noted above, while it is accidental to that which is known simply as known that it spark desire in the agent, it is not accidental to the nature of the agent to be ordered to that which is known as an end. So, some objects are naturally and objectively practical in the sense that their definition involves operation: for example, "seeking to do justice" is by nature and objectively a practical object. Yet, for this practical object to exist is something strictly derivative from the appetition subsequent on a knowing that is naturally speculative.

Further, even an objectively practical object may be considered in a speculative manner, that is, not in order here and now practically to augment action toward the end of the operation considered, but rather instead simply to contemplate the nature of the ordered whole of the good life. Hence one may contemplate the practical life in a speculative manner, and this contemplation will then subsequently *enrich* one's practical agency by providing a firmer and more rational context for action that may inspire one by entering into one's motivation.

In any case, the naïve insistence upon a dichotomy between nature and the good, between "fact" and "value" is a philosophically unsustainable position.[5] Moreover, it is very clearly a position that St. Thomas Aquinas never

---

properly speaking, when by his intention he ordains the principles of the work to operation as an end. In this way, as Avicenna says, medicine is divided into theoretical and practical. *It is clear that the practical knowledge of an artist follows his speculative knowledge, since it is made practical by applying the speculative to a work. But when the practical is absent, the speculative remains*" (my emphasis—SL). These remarks once more indicate that for St. Thomas Aquinas practical knowledge always presupposes this underlying speculative element: precisely the point at issue in the discussions with the theorists of the New Natural Law Theory.

[5] It is good to see certain analytic thinkers—after generations of analytic thought largely saturated with such errors—gradually breaking free of them. As a historical matter, the anti-teleological divorce of nature and good is of Humean provenance, and it should not be denied that this teaching has, until only comparatively recently, been of disproportionate influence within English analytic thought— where it still exerts a strong fascination. To deny this would be simply historically and doctrinally incorrect. Yet it is a good sign that recent analytic theorists such as Hilary Putnam (*The Collapse of the Fact/Value Dichotomy* [Cambridge: Harvard University Press, 2004]) now oppose such absolute dichotomization of "is" and "ought." Of course, one ought not forget that Putnam also is the author of *Ethics Without Ontology* (Cambridge: Harvard University Press, 2005). And surely this

held, and which hence can only be imputed to him by superimposing alien philosophic presuppositions upon his text and teaching. Although books can, and have, been written about these subjects of the relation of being and good,[6] and on the fundamentality of natural teleology for ethics,[7] for the present this must be our last word. But after all, how could an ought *not* be a species of *is*? Because, there truly is moral virtue, excellence, and obligation; there truly are ends to which human nature is ordered and which are definitory of human perfection. Every practical ordering presupposes a prior *speculum*, like the bit of matter around which a pearl forms. Natural teleology is no more devoid of reasons for action, than natural desire consequent on knowledge is devoid of practical import, or than being is deprived of good. Indeed, the shoe is on the other foot: without natural teleology no reasons for action exist and in fact no action is possible. To grasp a reason for action is to refer, either normatively or privatively (in the case of appetites unrectified by reason which thus are disproportionate to the good) to natural teleology.

OBJECT, END, AND MORAL SPECIES

But we have yet to make the acquaintance of the principal guest at the feast, namely, the object of the moral act, and its relation to the end, and to the moral species of the act. It is to these considerations that we must now turn.

The Object

The teleological relation between what is known as the object of the moral act and the end of the moral act is so profound that without understanding

---

title takes one back to square one: for natural teleology is definitory for the ontology of nature. Hence implicitly to be told that ethics is not derived from natural teleology because not derived from the ontology of which this teleology is a part, is such as implicitly to put one back into the original Humean problem: wherein we lose sight of natural teleological order as morally normative. Hence, whatever the intention of the theorist, it is a serious error to divorce good from being, to divorce teleology from ontology.

6 Regarding being, one, true, and good, see Jan Aertsen's magisterial *Medieval Philosophy and the Transcendentals: The Case of Thomas Aquinas* (Leiden/New York: E. J. Brill, 1996).

7 Cf. Henry Veatch's brilliant work, *For an Ontology of Morals: A Critique of Contemporary Ethical Theory* (Evanston, IL: Northwestern University Press, 1971) and his likewise excellent *Swimming Against the Current in Contemporary Philosophy, Occasional Essays and Papers* (Washington, DC: Catholic University of America Press, 1990).

it, it is impossible to determine the moral type or "species" of an action. As the papal encyclical *Veritatis Splendor* reminds us (no. 79), "The primary and decisive element for moral judgment is the object of the human act." One can see, then, how critically situated the discourse of St. Thomas is which delineates the nature of the object of the moral act.

First, we should define our terms. While both the end and the means are in different respects spoken of as "objects" by St. Thomas, nonetheless Thomas uses this term "object" principally in a very specific sense. St. Thomas is very clear that the "object" of an act is "what the act is about relative to reason" and that it stands in relation to the act as its "form," giving the act its type or species:

> The object is not the matter "of which" (a thing is made), but the matter "about which" (something is done); and stands in relation to the act as its form, as it were, through giving it its species.[8]

There are two elements that together comprise "what the act is about relative to reason," and not only one: for "what the act is about relative to reason"[9] always materially includes the act itself and its integral nature. Yet, while it is true that the act itself and its integral nature can be generically known[10] in such a way that some acts are determinable to be objectively contrary to right reason merely by their genus, *the object of the act always includes a relation and proportion to the end sought.*[11] This is important in two ways: (1) clearly the object will always have a proportion to

---

8 *ST* I–II, q. 18, a. 2, ad 2.
9 See *ST* I–II, q. 18, a. 5, resp.: "Now in human actions, good and evil are predicated in reference to the reason; because as Dionysius says (Div. Nom. iv), 'the good of man is to be in accordance with reason,' and evil is 'to be against reason.' For that is good for a thing which suits it in regard to its form; and evil, that which is against the order of its form. It is therefore evident that the difference of good and evil considered in reference to the object is an essential difference in relation to reason. . . ." See also q. 18, a. 2, resp.: "And just as a natural thing has its species from its form, so an action has its species from its object, as movement from its term. And therefore just as the primary goodness of a natural thing is derived from its form, which gives it its species, so the primary goodness of a moral action is derived from its suitable object. . . ." See also *ST* I–II, q. 18, a. 10, resp.: "the species of moral actions are constituted by forms as conceived by the reason."
10 Cf. *ST* I–II, q. 18, a. 2.
11 Cf. *ST* I–II, q. 18, a. 4, ad 2; see also *ST* I–II, q. 1, a. 3, ad 1.

what it itself is naturally or *per se* ordered to; and (2) it will also always have some relation, whether *per se* or *per accidens*, to whatever further end the agent may seek through the act. The relation to reason is indeed a determination relative to the end sought by the agent, for this relation to reason is the formal aspect under which this particular act appears to be choiceworthy to the agent. Hence the moral object may be represented after the manner of a fraction:

$$\frac{\textit{relation to reason, which is to say that which makes an act choiceworthy to the agent}}{\textit{the act itself and its integral nature}}$$

The relation to reason is placed atop the act itself and its integral nature: this is because the relation to reason refers to the aspect under which the act in question is appetible to the agent and this, as such, is the more formal aspect of the object, for without it the act would never occur. Nonetheless, the material aspect of the object—the act itself and its integral nature—is also necessary to the object, and this, again, for the very good reason that *what the act is about relative to reason by its very nature can exclude neither the act itself, nor the integral nature of the act itself, both of which are materially included.*[12] The act itself and its integral nature are always materially included in the object.[13]

---

[12] Hence the choiceworthiness of the act to the agent—which is defined in relation to the internal act of the will—may be placed fractionally atop the object of the external act. Each of these is a hylemorphic constituent of the form of the whole act which is the object *simpliciter*. For the act is unitary, and the object of the act *simpliciter* is *the form of the whole* and not merely the form of the part. Thus, the relatively more formal part of the object of the act simply speaking is represented by a relation to the object of the interior act. This is referred to in the text above as the "relation to reason" because it is the external act's relation to this object of the internal act of the will which is the reason for the external act's appetibility and choiceworthiness to the agent. This object of the internal act is placed above the material part of the object which is the object of the external act (as Thomas says—*ST* I–II, q. 18, a. 6, resp.—the object of the internal act of the will is formal with respect to the object of the external act). Both are included in the object as such, which is the form of the whole unitary act, and neither can be excluded.

[13] Indeed, as St. Thomas puts it in *ST* I–II, q. 20, a. 2: "We may consider a twofold goodness or malice in the external action: one in respect of due matter and circumstances; the other in respect of the order to the end. And that which is in respect of the order to the end, depends entirely on the will; while that which is in respect of due matter or circumstances, depends on the reason: and on this goodness depends

It might be thought that the object of the act, being something *formal* in relation to the act, must be exclusively formal, that is to say, must exclude any material element whatsoever. Were this to be true, then the relation to reason alone would constitute the moral object, and the object would not include the act itself along with its integral nature. But while form is distinct from matter, essence itself is also spoken of by St. Thomas as formal—not as merely a part (for, to take an illustration, the essence of man includes matter as well as form) but in the sense of *most determining or defining*. In yet another usage of "form" St. Thomas will say that when the object is *per se* ordered to the end, the most *formal* moral type or species of the act is derived from the end of the act. In this use of "most formal" Thomas clearly means most determining and defining, and most universal, rather than taking form as merely a "part."

So too, when St. Thomas refers to the object as formal with respect to the act performed, this means that the object is most determining and defining with respect to the act, and not that the object lacks any material dimension. That is to say that the object of the act is formal in the sense of most determining and defining, but that *within* this object there is also a relative distinction in terms of a formal and a material part.

Likewise, essence—which is formal in the sense of most determining and defining—includes both form and the common matter of the definition. Since form is included in the essence, it is alike true that the *species of a thing* is known in the knowledge of its essence. Thus the object of the moral act, which defines and determines the act, includes a relatively more formal part—the aspect under which it is choiceworthy and appetible to the agent—and a relatively material part, namely the act itself and its integral nature (and *per se* ordering) which form the necessary substrate of the moral object.

In speaking of the object of the moral act, St. Thomas refers to the moral nature (or essence) of the act performed, that is, what is this act about relative to reason? The physical species or type of the act is not simply equivalent with its moral species or type. But by the same token, the

---

the goodness of the will, insofar as the will tends towards it." The "due matter" of the act is materially included in the object of the act, for it makes up part of the very definition of the act, and as such must be materially presupposed in the object as "what *the act* is about relative to reason" unless *the act* is in each particular case a placeholder standing for we know not what.

physical character of the act is one of the causal elements that enters into the constitution of the object and species of the act. The object includes not only the act itself and its integral nature, but, as proceeding from a rational agent, includes also the relation of the act to reason: a relation which is actually a relation to the end *in light of which* the act appears appetible or choiceworthy to the agent. Of course, St. Thomas's account of the moral object presupposes knowledge on the part of the agent, since the presupposition is that the agent acts voluntarily (without which the act would be, just so far as lacking in pertinent knowledge, other than voluntary and hence, morally speaking, not fully a human act).[14] So it is presupposed that the agent chooses the act for the sake of the end, knowing the nature of the act chosen as well as knowing what makes this act choiceworthy to himself in relation to the end he seeks.

Were either the relatively more formal, or the relatively material, aspects to be excluded from the object of the moral act, absurd conclusions would follow. Suppose that we thought that the relation of the object to reason— to that which makes the object seem to the agent to be choiceworthy—were not essential to an understanding of the object of the act as such? This reminds one of the old joke: a man who pushes an old lady *out of the way* of

---

[14] One philosopher of my acquaintance once raised the case of the man who, in one of Mozart's operas, made love with his wife under the misapprehension that she was really the maid. This, the philosophic critic thought, sufficiently indicated that the integral nature of the act is *irrelevant* to the moral object. But, of course, *we are presupposing knowledge in considering human volitional acts*—so far as one is accidentally ignorant of what one is doing, *just so far is the act not voluntary, and just so far—in that precise respect—is one not morally responsible for the act performed.* Of course, in the example given by the critic, the object would be "making love with a woman thought not to be one's wife, for the sake of gratifying venereal desire." The act chosen is wrongful—despite the fact that the agent is accidentally ignorant of the identity of the woman chosen—because *by the very nature of that which is chosen* the agent directs himself toward that which is incompatible with a good life. What defines *the very nature of that which is chosen* is not any further purpose of the agent, but rather the integral nature of the act of adultery. Yet it is true that the agent in this case is ignorant that it is actually his own wife whom he embraces: and just so far as the embrace with his wife is not voluntary, and he is not morally responsible of the innocent act of embracing his wife. So that which is good in the agent's act he never meant to choose; and that which is bad in his act is that which he meant to choose. Likewise, a man who flips the switch of a remote control supposing that he is setting off a bomb is innocent of the ordinary act of flipping on the remote control, but not of choosing to set off a bomb.

an oncoming bus and a man who pushes on an old lady *into the way* of an oncoming bus are both men *who push old ladies around*. Of course this is preposterous: because the "pushing around" isn't fully grasped in the context of human action without reference to *that for the sake of which* it occurs. Both are acts of pushing, but they seem to be chosen for markedly different reasons. If we omit relation to reason from the consideration of the object of the moral act as such, then we lose the very *ratio* under which the act enters into the action of the agent.

On the other hand, if we exclude from the object of the moral act the matter constituted by the very act itself and its integral nature, we run into problems of an entirely different kind. While there will be more to say about these problems later—chiefly because these problems are in fact the very ones engendered by certain popular treatments of the moral object—it is nonetheless worthwhile immediately to state the *prima facie* problem with this view of the object. That problem is as follows: since the relation to reason is chiefly a relation to the end in relation to which the agent finds an act choiceworthy, by reducing the object to the relation to reason, we reduce absolutely everything to the end principally sought by the agent. But because everything moves towards its end by reason of its form, it is obviously absurd to treat the form of our action as *nothing but* relatedness to whatever further end may be sought by the agent and lacking any nature of its own whatsoever. Were this to be true, then the object of the act could be altered merely by *redescribing* the act performed: "I'm not really strangling a child to death, I'm preventing dynastic civil war."

Rather, as the maxim cited above makes clear—everything moves to its end by reason of its form—*objects exhibit a per se or natural order toward certain ends, irrespective of the further purposes agents may thereby pursue*. Thus *some objects* may be known by this very teleological datum as objectively contrary to a good life and so not choiceworthy because they are defined in relation to morally deficient ends—no matter what *further end* one might thereby seek.

Suppose the case of a man in line to receive life-saving treatment, who has a prognosis of but three months to live, while the treatment he is seeking is given only to one person at a time; suppose, further, that there are three persons in front of our terminal patient in line for the treatment. When our man in line behind the three others decides to take two of the three patients in line ahead of him for walks in a dark alley, to plug them with a .44 caliber bullet, can he honestly say to himself: "what my action is really about is not wrongful homicide; what my action is really about, relative to reason, is removing impediments to the reception of life-saving therapy." Clearly the *end* for the sake of which he acts might indeed be to obtain life-saving therapy; further, he might genuinely and intensely *hate* the very idea of killing those who were in front of him in line, that is to say, he might have no desire for this in and of itself. Nonetheless, the very *nature of his act* includes such killing (the act performed is *per se* such as to terminate in lethal harm to the patients in front of him)—even though what makes the act choiceworthy to the agent is not this killing, but rather the removal of impediments to receiving life-saving therapy.

Take another example: this one derived from the commentary of an acquaintance aimed at expounding the teaching of the U.S. bishops with respect to care for terminal patients. I recollect hearing someone say that one could use, with terminal patients, "as much morphine as one wants." I objected to this formulation that it was truly impossible. "No," came the response, "one can use as much morphine as one wants to use in such cases." At this point, I asked: "May we take a 100-gallon can, and then, using a hose the size of a man's leg connected to a needle, connect that 100 gallon can directly to the heart?" The answer is (and was) obvious: "Of course not." Although we may use a quantum of morphine that we judge likely to attrite lifespan[15]—likely, let us say, to reduce the lifespan from three months to three weeks—we cannot reasonably use a dosage of morphine which we judge certainly to be immediately and proximately sufficient to kill. Why? Because *what we are doing relative to reason* is not merely the relation to reason—not merely the relation to what makes the act choiceworthy and appetible to the agent—but also includes the act itself and its integral nature. To deliberately and knowingly deliver to an innocent person a sufficient dosage of morphine immediately to kill is, by the nature of the case, to introduce *a new cause of death*, such that one is performing homicide. With serious reason doubtless we may attrite life. But this is something very different from deliberate and direct taking of life.

Since the person receiving the lethal dosage is neither assailing anyone (and so the act is not one of *defense*) nor being judged guilty and punished

---

[15] Cf. *The Catechism of the Catholic Church*, #2279.

(and so the act is not one of *justice*), the deliberate homicide is a *wrongful homicide*. And such an act is always wrong, always a *malum in se*, an act in itself evil, irrespective of the further end one may seek through such an act. But of course, if it were licit to define the object of the act merely in terms of its relation to reason, then we could say that the object of the act wherein one delivers such a dosage is merely *pain relief*. This is true of all cases of active euthanasia, where—unlike my rather absurd example—persons truly seek pain relief, persuaded that only death can provide it. Here the point becomes all the more important: for granted that such agents may be in truth devastated and horrified by the unremitting pain of a loved one, and motivated solely by the desire to end such pain, *nonetheless* active euthanasia by its very nature does more than end pain: it ends *life*. What is being chosen is thus not only pain relief; it is the relief of pain *by means* of relieving from life, such that the act is homicidal. Objectively speaking, then, these are not merely agents of pain relief, but homicidal agents. Nor will it do to suppose that mere redescription is sufficient to alter the nature of the object of the moral act, as we can redescribe the administration of a dosage of morphine sufficient to cause immediate death as mere "pain relief" with an accidental "by-product" of death.[16] If we choose to perform an act whose integral nature is *per se* ordered to be directly lethal to the patient, whatever else is in our minds, we have chosen a homicidal act.[17]

Of course, there are a variety of ways of arguing that the integral nature of acts need not be included in the object, while also trying to rule out the more absurd implications of this very view. But, for the present, permit it to be noted that it simply makes no sense for *what the act is about relative to reason either to exclude the act itself, or to exclude the integral nature of the act*. For this act performed by me, here and now, is not only an act that I have judged attractive and choiceworthy for some reason, but *it also has a*

---

[16] But, of course, in the case where more pain relief is necessary, if one prescribes a dosage of morphine that runs a higher risk of inflicting death, that is entirely different than prescribing a dosage of morphine in and of itself knowably sufficient immediately to kill.

[17] As will be seen below, in the section regarding applications, the difficult issues often hinge precisely on whether an act is *per se* or only *per accidens* ordered to harm: for this matters. Cf. the case of Mary and Jodie, in the Appendix, "Particular Applications to Difficult Cases."

nature and per se ordering, and indeed without the act itself and its integral nature there is no human act at all. It follows with clear and absolute necessity that the act itself and its integral nature must be included as the relatively material aspect of the object of the act, with the more formal aspect being that which makes it choiceworthy to the agent, the *ratio* of its being at all attractive to the one acting. The object of the act is this *defining form of the whole act*, inclusive of both the relation to the end which is sought by the agent and in terms of which it is choiceworthy, *and* the act performed itself with its integral nature and its *per se* teleological order.

It might be objected that if the act itself and its integral nature are necessarily materially included in the object that then an absurd implication follows: that one may simultaneously intend one thing as one's end, while the object of the act one chooses may by its nature be contrary to what one intends. Would this not be absurd, postulating an act whose very nature were such as to undercut what the agent actually sought by the action? Yes, it is absurd, but the absurdity is not that of insisting that the act itself and its integral nature must be materially included in the object of the act. Rather, the absurdity consists in choices which lack wisdom, wherein we implicitly seek one thing in a way wholly inconsistent with such intent.

For example, a young woman wishes to be popular and respected, and chooses as means a promiscuous style of life. She may indeed become popular, but the odds are against her being respected: her failure to discriminate these as distinct objectives, and to realize their relative significance, is not the failure of a philosophic theory of the nature of moral action, but the reality of fallible and fallen human nature.

Or, suppose the instance of an abusive relationship, in which one party, who is jealous, strikes another in a desire not to lose the affection and presence of that person in his life. Yet one might argue that the end sought is actually materially contradicted by the natural *per se* effect of striking: inflicting harm naturally will tend to contradict the purpose of sustaining affection. Here too the failure is not that of a philosophic theory of moral action, but of fallible and fallen human nature. What an act is about relative to reason always implicitly and materially includes the act itself and its integral nature, even should this integral nature of the act tend toward effects contrary to the end sought. Further, to suppose that it is absurd for the object to include a formal and a material part, on the ground that matter is not form and that therefore this causes the object to be self-contradictory, is tantamount to saying that because essential human nature includes both form and matter that therefore it is self-contradictory. Rather, the relation of act to potency is clear, as is the hylemorphist account of form (act) and matter (potency). There is no theoretic inconsistency, but rather the nature of human action is such that weakness, imprudence, and sinful proclivities may cause a person to choose an act for the sake of an end even when the act chosen is by its nature inappropriate for the attainment of the end sought.

While the moral object of the act as such includes both the more formal aspect of the relation to reason, and the more material aspect of the act itself and its integral nature, we can consider the object of the act *in precision* from its total concrete ordering in any particular act. That is to say, we can consider the object in a generic way, apart from any further ends sought by the agent—but not apart from the in-built *per se* ordering of the acts themselves[18] which is why we can say that some of these fall under negative precept, even apart from consideration of further ends to which an agent might order them.

This merely generic consideration is possible precisely owing to the integral nature of the object: certain objects are by their very nature deeds that ought not to be performed because always contrary to the human good. Yet to grasp the nature of such acts requires teleological knowledge. Thus we know antecedent to any knowledge of the further particular ends sought by an agent that the agent ought not to murder, because we understand what the act of murder *per se* terminates in, namely a killing contrary to justice and law. This knowledge of the *per se* terminus of the act of murder does indeed imply that one has discriminated that the act in question is not the military act of a soldier defending his post, or an act of just private defense, or the imposition of a just penalty. For murder as such is known not to be *per se* ordained to these ends.

So it remains true that we ought never to murder—irrespective of the full specifying relation whereby murder may seem attractive and choiceworthy to a particular agent (but note that we do not say that one ought

---

18 For again, as *ST* I–II, q. 18, a. 4, ad 2 makes clear, "A relation and proportion to the end is included in the object of the external act."

never to kill, for killing is indeterminate as to moral species without further knowledge—although we can say that in the absence of the form of just penalty, or just war, or just defense, we ought not deliberately to kill).

The moral act has its first and primary goodness from its condign object. Clearly, if an act be such generically as to fall under negative precept, it will not matter what further intended purpose makes the act appear choiceworthy to the agent. Such an act will simply be wrong by reason of its object. But to know what types of acts to avoid will not spare us from the need to identify the nature of the acts being performed, and this involves reference to the teleology of the act. Indeed, it is *because* we implicitly understand something of the generic teleology of certain acts that we realize that acts of those types are not by their nature ordered toward good ends.[19] In short, we can generically recognize a certain *per se* teleology which enables us to make judgments about the object.

Such a merely generic consideration of the object, in precision from its further ordination within the action of any particular agent, serves to highlight the truth that what is in one respect material, may be in another formal; what is a potential principle in relation to a subsequent act may be an actual principle in relation to a prior act. In relation to the complete *ratio* of the agent's action here and now, the object of the chosen act may be material, for it may be chosen only in relation to a yet further end desired by the agent to which it is only *per accidens* ordered, and this *per accidens* ordering may be the only reason that the agent finds this act choiceworthy. Yet, in relation to the act of murder itself, the *per se* terminus of this act is something actual, formal.

One can imagine a case in which murder may be desired by someone as the path to obtaining a good opportunity as a standup comic—a *per accidens* ordering if ever there was one. In relation to this end, the object "murder" is as it were from the standpoint of the one doing the act a material means which is informed by the most formal desire of obtaining a good opportunity. But we do not define murder as the act whereby one obtains a good opportunity as a stand-up comedian, for we grasp that this act of murder has its own *per se* terminus: the unjust killing of an innocent

---

[19] A "bad end" being the object of disordered appetition by the agent, whose desire is deprived of right reason, as contrasted with the normative order of the hierarchy of ends as principiating prudential judgment.

or of one awaiting sentence by higher authority. Murder, as such, exhibits *its own teleology*, a certain *per se* order toward the taking of another's life contrary to justice and law—either the taking of the life of an innocent or of that of a guilty person awaiting sentence by higher authority. And so taken generically and abstractly we can indeed see that certain actions by reason of their objective nature should simply never be performed, irrespective of whatever further ends might thereby be sought. That is, they are such that by their nature they involve serious deprivation of right reason, and as such are not suitable constituents for action.

But does this not contradict what we were just saying? Does it not contradict the proposition that the object of the act *qua* object of the act entails both a relatively more formal aspect (the relation to the agent's reason, which is a determination with reference to the end sought by the agent) and a relatively more material aspect (the act itself and its integral nature)? Are we not implicitly leaving the relation to reason, which in reality is a determination made in relation to the end, out of the picture? No. *The reason is that even generically considered—thus leaving out the full design and any further per accidens ordering of the object by the agent—our knowledge of the object of the moral act must implicitly include sufficient reference to its per se end to place the act in its moral species,*[20] *without which we are in no position to hold that certain acts of their very nature fall under negative precept.* Indeed, it is this truth which alike points to the centrality of the normative or *per se* instance of the moral act as the instance wherein the object of the act is *per se* ordered to the end (about which much more will be said below). For the generic intelligibility of objects presupposes precisely this case of the human act—for example, the case wherein the object as such is *per se* ordained to the end.

One does not escape the truth that the choice of an action involves the willing of an act of a certain *nature* known by its *per se* order to the end whence it is denominated the type of act it is. Recollect the truth that efficiency is not so much as susceptible of definition apart from reference to the end to which it is ordered. What is snow shovelling? The movement of snow with a shovel or shovel-like implement. Hence it is because we know that to which acts of certain types are *per se* ordered that we can possess

---

[20] Cf. *ST* I–II, q. 1, a. 3.

generic knowledge of the objects of such acts, even apart from their further context within the full scope of the agent's desires.

While the generic consideration naturally does not supply the multifarious contexts and particular further specifications with which the moral object will be found in particular acts, *it must retain a certain abstract reference to the end.* This is what we illustrated above with respect to murder. For we know murder to be wrong, irrespective of the motive for which it may be performed. But this generic knowledge of the object "murder" involves a certain abstract reference to the end sufficient to exclude from the end such designations as that the *per se* end of the act be honorable military service in a just war, or just private defense, or the just imposition of a judicial sentence of death. All these are implicitly excluded by the generic knowledge of the object "murder," which is not such as to be *per se* ordered to honorable military service in just war, or just private defense, or the just imposition of a judicial sentence of death.

Likewise, a firefighter who places 100 gallons of water on a fire in a church sanctuary to subdue a dangerous blaze is not committing sacrilege; whereas, one can imagine a person performing such an act for no good reason, which would be a sacrilegious act. We say that sacrilege is generically wrong: but even for this generic knowledge we presuppose a certain abstract understanding of the end, and of what is excluded from the end (as we would say that the desire of a firefighter to save lives in a church by pouring water on a dangerous conflagration is excluded from the generic sense of the end entailed by the object "sacrilege"—lifesaving is not essentially sacrilegious). We know already that lying and adultery are not *per se* ordered to improving one's prayer life; we know that murder is not *per se* ordered to developing a harmonious personality; we know that bestiality is not *per se* ordered toward improved proficiency in calculus. Rather we know that the act of lying is *per se* ordered to the inversion of truth; that the act of adultery is ordered toward lust, betrayal, and the violation of marriage; that the act of murder is ordered to kill someone contrary to law and justice who is either innocent or who awaits sentence by higher authority; and we know that the act of bestiality is ordered to the unnatural degradation of the person and of the dignity of the person's procreative powers through a satiation of lust that is degraded far below even the evil of simple fornication.

Of course, it remains the case that full consideration of the moral object *qua* object *of a particular act*, requires not a generic but a specific reference to the relation to reason, inclusive of any *per accidens* further ordering of the object of an act by the agent. Yet we may consider the object merely generically and hence in abstract relation to myriad possible acts and in accord with an immediate and *per se* knowledge of the teleological order that defines the object. Thus we define "theft" as "the taking of what is not one's own," while knowing in fact that there are occasions when taking what is not one's own *may be required by justice or by charity to one's neighbor*. Yet our definition of theft is not wrong, but its understanding merely implicitly requires a strong tacit apprehension of the *per se* teleology of theft, because implicitly we understand this definition as meaning a taking of what is not one's own such that it is not for the sake of the common good. A taking of what is not one's own that is for the sake of the common good might occur, for instance, when someone saves a life by breaking into a shop to obtain a tool to free a trapped person in a burning vehicle before the vehicle explodes: surely this is not an act of theft, not even if the one taking the tool is a pauper who cannot later pay for the tool. We clearly *exclude* such instances from our generic understanding of theft—it is understood that what we mean by theft is an act which is not susceptible of *per se* ordering to the common good. *The apprehension of the per se order of the object of the moral act is such that we know that a whole array of ends are excluded from this per se order, without which knowledge we could not properly be said to possess generic knowledge of the object.*

Thus even the generic consideration of the object requires a certain reference to the end, and it cannot avoid such reference for the following reason: *action as such makes reference to an end, because action as such is teleological.* Indeed, efficient causality is unintelligible apart from teleology, and human action is a species of efficiency whose sources of course rise higher than the physical order, reaching to intellect and will. Hence the impossibility of definitive abstraction from all teleology while keeping even generic knowledge of the object, for the object of a simple act is such that it itself is ordered *per se* to some ends and not to others (and a complex act is a composite of simple acts, one of which is most desired by the agent with the others serving as means, as shall be considered below).

Hence the generic consideration of the object is abstract (in the sense of being abstracted from the full context and any *per accidens* further ordering by the agent) and in a sense does not consider it *qua* object *of a particular act*, but rather as possible object in myriad acts all defined by the same type of end. Understood in this way, lacking the further specification in concrete act, such a consideration will be adequate in one respect (with regard to the genus) and inadequate in another respect (with regard to any further specific determination of the act in relation to reason and the end beyond the immediate *per se* ordering of the object).

Such a generic consideration with its abstract but adequate sense of the type of end necessary for the definition of the object enables us to say that murder is always wrong. Yet the merely generic character of the object (with its abstract sense of the end requisite to this generic definition) needs to be specified more fully *in relation to the reason of the agent and the end sought by the agent* in order to grasp the full moral intelligibility of the action undertaken by the agent. Hence, even to know that an act falls under negative precept does not provide us with all the moral intelligibility we seek. Yes, this act is a forbidden act of murder—but, perhaps it was done for greed, perhaps for love, perhaps in the hope of saving others from death, perhaps from dangerous ideological fanaticism. These will add to our awareness of the moral character of the agent and the full character of his action, even in the case where we know certainly that the act is gravely wrongful.

Here it is only reasonable to state again, what has been iterated above several times: that even the generic knowledge of the object of the moral act implicitly involves an abstract and minimal sense of the end to which it is *per se* ordered, such that certain ends are excluded on principle as being natural or *per se* termini for certain objects. And so "murder" excludes *per se* the just imposition of the death penalty, as "bodily mutilation and torture" excludes *per se* "heart surgery to heal the sick." This brings us to an implication concerning the more formal part of the moral object—*the relation to reason. For the relation to reason is a reference to that which the agent finds choiceworthy in the act, and this is necessarily therefore a determination relative to the end sought by the agent. If even the merely abstract and generic consideration of the object implies a minimal definitory awareness of teleology, it is obvious that neither object nor moral species will be knowable without reference to teleology.* Further penetration into the nature of the moral act will then require contemplation of the teleological grammar, which—according to St. Thomas Aquinas—governs the constitution of the object and species of the moral act.

The Teleological Grammar Governing Object, End, and Moral Species

We have thus far spoken of the object as the primary source of the goodness (or badness) of action, because the object of the act—that which "most defines" the action—is that which our action proximately concerns. Yet, as St. Thomas clearly argues in *ST* I–II, q. 18, a. 4, ad 2, despite the fact that in a sense the end is extrinsic to the object, *nonetheless a due proportion and relation to the end is inherent in action.* As was seen above, this is precisely why even generic knowledge of moral objects implies at least abstract teleological reference. As we know already, for example, that theft is not *per se* ordered to salvation, or adultery *per se* ordered to education, and this knowledge of the end is implicit in our awareness of certain objects as good or evil; so, for the full analysis of the concrete act, reference to the end, and the relation to the reason of the agent, is most formal. Whether considered abstractly and generically, or fully in particular context and specification, the relation to the reason of the agent is the more formal aspect of the object. In the first case (generic knowledge of the object) the reason of the agent is considered only minimally and generically, whereas in the second case it is considered fully in the context of particular action.

The understanding of the relation of object and end is of paramount importance in understanding the moral species or type of the action. This is because, as St. Thomas puts it most clearly in *ST* I–II, q. 18, a. 7 (the whole article is devoted to this), that where the object is *per se* ordered to the end, the most formal, containing, and defining moral species is derived from the end (and the species derived from the object is then, as it were, simply a specific difference contained within and derived from the moral species derived from the end). It follows that to know the fundamental *type* or *moral species* of any particular action, we must *first* know whether the object is, or is not, naturally *(per se)* ordered to the end.[21] For if, and only if, the object is naturally *(per se)* ordered to the end, will the

---

[21] It is important to realize here that what is in question is whether the object is *per se* ordered to the end sought by the agent. This end sought by the agent may, owing to unrectified appetite on the part of the agent, be deficient. But it will still be true to say that an object is *per se* ordered to an end or not—for example, adultery is evil, but this does not mean that some objects are not *per se* ordered to adultery. The sense of *per se* order to the end is not presupposing rectitude on the part of the agent with respect to the end—both virtuous and vicious agents perform acts essentially ordered to the ends they seek, while only the virtuous rightly order themselves and their

moral species derived from the end be most formal and most containing and defining, such that the moral species derived from the object is merely a specific difference of that species.[22] Of course, here the object is taken generically, that is, when one asks whether this object is *per se* ordered to the end, one is considering the object generically (for, as specified in the act, it is related to reason, which relation indicates that in the act whereby it is choiceworthy to the agent, which of course is always in terms of the *ratio* toward the end). For example, there is nothing about playing chess that is *per se* ordered to theft, whereas for one private party to coerce another into giving money or property to him is *per se* ordered to theft. Here we see, again, that efficiency cannot even be defined apart from teleology. Either the object is *per se* ordered toward the end sought by the agent, or it is not. For example, playing cards is not *per se* ordered toward repulsing the attack of enemy troops, whereas machine-gunning them is.

This kind of action, wherein the object is essentially ordered to the end of the will, is the very *unit of currency* for Thomas's consideration of human acts. Let us be clear: the basic unit of action is the case where an object is essentially ordered to the end of the will, whether the end of the will be the normative natural end (and thus the action good) or the end of the will be, in some case, deprived of right reason owing to unrectified appetite and so wicked (and the act accordingly contrary to reason). It is the *unit of currency* of St. Thomas's analysis, because this is the nature of simple as opposed to complex acts, and before we understand complex acts we must understand simple ones, for complex acts are composed of simple acts. The act wherein object is *per se* ordained to the end is indeed the *per se* instance of the human act as such.

What is a complex act? To provide an illustration, let us take the case of someone who steals in order to fornicate. Clearly there is nothing about stealing that by its nature essentially implies or causes fornication, nor

---

actions to the end of a good life. Hence the double primacy of natural teleology: both in defining the normative order of ends, and also in determining the moral type or species of actions, following upon the particular ends sought by agents, howsoever deficient these may be in terms of the normative order of ends.

22 The case where the object is not naturally or *per se* ordered toward the end, is in reality a complex act made up of two simple acts, one of which is accidentally ordered for the sake of the other—as, to take the classic example, one might steal in order to fornicate. This example, and the nature of complex acts, are treated almost immediately below yet within this section.

anything about fornication that essentially requires stealing. One may steal without fornicating, and fornicate without stealing, and there is additionally nothing about stealing that of itself tends toward fornication. *For natural or essential order is discernible both in the case wherein the achievement of* X *by its very nature requires the performance of* Y, *and in those cases where, although there is perhaps more than one way to achieve* X, *nonetheless* Y *of itself and essentially tends toward* X. Clearly neither of these is true of theft and fornication—theft is neither essentially necessary for fornication nor does it tend by its own nature toward fornication. It follows that theft is not naturally or *per se* ordered toward fornication.

When some agent then steals in order to fornicate, we have a *per accidens* order, not a *per se* order, and thus we have a complex act, an act made up of two very different simple acts which have very different moral types or species: the moral type or species of theft, and the moral type or species of fornication. Now, since the agent *per accidens* is ordering theft to the further end of fornication, which latter is what the agent most desires (it is simply speaking what the agent is aiming for), we can say that the agent is more fornicator than thief. Likewise, since theft is not *per se* ordered to fornication, we see that theft is not contained *within the moral species* of fornication. Rather, there are *two moral species here*, and really *two simple acts*. But because of the agent ordering the one act to the other, we can, in a sense, view the one simple act as an object (theft) and the other as an end (fornication). Yet, in truth, we have two simple acts, one of them further ordered in the mind of the agent to the other, which is "more formal" inasmuch as it is, for the agent, the principal end sought (e.g., the one who steals to fornicate is more fornicator than thief; the jewel thief who, simulating intimacy, fornicates in order to gain access to the mark's private apartment and enclosed safe is more thief than fornicator).

Note that we must understand the teleological ordering of object to end even to be able to account for complex acts, and that only this understanding permits us to determine the moral species of the act (for in simple acts the most defining and containing species is from the end; whereas complex acts are really combinations of simple acts related to one another *per accidens*, in which we view one simple act as a moral object in relation to another act because that other act is the end which is most desired by the agent and the very reason for the agent's action). So, whether the end sought by the agent is the good and proper end, or is defective owing to the unrectified appetite of the agent, the determination of moral species *requires* that we understand the teleological relation of object and end. For only in the case wherein the object is naturally, essentially, *per se* ordered to the end, is the most formal, containing, and defining species derived from the end.

Let us take another example to illustrate. There exist characters who, like Jack the Ripper, are fond of opening up people's chest cavities. There also exist surgeons, who open chest cavities because only this means by its very nature suffices to gain access to the heart for purposes of its surgical repair. Now, clearly, insofar as the end of surgical repair of the heart cannot be achieved without the opening of the chest cavity, the opening of the chest cavity is *per se* ordered to this end. For one thing is said to be *per se* ordered to the other either if the achievement of one thing is absolutely required for the achievement of the other, or if one thing simply by its nature tends toward the achievement of another. In the case of surgery, accordingly, we do not say that there are two simple acts with two distinct moral species: We do not say that first there is an act of opening the chest cavity (with the moral species of butchery) followed by an act of surgery (whose moral species is that of a medicinal or healing act)—but only one act, with one medicinal species. This is because where the object is *per se* ordered toward the end the most defining moral species is derived from the end. Since the end is medical, and since the object is naturally ordered to it (in this instance, naturally ordered in the sense that absolutely speaking one cannot gain access to the heart for the purposes of surgical repair without opening the chest cavity), the most formal species is derived from the end, and the moral species derived from the object is contained within the species of the end, that is, this opening of the chest cavity is *medical.*

It is impossible to overstress how foundational this analysis is for St. Thomas Aquinas. Contemporary authors rightly stress that, since the will in moving out to the end also moves out to the means to the end and the object of the act, that in a sense the object is a "proximate end." However, this is strictly *analogous* language. Why is this so? First, because—as Thomas says everywhere—*intention is chiefly of the end*, and moreover, one may have *intention of the end* even prior to the determination of means, and before any act with its objective character is chosen. For St. Thomas that which primarily is spoken of as being "intended" is the *end*, whereas the object of one's external act (which is as means to the end) is primarily spoken of by St. Thomas *qua* means as "chosen." Hence the following words of St. Thomas:

> Accordingly, insofar as the movement of the will is to the means, as ordained to the end, it is called "choice"; but insofar as the movement of the will is to the end as acquired by the means, it is called "intention." A sign of this is that we can have intention of the end without having determined the means which are the object of choice.[23]

Granted that, inasmuch as we will the means for the end, we can speak of the means as a more proximate end, this is wholly secondary, derived, and analogical language, because absolutely and simply speaking the movement of the will to the means as ordered to the end is called "choice," whereas "intention" pertains both to the end prior to determination of means, and also to the end as acquired by the means. Why is this terminological issue important? It is important because confusion here will lead to a failure to understand the basic unit of analysis of St. Thomas's action theory; it will lead to the failure to understand the most primal sense of "human act" as the case in which the object is *per se* ordered to the end. If we use *end* indifferently, both for the end in this simple case, and for the object, we confuse the matter.

It might be pointed out that in the case of a complex act, one of the simple acts is further ordered to another, which subsequent act is the one more desired by the agent. Clearly here, precisely because the "object" of the complex act is truly a distinct simple act with a distinct moral species, we do have a genuine "end." But the reason for this is already clear: we have a genuine end because the first part of the "complex act" is truly a simple act with its own intelligible structure, with an object *per se* ordered to the end. The convenience of conceiving of complex acts wherein one simple act is *per accidens in the mind of the agent* further ordered to another act for the sake of which the first act is undertaken, presupposes the prior and simple instance of the analysis of simple acts, acts wherein the object is naturally ordered to the end. This issue of *per se* order indicates that whereas most contemporary theories of human action are overly ideational and

---

23 *ST* I–II, q. 12, a. 4, ad 3; see also *ST* I–II, q. 12, a. 1; *ST* I–II, q. 12, a. 3.

logicist—indeed angelist—in their exclusion of reference to natural teleology, St. Thomas's teaching is *intelligibly saturated* with natural teleology.

According to the teaching of St. Thomas Aquinas, we cannot so much as determine the moral species of an action unless we first know the answer to this question: is the object of this action naturally ordered to the end? If the object is ordered to the end then, whatever else may ensue on the part of the object, we will know that the most defining species is derived from the end willed (of course, again, all this presupposes knowledge, since simple ignorance makes an act, just so far considered, to be other than voluntary). If, on the other hand, the object is not naturally ordered to the end, then we will know that we have a complex act, that is to say, that we are dealing with a case wherein one simple act with its own *per se* ordering of object to end is itself *per accidens* further ordered to another simple act with its *per se* ordering of object to end: as a simple moral act of theft (with *per se* ordering of action ordered to stealing) may *per accidens*, in the mind of the agent, be further ordered to the end of the simple moral act of fornication (with its *per se* ordering of actions that by nature are fornicative), such that we may speak of the first act as being like an object, and the second as being like an end. And yet, absolutely speaking, although one can see the point of speaking of this *per accidens* linkage as a complex act—because this does indeed describe what is going on in relation to the reason of the agent—nonetheless, absolutely speaking, it is a sequence of simple acts with their own distinct moral species, joined only by the *per accidens* judgment of the agent. For theft is not *per se* ordered to fornication, even though this act of theft here and now occurs because someone steals for the sake of having funds for use at a brothel.

The *per se* unit of analysis of moral action, then, is the simple case wherein the object is naturally ordered to the end,[24] and wherein the most

---

[24] Of course, as is noted in note 9 *supra*, by "naturally ordered to the end" we speak of the natural order of the object of the act to that which is sought by the agent, even though this latter may be rationally deficient owing to the cause of unrectified appetite. Hence, we can say that some acts are "naturally ordered" to theft, to seduction, to murder, as well as say that some acts are naturally ordered to friendship, or study, or wisdom—the ends need not, *simpliciter*, be "natural" in the normative sense for them to be sought by agents. Nor must the ends be in the normative sense "natural" in order to be such that certain acts either tend toward them or are required by them: for example, to "naturally" be the termini of certain acts. But of course, fully to understand the moral species of a bad act will be to discern the respect in

containing, formal, and defining moral species is derived from the end, and the species derived from the object is contained within the more formal species derived from the end and in relation to which it constitutes a specific difference. When Thomas speaks most formally, it is this unit of analysis to which he refers. He does so for the very good reason that, absolutely and naturally speaking, the *per se* is prior to the *per accidens*, and derivatively, the understanding of complex acts depends upon a prior analysis of simple ones.

A Brief Note on the Integral Good

It is worth pausing here briefly to observe yet another reason for the importance of the foregoing analysis. St. Thomas teaches that good acts flow from integral causes, and that any defect will yield a correspondingly deficient act. That is to say, an act has a certain entitative goodness that flows from its very being; it has a goodness that derives from the species derived from its object; it has a goodness that flows from the circumstances, or as it were the accidents, that pertain to the act; and lastly, it has a certain goodness "from its end, to which it is compared as to the cause of its goodness."[25] As St. Thomas puts it, "However, an action is not good absolutely, unless it is good in all those ways; for evil results from any single defect, but good from the complete cause, as Dionysius says."[26]

We have already treated the form and the end, and the being of the act itself is clear enough. It remains, then, to say a brief word about circumstances. For according as it is related to reason, a circumstance can sometimes be the essential difference of the object and thus specify a moral act; indeed in this way a circumstance can actually change the species of an act.[27] This seems odd: how can something *accidental* to an act determine its *essential nature*—in this case, determine its essential moral type or species? The answer is, of course, that what is accidental in one respect may in relation to reason be essential in another. For it is not *qua* circumstance that it specifies an act, but as a principal condition of an object: that is, in one respect it may be an accident, but in another, it is not.

---

which a vicious act is deprived of right reason and inconsistent with the normative hierarchy of ends.

[25] *ST* I–II, q. 18, a. 4.

[26] Ibid., ad 3.

[27] *ST* I–II, q. 18, a. 5, ad 4.

Physical species are not a function of the relation to reason—a cow is a cow is a cow, no matter the relation to reason, and the accident that it is muddy, or wet, or slow will never enter into the definition of its species. But human acts are judged essentially moral or not on the basis of their conformity with right reason, and right reason demands that actions be integrally good, that is, that they be seriously defective in no way. The object of an act is as such partially constituted in relation to reason. Thus when a circumstance becomes a principal condition of the object of an act it specifies an act.[28] To take a simple instance, the nature of moral transgression is altered from mere theft to sacrilege when what is stolen is a sacred object.

Not every circumstance introduces a change in relation to right reason and so with respect to the morality of an act, but clearly a circumstance can do so—as the case of returning a borrowed firearm to a neighbor who happens to be in a drunken homicidal rage serves to indicate. From the point of view of returning borrowed property, it is an accident whether the one to whom it is returned is or is not in a drunken homicidal rage; but from the vantage point of the relation to reason, the very nature of the act is changed if under the aspect of returning borrowed property one knowingly makes a direct and material contribution to wrongful homicide. Thus, this circumstance forms a principal condition of the object, such that returning the borrowed property would be not prudent and responsible, but contrary to reason. This is a function of the relation to reason, a relation, again, that is essentially important with respect to the moral species, for the moral species pertains to the conformity of action to right reason. By contrast, the physical species is what it is, and its definition does not vary on the basis of what is accidental or circumstantial.

To take a more complicated instance, an act of theft becomes something different when it is prosecuted by the agent chiefly and primarily not for the sake of stealing but because circumstances are such that it will aid in the murder of an innocent. It is accidental to theft that it aid murder, but if murder is uppermost in the mind of the agent, this circumstance (in relation to the moral species of theft) is a principal condition of the object (because the entire act of theft, in a complex act, is as object to the *per acci-*

---

28 *ST* I–II, q. 18, a. 10, resp. & ad 1–3.

dens end of murder). An act can likewise fall under more than one moral species, precisely because different moral conditions can pertain to it.[29]

Thus, goodness is from integral causes, and moral defect or evil enters in with any defect in being, object, circumstance, or end. An act which is good in one way, may be evil in another: perhaps the end is good, but the object is defective; or the object is good, and the circumstances too, but the end sought by the agent is not. This serves once more to highlight the importance of a right understanding of object and end, which are essential elements in the equation—and indeed, the more essential, when it is realized that only when a circumstance forms a principal condition of the object does it specify the act.

THREE STRATEGIC ERRORS

In the latter part of this chapter it should be seen that we have considered three foundationally grave errors whose occurrence necessarily vitiates all ensuing moral analysis. Considering them in the inverse order of their discovery, these are:

1. That any understanding of moral action which overly abstracts from natural teleology will be incapable of understanding the moral species of actions: for only knowledge as to whether the object is *per se* or *per accidens* ordered to the end of the will suffices to yield sufficient knowledge of the moral species. Granted that there is generic knowledge of the species of the object; this generic knowledge, while adequate generically, is by definition specifically incomplete. As St. Thomas puts it, human actions "have a measure of goodness from the end on which they depend, in addition to the goodness which is in them absolutely,"[30] and again, he says of the end that it is "last in execution, but first in the intention of the reason, according to which moral actions receive their species."[31] Indeed, as we have seen, only when the object is *per se* ordered to the end is the most containing and defining species derived from the end. This matters tremendously, as in the case of *per se* order it discloses the fundamental character of the

---

[29] *ST* I–II, q. 18, a. 7, ad 1.
[30] *ST* I–II, q. 18, a. 4.
[31] *ST* I–II, q. 18, a. 7, ad 2.

act, in relation to which the object introduces merely a specific difference. Further, only this teleological knowledge enables us to discriminate the case of the complex act, with all that this implies, from a simple act. St. Thomas's account of object, end, and moral species, is *absolutely saturated* in natural teleology. Only implicit logicist, idealist, or cognate presuppositions seem able to account for interpretations of St. Thomas's text which treat natural teleology as virtually irrelevant to moral analysis.

2. Likewise, it will be a mistake to eviscerate the moral object of the act itself and of its integral nature, treating the object of the moral act solely in terms of the relation of the act to reason. This is a mistake for five reasons. First, the object is formal not merely in the sense of form as a part, but rather of the form of the whole or essential nature as defining and determining the character of the act. Second, were the object merely the relation to reason, then it would be impossible to speak of the object in a merely generic fashion and in precision from its further specification in the concrete act in relation to reason, because minus the relation to reason there would then be nothing left to consider—so that we could not, generically, say that certain types of action are objectively wrong irrespective of the reasons an agent might find them choiceworthy. Third, were the object of the act merely the relation to reason, the object of the act—that which defines the act—would be wholly ideational rather than having any natural component whatsoever: but clearly our moral actions have a natural component (e.g., we are said to murder someone when we inflict death on an innocent, and death is not merely an idea but a physical state). Fourth, were the object of the act merely the relation to reason, it would also follow that we could alter the object of the act in toto merely by *redescribing the act* in relation to reason, whereas to the contrary objects have a generic intelligibility even considered without their specifying completion in relation to reason and the end sought by the agent. Fifth, and perhaps most formally, *because it is plainly the case* that *what an act is about in relation to reason by its very definition materially presupposes the act itself and the integral nature of the act itself,* on pain of becoming the following formula: "The object of the moral act is what the unknown and unknowable is about rela-

tive to reason." The phrase "relation to reason" implies *two terms* and not merely one: *something*—something not simply reducible to reason—is in relation to reason. *What the act is about* in relation to reason materially includes the act itself and its integral nature. That—as the objection dealt with earlier argues—this implies that one and the same agent may contradict his own intention by his choice of action, displays that the object includes a more formal part (the relation to reason which is in reality a relation to the end) and a material part (the act itself and its integral nature). And so it is not seldom the case that persons seek an end which is vitiated by the nature of the act they choose, precisely because the aspect under which the act commends itself to their reason is not all there is to the matter. For there is also the act itself, and its integral nature, which are not reducible merely to the relation they bear to a desired end—a situation most clear in the case of complex acts (for example, as earlier noted, the case of the person who seeks to relieve a patient from pain by relieving the patient of life, an act which only *per accidens* can be said to relieve from pain— it also relieves, for instance, of singing in the opera, of counting money, of eating lunch, and of indefinitely many other terrestrial experiences—in the course of "relieving" the patient of life itself).

3. Finally, it will be an error to suppose that a complete analysis of the object of the moral act as such is possible in abstraction from the relation to reason (which, implicitly, is the relation to the end, desire for which moves some agent to find a particular act choiceworthy and appetible). For, although a merely generic intelligibility may be affirmed of the object of the moral act, and although some acts are such that they objectively fall under negative precept, nonetheless, in the concrete action the object will always involve *more* than its merely generic intelligibility. And so, some things which are generically innocent may become illicit because of their relation to the reason of the agent and the end desired by the agent; and some things which are wrong in themselves, although they cannot become rightful in themselves, yet in their relation to the reason of the agent may become worse yet. Hence as to the first, almsgiving is generically good, but becomes illicit when performed principally to mislead government investigators who inquire about one's character. As to the second,

wrongful homicide is made worse when chosen for the sake of further-ing the illicit purpose of a vendetta, as opposed, say, to the choice of murder in the hope that this evil act may spare many others from wrongful death (this act is of course still a *malum in se*, but *not because one seeks the end of sparing others from wrongful death but because one knowingly performs a murder*).

Of course, the fact that consideration of the object of the moral act as such requires the relation to reason does not prevent the generic goodness or otherwise of the object from being known; but it does prevent knowledge of the complete *ratio* of the object of the act as such from being known. This is because merely generic knowledge prescinds from full, definitive specificity with respect to any further purpose of the agent (who may desire the act solely for some *per accidens* purpose, as for instance the one who murders to obtain a good opportunity to be a standup comic). This third error—the error of supposing that the relation to reason is irrelevant for a fully specific account of a moral act—is a mistake which virtually no one makes. Yet it is the only error that would properly be worthy of the name of physicalist or perhaps better "objectivist"—whereas, the first two errors are made by many well-known moral philosophers and theologians. It follows from what has been said above that we should respond to these errors not only in general, but in application of the general truths about the relation of object, end, and moral species to particular moral questions.

However, before proceeding to particular applications of the Thomistic account of object, end, and moral species, it is worth first applying our-selves to the critical proving ground of the case of private defense. For it is in the case of private defense, expressly taken up by St. Thomas Aquinas in *ST* II–II, q. 64, a. 7, that these first two errors about object, end, and moral species cause the most amazing and total incapacity to yield forth any reading of Thomas's text that conforms to moral common sense or even to the legal customs of Thomas's day. Accordingly, it is worthwhile to show how St. Thomas's actual account of object, end, and species yields, in *ST* II–II, q. 64, a. 7 a completely intelligible moral account that con-forms to right reason and common sense. Only after addressing this strate-gic example will the questions of double effect, and further particular applications of St. Thomas's teaching, be addressed.

REGARDING NORMATIVE TELEOLOGY

While understanding St. Thomas's account of the teleological grammar for the constitution of the object and species of the moral act is of critical importance, this natural teleology itself in its wider normative dimensions includes reference to the transcendence of the common good. For not only acts deprived of right reason, but acts subject to it, are performed, and the difference between these is a function of normative teleology. Yet there is in a secondary sense pertinent to the assignation of species a natural order even with respect to vicious acts (some acts are by their nature ordered toward vicious ends: e.g., some acts are by their nature acts of torture, some acts of murder, etc.).

In respect to the normative hierarchy of natural ends, the transcendence of the common good is of prime importance. Higher or common goods testify to the unique dignity of the human person. For the person is not only ordered toward individual goods or ends, but is ordered toward ends which, while good *for* the person, do not belong as merely individual or private goods to the person: such are the essentially more diffusive, rational, and universal goods or ends known as "common" or "higher" goods. If one eats a piece of pizza, another does not; but many can share the same insight into the truth without any diminution, and if one does justice to one person, one need not then do injustice to another to compensate.

The essential hierarchy of ends includes a hierarchy of "common"—essentially more diffusive, rational, and universal—ends, from the common good of civil society all the way to the common good of the celestial city in the essentially supernatural beatific vision of God. Natural teleology is of importance in more than one way, and—while it is critical for understanding the object and moral species of any voluntary human act—it is most of all critical in understanding the order obtaining amongst ends. It is in relation to this order that acts are denominated as virtuous, continent, incontinent, or vicious.

The *vulgarization* of the right maxim states that "the end does not justify the means." But of course, if the end does not justify the means, what does? The *unvulgarized* correct maxim states that "the end does not justify simply any means whatsoever." In other words, *correct proportion to the end* defines rectitude of action, where by "end" we mean *normative end*—not merely anything that may be desired as an end by unrectified appetite, but that which essentially constitutes and defines human perfection: *the norma-tive object of wish* as distinct from *the merely factual object of wish* (for people can wish for things that will not be good for them). When our acts are well formed, then they are well-proportioned toward the end of the good life as an ordered whole. But the end of the good life not only does not, but indeed *cannot*, justify any action whatsoever. One may not do evil that good may come, because evil is such that by means of it one *cannot* achieve the end of a good life, any more than one can *melt* a substance by *freezing it*.

However, our aim at present is to exhibit the degree to which natural teleology saturates St. Thomas's account of the object and species of the moral act. It is an important illustration of this thesis that St. Thomas's account of the moral object and moral species does not, in conjuncture with his account of private defense, yield up conclusions that seriously fail to harmonize with reasonable moral perceptions.

For years, interpretations of St. Thomas's teaching about object, end, and moral species have yielded accounts that make serious hash out of *ST* II–II, q. 64, a. 7. Surely one attribute of a correct Thomistic account of moral action should be that—in conjunction with the teaching of *ST* II–II, q. 64, a. 7—it should imply conclusions about private defense that are morally intelligible. To the proving ground of this central illustration I will now turn.

CHAPTER TWO

■ ■ ■

Object, End, and Moral Species: The Case of Private Defense

THE PROVING GROUND OF LETHAL PRIVATE DEFENSE

I HAVE WRITTEN elsewhere considering, in detail, the famed treatment given by Cajetan to *ST* II–II, q. 64, a. 7.[1] It is, historically speaking, with Cajetan's brilliant yet subtly askew rendering of this article that the first significant break with Thomas's account of the moral object occurs amongst those whose central intent is clearly to interpret, explain, and defend the teaching of St. Thomas Aquinas. However, what is a minor but real anomaly in the treatment of Cajetan on the issue of private defense, becomes with the passage of time and the exaggeration of the elements involved a more and more substantial departure from St. Thomas's teaching, until today the issue of lethal private defense is often highlighted by critics to show the inconsistency of those who prevalently insist that the integral nature of the act is included within the moral object, but in the case of private defense deny this.[2] That there is positively no reason to deny this

---

[1] Steven A. Long, "A Brief Disquisition Regarding the Nature of the Object of the Moral Act According to St. Thomas Aquinas," *The Thomist* 67 (2003): 45–71.

[2] Cf. John Finnis, Germain Grisez, and Joseph Boyle, "'Direct' and 'Indirect': A Reply to Critics of Our Action Theory," *The Thomist* 65 (2001): 1–44, and especially p. 28, where the authors defend the licity of craniotomy—crushing the skull of the *conceptus* in order to save the life of a mother when the child cannot be birthed otherwise— saying of the criticism that this is directly harming the *conceptus* as opposed to indirect killing of the sort that might occur in the removal of a gravid cancerous uterus that "this difference does not show that craniotomy is direct killing. A counterexample makes this clear. All those acts of self-defense of the kind that Aquinas shows need involve no intent to kill and no direct killing are nonetheless performed

inclusion of the integral nature of the act performed in the case of just private defense effected through knowably lethal means, and that it is the contrary view which fails to read St. Thomas's own express doctrine on this matter clearly, is the object to whose establishment this chapter is directed.

The position of St. Thomas Aquinas regarding private defense is articulated in the answer of *ST* II–II, q. 64, a. 7 to the question "Whether it is lawful to kill a man in self-defense," as follows:

> I answer that, Nothing hinders one act from having two effects, only one of which is intended, while the other is beside the intention. Now moral acts take their species according to what is intended, and not according to what is beside the intention, since this is accidental as explained above. Accordingly the act of self-defense may have two effects, one is the saving of one's life, the other is the slaying of the aggressor. Therefore this act, since one's intention is to save one's own life, is not unlawful, seeing that it is natural to everything to keep itself in "being," as far as possible. And yet, though proceeding from a good intention, an act may be rendered unlawful, if it be out of proportion to the end. Wherefore if a man, in self-defense, uses more than necessary violence, it will be unlawful: whereas if he repel force with moderation his defense will be lawful, because according to the jurists [*Cap. Significasti, De Homicid. volunt. vel casual.], "it is lawful to repel force by force, provided one does not exceed the limits of a blameless defense." Nor is it necessary for salvation that a man omit the act of moderate self-defense in order to avoid killing the other man, since one is bound to take more care of one's own life than of another's. But as it is unlawful to take a man's life, except for the public authority acting for the common good, as stated above (A3), it is not lawful for a man to intend killing a man in self-defense, except for such as have public authority, who while intending to kill a man in self-defense, refer this to the public good, as in the case of a soldier fighting against the foe, and in the minister of the judge struggling with robbers, although even these sin if they be moved by private animosity.

One notes the critical elements of this response: first, that "Nothing hinders one act from having two effects, only one of which is intended, while

---

'upon' the person killed." In other words: if the integral nature of the act is included as the matter of the object in other cases, then it should be included in the instance of defense, a conclusion which many do not wish to hold: so, should not the matter of the act then always and on principle be excluded from the object of the moral act?

the other is beside the intention." Now we see that it matters what the primary sense of "intention" is. One grants that one may, in a secondary and analogous sense, affirm that the means to the end is intended, because the will goes out to the end through the means. Nonetheless, the primary sense of *intention* pertains *to the end*, and pertains to the end even prior to the determination of the means. One recollects St. Thomas's words:

> Accordingly, insofar as the movement of the will is to the means, as ordained to the end, it is called "choice"; but insofar as the movement of the will is to the end as acquired by the means, it is called "intention." A sign of this is that we can have intention of the end without having determined the means which are the object of choice.[3]

One should carefully observe that according to St. Thomas "we can have intention of the end without having determined the means which are the object of choice." *Per se* the term "intention" for St. Thomas designates either the end *simpliciter*, or the end as acquired by the means, but in either case principally *the end*. Whereas, *per se*, for St. Thomas "choice" designates the movement of the will to the means.

Of course, *in a sense,* even in a simple act, wherein the object is naturally ordered to the end, one may say that because the will goes out toward the end *through the means* that the will "intends" the means: but this is a secondary and analogous use of "intend." For there would indeed *be no means* were there not first, and as a condition of having such means, *intention*.

Likewise there is, of course, the case of complex acts, wherein one act with its own *per se* ordering to the end and moral species is ordered by someone to a further distinct act with its own *per se* ordering to the end, and moral species, such that the first act may be viewed as the object and the second the end. But all this presupposes that we can first *distinguish simple and complex acts*, and that we can *place each simple component act of the complex act in its moral species*. These prior discriminations cannot be achieved without (a) discerning the teleology of object to end—whether the object is *per se* ordered to the end, or not; (b) understanding that in the case where object is *per se* ordered to end that the most formal, defining, containing moral species is derived from the end; and (c) finally,

---

[3] *ST* I–II, q. 12, a. 4, ad 3; see also *ST* I–II, q. 12, a. 1; *ST* I–II, q. 12, a. 3.

grasping that the case wherein the object is *per se* ordered to the end *is the per se case of moral action*, such that understanding all other and more complex acts presupposes understanding the simple case wherein object is *per se* ordered to end. This makes clear the truth of the proposition that we must be in a position to distinguish intention of the end in the simple case from the object, even though in a secondary sense the object is of course in the *per se* case of human action analogously said to be intended. Because the will moves toward the end through the act as chosen means, the will does move toward the means: but it moves toward the act as chosen means *as caused* by the intention of the end for the sake of which the act is chosen. For this reason—that the primary intention is the cause of the choosing of the act—the motion of the will to the means is only in a secondary and analogous sense spoken of as "intended."

Likewise, granted that what is end in one respect is means in another, such a framework is impossible unless there is a natural end: both a *finis ultimus*, which is in no way "means," and also (and for our specific purpose here more importantly) a simple case of "end" in the case wherein object is *per se* ordered to end, even though the simple case can be *further ordered* and as so ordered then is viewable as a means in relation to some other end. For the fundamental proposition is the following: if we are rightly to understand complex acts in which a simple act is further ordered to another act, we first must be able to distinguish the two cases (simple from complex act), *and also and absolutely speaking we must be able to determine the moral species of the simple act.*

So, to repeat, there is a *per se* case wherein act as chosen means is strongly and clearly distinguished from end as principal object of intention, and wherein the object of the act is *per se* ordered to the end. This is the *per se* instance of the human act, without which no further analysis of human acts will prove possible. When Thomas speaks most formally about human action, it is to the *per se* case of human action that he refers: the case wherein object is naturally, *per se*, ordered to the end. This becomes apparent very quickly as we read further in the *respondeo* from *ST* II–II, q. 64, a. 7: "Now moral acts take their species according to what is intended, and not according to what is beside the intention, since this is accidental as explained above." Now, this is manifestly the case in the *per se* instance of human action: where an action is naturally, *per se*, ordered to the end, the most formal, defining, containing species is derived from the end, and the species of the object merely further specifies the act *within* this fundamental moral type or species. So: of course, moral acts, speaking most formally, that is, in what I am calling the *per se case of human action*—the case in which object is naturally and *per se* ordered to end— take their species according to what is intended (the end) and not according to what is beside the intention (that which is not the end). In the *per se* case of human action, the species of the object is contained within that derived from the end, but the defining and containing species is indeed *from the end*, and the object *is not the end.*

The object is, literally, *praeter intentionem* in the sense that in the *per se* case of human action, the object is "other than" the end, even while the *species* of the object is *contained in the species derived from the end.* In the *per se* case, *moral acts take their species according to what is intended—from the end*—and not elsewhere from what is beside the end "since this is accidental, as explained above." But the species derived from the object is only, in the *per se* case of human action, an *accidental modification* of the most formal, defining, and containing species *which is derived from the end.* It is not the object which is giving us the basic moral character of the act in the *per se* case. Rather, it is the end which in the *per se* case of human action gives us the basic moral character of the action, in relation to which the object introduces only a *per accidens* specification. Naturally, by "*per accidens*" here we mean not *per accidens* relative to the choice, but *per accidens* relative to *the moral species derived from the end*: as, for example, it is accidental to a partic- ular act of dental hygiene that it be pulling out a "wisdom tooth," although it is not accidental to *this act* that it be pulling out a "wisdom tooth." It is accidental to "traveling to Cleveland" that it be an "automobile trip," but it is not accidental to *this trip* that it be an automobile trip. Relative to *the species* derived from the end, the species of the object is as such *per accidens.* When we ask, of a simple or *per se* instance of the human act, "what type of moral act is this," the answer will be derived from the end; and, in relation to this fundamental moral type, the further specification provided by the object is quite literally accidental. So, again, for example, one asks "What kind of act is this?" Suppose the answer is: "an act of theft." It is, then, accidental to being an act of theft that it is this or that particular type of theft: although to repeat it is not accidental to *this act* that it be chosen as the act it is.

Let us consider the next lines: "Accordingly the act of self-defense may have two effects, one is the saving of one's life, the other is the slaying of the aggressor. Therefore this act, since one's intention is to save one's own life, is not unlawful, seeing that it is natural to everything to keep itself in "being," as far as possible." Two effects of one act are identified—saving one's life and slaying the aggressor—and this act "is not unlawful" since *one's intention is to save one's own life"* and "seeing that it is natural to everything to keep itself in 'being,' as far as possible." The intention is of the end, and the end is "saving one's own life." Presuming that one has a justification for saving one's own life (there would be cases wherein doing so could be the sin of strife, say, in the instance of resisting just punishment of death), and that the defense is elsewise proportionate or moderate (e.g., does not unduly risk the lives of other innocents), then this intention of the end will provide the defining moral species of the act *if and only if* the object is *per se* ordered to this end. Since Thomas wishes to define the case wherein lethal self-defense is licit, it is this case that he is explicating (the question, one recalls, is "Whether it is lawful to kill a man in self-defense").

With respect to this question, one might identify three cases: case 1—the killing is wholly accidental to the particular act of defense because it was a wholly unforeseen and unforeseeable effect of the defense (and the supposition of this case is that there is justice in the end of the defense in question, which might not always be true); case 2—the killing is chosen as the only or the best means available for a particular defense because other means are unavailing or inefficacious, so that the natural preference not to kill is surmounted by the need to defend and the existence of only one likely efficacious means (but note: the killing is not *the end*, for the end is *defense* and the agent has no intention to kill the assailant simply taken as an end in itself, but only to defend against the assailant); case 3—the agent *intends* to kill the assailant using the assault as a mere *pretext* or occasion to perform homicide, which is what the agent seeks as an end from the beginning and in its own right. St. Thomas's account is such that, if defense is warranted and the only or assuredly the best means of defense is lethal, and—supposing the end of defense is just to begin with, and that others are not unduly threatened—the first two cases count as licit instances of self-defense. He himself says that the act is not unlawful since the *intent* is to save one's life. Yet, even given such an intention:

[A]n act may be rendered unlawful, if it be out of proportion to the end. Wherefore if a man, in self-defense, uses more than necessary violence, it will be unlawful: whereas if he repel force with moderation his defense will be lawful, because according to the jurists [*Cap. Significasti, De Homicid. volunt. vel casual.], "it is lawful to repel force by force, provided one does not exceed the limits of a blameless defense." Nor is it necessary for salvation that a man omit the act of moderate self-defense in order to avoid killing the other man, since one is bound to take more care of one's own life than of another's.[4]

So the act of defense must be in proportion to the end of defense: if other acts are more than adequately defensive, there is no need to kill; likewise, if an act of defense involves undue risk to others, it loses its proportion to the end, all the more so if harm to the common good is knowably entailed by the defense. Yet one need not omit moderate self-defense to avoid killing "since one is bound to take more care of one's own life than of

---

[4] *ST* II–II, q. 64, a. 7. It is noteworthy that St. Thomas puts forward the proposition that "one is bound to take more care of one's own life than of another's." How, one might ask, does this square with "Greater love than this hath no man: that he lay down his life for his friend"? But in relation to what does one define the love as objectively so great, save that what man is chiefly and proximately entrusted with is his own life? Moreover, formally speaking, one can only guarantee the rectitude of *one's own* actions, and in this sense all who seek to act rightly realize the need to "take more care of one's own life than of another's." But the chief sense of St. Thomas's proposition is clearly teleological: one has governance of *one's own* acts only because of the gift of life bequeathed to one, for the right use of which one answers to God. Hence a man is bound by positive precept to care for himself—not, for example, by way of the omission of obligatory discretion to harm his own health. And so there will be cases—especially when others whom one is bound to care for depend upon one for their good—when one is obligated to defend oneself against wrongful assault and perhaps even obliged to the deliberate use of deadly means for the sake of stopping the assault. For one's life is in one's own care, the good of others who depend upon one depends on that care, and so frequently there is no justification for neglecting one's own defense. Of course if others do not depend upon one, and one is inspired by God to be martyred for the glory of God and the good of souls; or if one is a vowed religious who has definitively eschewed killing, then the circumstances are different. But in these latter cases, it is not that one is encouraged to omit necessary care for one's life, but that a greater and nobler end is entrusted to one's care, for the sake of which one may lose one's life. This case does nothing to alter the fact that normally a layman will be obliged to defend himself, both because this is his obligation with respect to the gift of his own life, and because and insofar as others may depend upon him for their well-being.

another's." Nothing in this excludes the case wherein only lethal means bear the necessary proportion to the end.

What is meant by saying that it is not necessary for salvation that one omit the act of moderate self-defense "in order to avoid killing the other man"? One might read this as "in order to avoid *any accidental killing* of the other man," that is, any killing which is unforeseen and unforeseeable with respect to one's choice of defense. Yet St. Thomas does not say this. Indeed, there is no particular reason why the passage should be read in this way unless we misunderstand what the term "intention" signifies in the *per se* case of the human act. For if the act of moderate self-defense is *per se* ordered to defense—is proportionate rather than disproportionate— then its defining and determining species will be that of defense. There is no reason in advance of prudence for claiming that every case of moderate defense can include killing only by way of unforeseen and unforeseeable consequence rather than by way of foreseen means. Why should not some defense be such that it cannot be achieved without the deployment of a lethal means? One is about to be cut down with a sword, and will be, unless one makes the sole move that can stop the effect from ensuing, a lethal thrust to the heart . . . and so on. Both the first and second cases are cases of moderate, proportionate defense.

St. Thomas continues:

> But as it is unlawful to take a man's life, except for the public authority acting for the common good, as stated above, it is not lawful for a man to intend killing a man in self-defense, except for such as have public authority, who while intending to kill a man in self-defense, refer this to the public good, as in the case of a soldier fighting against the foe, and in the minister of the judge struggling with robbers, although even these sin if they be moved by private animosity.[5]

"As it is unlawful to take a man's life, except for the public authority acting for the common good, as stated above, it is not lawful for a man to *intend* [my emphasis] killing a man in self-defense, except for such as have public authority, who while intending to kill a man in self-defense, refer this to the public good." So, a private citizen may not *intend* to kill in self-defense. Since we are speaking of a *per se* case of human action—the case

---

5 *ST* II–II, q. 64, a. 7.

wherein the object is *per se* or naturally ordered to the end, and where the most formal and defining species is that of the end—we are being told that the very purpose of such justifiable action cannot be merely the killing of someone. For the aim of defense is not simply to kill, but to ward off an assault and secure life and safety from harm.

Hence, St. Thomas is clearly teaching here that by the very nature of the case a private citizen cannot, in the course of self-defense, simply intend as an end, independently of any defensive purpose, the killing of an individual. Rather, for the act to be one of defensive homicide, it must be such that it is proportionately ordered to the end of defense, to the warding off of assault and securing of life and safety from harm. For example, the private citizen is seen to seek the end of defense if, when he threatens the use of lethal force and the assailant surrenders rather than persists in assault, the defender does not then proceed to kill him: the *end* is defense, rather than killing.

But those with public authority, who can order slaying as such to the common good, may indeed "intend" to kill. That is to say, when the posse chases the criminal, the posse might be legally empowered for the sake of the common good, as historically has been the case, to kill on sight. Or, the posse might be legally empowered to kill those sought for arrest and trial if these resist arrest, a purpose not purely defensive—that is to say, that the end sought can actually be to kill a malefactor. A gang might have every desire to avoid fighting with armed police, preferring to assail unarmed innocent citizens. But the police, seeking to stop them, might be empowered (and in some legal regimes have been empowered) either to kill such malefactors on sight, or to kill malefactors on the condition of their attempting either flight or resistance, such killing being ordered to the purpose of protecting the realm and punishing their evildoing. Whereas police may intend to kill, however, the private citizen can concern himself only with proportionate, moderate defense, and may kill if and only if lethal means are the sole, or assuredly the best, means available to ward off unjust assault.

Precisely what St. Thomas does *not* mean by saying that the private citizen may not intend to kill in self-defense is that he may never deliberately *choose* lethal means as ordained to defense: for intention and choice are distinct. Nor does St. Thomas mean that a private citizen may kill in self-defense only by accident and not "intentionally." That is, he does not mean that if killing should follow from a moderate defense in a way that is unforeseen and unforeseeable that this is permissible, but that in the case wherein only a lethal means can defend the private citizen that the private citizen must abjure its deliberate use: for he has already instructed us that the citizen is not obliged to "omit the act of moderate self-defense in order to avoid killing the other man," and no reason has been supplied as to why a deliberately lethal defense must be by nature disproportionate. Rather, what is disproportionate is *intentional slaying*, for example, seeking as an end the death of the person rather than seeking defense as an end which may, in some case, imply use of a knowably lethal means.

It will be said that in a deliberately chosen lethal act of defense that the homicidal object is intended because the object is a "proximate end." To which it should be responded, that this is analogous language not favored by Thomas in the *per se* case of the human act, and that strictly speaking and causally *intention* is of the end and *choice* of the means. If it is noted that what is in one respect an end may be in another a means, it should be noted that it is true that in diverse respects something may be end in one respect and chosen means in another. Yet this alters nothing of the proposition that where an object is *per se* ordered to the end the most formal and defining species is from the end; hence this likewise alters nothing of the conclusion that where the object of a lethal act is proportioned to defense (such as to kill solely for the sake of defense and for no ulterior reason) the act is *defensive* in its fundamental moral character: a defensive homicide. As such, and only as such, is deliberate choice of lethal means warranted: as proportioned to defense in the case wherein defense is just and wherein either there are no other means, or the other means are knowably insufficient or far likelier to fail. For "one is bound to take more care of one's own life than of another's," and all the more is defense warranted when what is at stake is one's obliga- tion to an innocent who cannot care for himself, for example a mother's or father's defense of a child. Of course if there are less destructive means that also will effectuate defense, one is obliged to use these rather than a more destructive means. But inasmuch as killing the assailant always or for the most part stops the assault, it may be seen that in some cases—those wherein otherwise the defensive end would be either knowably or highly probably unattainable, and wherein no threat is posed by the defense to innocents— the deployment of lethal means can be undertaken owing to the natural proportion between such means and the end of defense, with the agent bearing absolutely no independent desire to kill as an end. On St. Thomas's account this type of deliberately lethal defense is, in such circumstances, wholly consistent with the end of a moderate defense. But of course this reading will be impossible to those who have not first discriminated that there is a *per se* instance of the human act, and that *intention* is used only *analogously* as between its primary and proper usage regarding the end, and its secondary and derivative usage regarding the means or the object of the act.

That St. Thomas takes himself to be concerned with a *per se* instance of the human act is shown both by his insistence that what is beside intention does not give species, by the reasoning we have just considered, and also by his response to the fourth objection, which poses the issue why, if one may kill in defense, one might not also commit fornication or adultery in an effort to save one's life. He answers that "The act of fornication or adultery is not necessarily directed to the preservation of one's own life, as is the act from which sometimes homicide follows."[6] That is to say, fornication and adultery are not *per se* ordered to defense: defense is neither such that it always requires fornication or adultery, nor are fornication and adultery such that by their nature they are ordained to defense. Whereas, to slay an assailant is always or for the most part to stop the assault, and so such slaying is *per se* ordered to defense when it is chosen precisely under that *ratio* (for one might deliberately provoke an attack in the hope of being able to slay someone, which clearly is not a defensive act but rather the pretext for wrongful homicide).[7]

How may homicide "follow" from the act of defense? As has already been indicated, in two ways: (1) purely by way of consequence, and (2) by way of deliberately chosen lethal means in the case wherein only such means are liable to be effective. As the first option indicates, it is possible

---

6 Ibid., ad 4.

7 Of course, one may hypothesize the case wherein the assailant somehow manages to wirelessly link an atomic bomb to the beating of his heart such that when his heart stops, the bomb goes off: then, to kill the assailant, would be to trigger an even worse assault! But the fact would remain that the initial assault was stopped albeit at the cost of triggering a worse, and so it remains that always or for the most part the killing of the assailant stops the assault. While technology adds complications, the closer one is to an instance of bodily assault, the more applicable the proposition would seem to be that killing the assailant always or for the most part stops the assault.

to mount a defense in which a lethal effect is merely a consequence of defense and not a function of the deliberate antecedent choice of lethal means under the *ratio* of the proportion of these means to the end of defense. In such a case, we do indeed have the standard case of double effect, about which more is to be said in the next chapter.

Such defenses from which unanticipated or at least unplanned harm or death unexpectedly occur by way of wholly unintended consequence are easily comprehensible. There is a scuffle, one shoves aside an assailant, and the assailant receives a contusion which causes internal bleeding and subsequent death. Even if one *knew* that this effect were likely to follow from one's act of merely pushing aside the assailant (owing to some bodily weakness of the assailant), that would not make one's act to be *per se* ordered to or aimed toward this effect, or to be undertaken with the hope of this effect, and indeed in such a case it would be but a partial cause (for were there no assault, then there would be no defense which accidentally but predictably kills).

But St. Thomas's formulation also pertains to the case in which killing is not a mere consequence, but in which a *deliberately and per se lethal means is chosen because it alone is proportionate to the end of moderate defense.* In this case, we do not have a mere consequence, not even a *foreseen* consequence, but a clear and deliberate judgment that only a stroke which is of its nature lethal—*per se* lethal—will suffice for the defensive purpose. For example, the felon's axe-bearing hand descends toward the neck of one's child, and there is only an instant to stop him; none other but a shot to the head will so incapacitate the nervous system as to assure that the axe does not slay or maim one's daughter. One knows that such a shot to the head is by its very nature, *per se*, ordered to kill. But one's selection of the lethal act is owing to its essential proportion to the end of defense, without which one's daughter will not be adequately defended. Because the act itself and its integral nature are always included in the object of the moral act, we must say that this is indeed a lethal act, but because the lethality here is chosen under the *ratio* of defense, to which it is *per se* ordered, the most formal, defining, and containing moral species is derived from the end. Hence we say this is fundamentally a *defensive act* and the difference (accidental with respect to this fundamental species from the end) which is introduced by the object is: homicidal or lethal: this is a defensive homicide.

Of course the means are not in the primary and proper sense of the term said to be intended but *chosen*, and are only analogically said to be *intended*. Indeed, it is only because of the prior intention of the end that the will moves out to the means at all, and this makes clear the sense in which the "intention" of the means is analogical and secondary in nature. It also makes clear why, in such a case, it is true to say that killing is not *intended*, because the defender's will does not move toward killing independently of the proportion of the act to a strictly *defensive end*: what is in the strict sense intended is *defense* and the acts proportionate to defense.

Since St. Thomas *nowhere* defines proportionate or moderate defense as necessarily non-lethal, it must be asked, Why, then, do so many interpreters of St. Thomas read his teaching as proscribing any deliberate choice of lethal means in the case of private defense? The answer is a failure to grasp that St. Thomas, in speaking of two effects, one being *praeter intentionem* and accidental with respect to the species of the act, is speaking of the *per se* instance of the human act. For example, St. Thomas is speaking of the case wherein the object is *per se* ordered to the end, and hence *per se* discriminable and distinct from that end, and where the most formal and containing species derives from the end in relation to which the species introduced by the object is merely an accidental further specification within the given type derived from the end.

Some authors also misread St. Thomas here because they believe that the integral nature of the act is not included within the moral object, and so they will hold that lethal defense is permissible but only because they wish to say that the moral object of a proportionate defensive act is never such as to deliberately include the use of knowably lethal means—*not because one may not use such means, but simply because on this view they would not be included in the object*. But, *sed contra*, if such means are deliberately used they not only accidentally diversify the fundamental moral species (defense), *they also essentially enter into the object of the act as such*. This lethality can licitly enter into the object of the act as such because killing is not absolutely speaking an act under negative precept, but is only under negative precept where it does not fall under the form of just punishment, the form of just war, or the form of just defense.

Hence erroneous readings of *ST* II–II, q. 64, a. 7 showcase the ways of getting St. Thomas's account of the human act wrong. One may not understand that teleology is necessary to determine moral species, and that there is a *per se* case of human action necessary to understand further complex acts, namely that case wherein the object of the act is naturally ordered to the end. Or, one may erroneously eviscerate the integral nature of the act from the moral object, owing to a failure to realize that the *formality* of the object is one of *determination and definition* but not of *part to whole* (as, analogously, essence abstracted as a whole is formal with such formality of determination and definition but not formal merely as a part vis-à-vis the whole). For the object of the moral act—what an act is about relative to reason—always includes, materially, the act itself and its integral nature. What then, is the object of a moral act in which a defender in a just and proportionate defense deploys knowably lethal means? The object is "defensive homicide," not wrongful homicide.[8] But homicide is materially included in the object of the act.

---

[8] A few years ago I made the happy discovery that, in essentials, this is also the interpretation held by the great Dominican commentator Francisco de Vitoria—oft lauded as the founder of international law—in his commentary on the *secunda secundae*. Speaking of defense, he follows Thomas in underscoring the difference between choice and intention. As intention pertains to the end, he argues that where there is a defensive end, no simple desire to kill, and no other proportionate means of defense save a lethal means, one may in a just defense deliberately deploy the lethal means. The lethal act that is necessary to defense is licit to will but not to intend (defense must be the intention). Hence Vitoria writes: "Si enim qui se defendit non habeat alia arma sino un arcabuz, tunc clarum est quod non potest se defendere non habeat alia arma sino un arcabuz, tunc clarum est quod non potest se defendere nisi occidendo. Ergo etiam licet velle occidere. Et quando ultra arguitur: ergo licet intendere: nego consequentiam, quia differentia est inter electionem et intentionem, quia intentio est ejus quod *per se* intentum est us finis. Sic ergo non licet propter se intendere mortem alterius, sed solum facere totum quod probabiliter potest ad defensionem suam. Sic etiam infirmus propter salutem vult abscindere brachium, sed non hoc intendit, cum non vellit de *per se* quod abscindatur brachium. Et breviter, ne in hoc maneat scrupulus, dicimus quod totum quod est necessarium ad defensionem, totum illud licet velle, sed non intendere" (Francisco de Vitoria, O.P., *Commmentarios a la Secunda secundae de Santo Tomas, Tomo III: De Justitia* [q. 57–66], ed. Beltran de Deredia, O.P., *Biblioteca de Teologos Espanoles,* volume 4, dirigida por los Dominicos de las Provincias de Espana). I am indebted for this discovery to the congenial erudition of Dr. John Boyle of the University of St. Thomas, most famed of course for his magnificent work bringing out the critical edition of St. Thomas Aquinas's *Second Roman Commentary.* Thomas Aquinas, *Lectura romana in primun sententiarum Petri Lombardi,* ed. Leonard E. Boyle, O.P. and John F. Boyle.

THE SOLUTION OF "DEPUTIZATION"

It is helpful here to consider the suggestion that a theory of state deputization be applied to justify private defense, thus bypassing St. Thomas's teaching in *ST* II–II, q. 64, a. 7. This is the idea that Thomas's principles will in fact allow for defense using lethal means—but only if one imports a theory according to which just private defense always occurs as *deputized* by state authority, an idea not to be found in St. Thomas's express treatment of the question of private defense in *ST* II–II, q. 64, a. 7. *The idea of deputization is a perfect brief illustration of a theory generated precisely in order to avoid applying what is taken for St. Thomas's object theory to his words about defense (for such application cannot logically escape conclusions contrary to reason).*

Of course it may indeed be quite reasonable to speak of private defenders being implicitly deputized to act for the state in certain specific circumstances. Yet *whatever the contingent arrangements of political regimes* may be, a "blameless defense" is by the nature of the case morally permissible. It is here that we must hold *either that in every case, or in some alone,* deputization is the solution to how Thomas can simultaneously hold (a) that no private citizen can as such rightfully deploy lethal means (for this is how *ST* II–II, q. 64, a. 7 is frequently and incorrectly interpreted), and (b) that the private citizen may nonetheless at times deploy lethal means because implicitly deputized by the state.

But if deputization *always* occurs, why did St. Thomas not note it in the article in which he treats this question? And if it only *sometimes* occurs, the following problem ensues. The problem is that in some cases wherein reason commends lethal defense the contingent arrangements of the state could, on an account that refers to contingent deputization, justly prohibit it.

The options are:

1. *The deputization is universal and all just defenses are cases of deputization:* but this is an odd thing for Aquinas to have omitted from his article on the subject; and it is also a proposition that if true would *actually wholly remove the category of just private defense, since all such defense would then automatically become public.* Then why, if this is St. Thomas's teaching, does he have an article that refers to the conditions for just *private* defense, if all just defense by private citizens is in truth *not private* but rather public because officially deputized by state authority?

2. *Only some just defenses deploying lethal means are permitted and others are not:* but then Aquinas would be holding that the state can justly do injustice—by prohibiting a blameless defense—and this is nonsensical. In any case the reason for the justice of private defense would not be that it is deputized by the state.

With respect to private defense, one might wonder how anyone other than a principled and consistent pacifist could fail to see that if a parent must deploy knowably lethal means to save the life of a child from unjust assault that such an act is *defensive* homicide and so—as defensive—not wrongful? Yet similarly unrealistic is the supposition that parents do not suitably defend their children save when they act in public *persona*.

In *ST* II–II, q. 64, a. 3, ad 3, St. Thomas considers the issue of the deputization of private citizens to act in behalf of the common good. He writes:

> It is lawful for any private individual to do anything for the common good, provided it harm nobody: but if it be harmful to some other, it cannot be done, except by virtue of the judgment of the person to whom it pertains to decide what is to be taken from the parts for the welfare of the whole.

Now clearly, lethal defense is not an act that harms "nobody"—it kills somebody. And, if it harms somebody, then it can only be taken "by virtue of the judgment of the person to whom it pertains to decide what is to be taken from the parts for the welfare of the whole." We may be tempted to think that because very frequently authorities would find it helpful to the common good to authorize lethal private defense in those cases where elsewise the innocent would perish, that we need no further principle to account for lethal private defense. Indeed, we might wish to interpret the common practice of the police examination of cases of private defense, and of formal court inquiry regarding the same, as confirming that when such defense is permitted this is a function of express deputization of private citizens in the service of the commonweal. Yet this will do neither as a reading of St. Thomas nor as a speculative answer to the question.

First, it will not do as a reading of St. Thomas. To reiterate, surely if he held that every case of just and lethal private defense were deputized by the state, he might have seen fit to mention that fact in his express treatment of the question of private defense? That he does not mention it is rather a great inconvenience for the idea of deputization as a way of saving St. Thomas's putative theory from disrepute.

Further, as has been noted above, if every case of just private defense—much less just *lethal* private defense—is a case of deputization of the private citizen by public authority, *then there ceases to exist any such thing as a just private defense—for a deputized act is precisely an act in public rather than private persona.* How odd, then, that St. Thomas refers to acts of private defense in *ST* II–II, q. 64, a. 7, and even refers to some acts of private defense which one need not for one's salvation omit despite their lethality? Clearly these are viewed by St. Thomas as private acts as distinct from acts of public authority: for he instructs us that public authority can *intend* to inflict death as part of justice, whereas private persons can only intend *defense*.

It is clear that the distinction between public and private acts of defense is in great prominence in *ST* II–II, q. 64, a. 7—and this is only four articles after the article containing the lines we have quoted above regarding private individuals authorized to perform acts that may harm somebody by "the judgment of the person to whom it pertains to decide what is to be taken from the parts for the welfare of the whole." Clearly, then, St. Thomas is not teaching that every case of just private defense, nor every case of just private *lethal* defense (for one is not obliged to withhold moderate defense lest one kill the assailant), is actually a case of the private citizen as deputized to serve the common good.

Of course, St. Thomas clearly makes deputization a function of the judgment of an official person: but is the justice or otherwise of an act of lethal private defense merely a function of official authorization? Is this not rather a question of *substantive justice*? Let us suppose, for a moment, that there is a state which prohibits the use of lethal force to defend innocent children from unjust deadly assault. Can such a prohibition be just? Can it actually be the case that a parent has a just claim to defend an innocent child under assault if and only if some official personage expressly gives the parent authority to do so? This seems extravagantly wrongheaded both in itself and as a reading of St. Thomas's text.

One concedes that the state must exert itself to be sure that private lethal defense is just rather than disordered or a pretext for murder. But this is *after the fact*, in an effort to be sure that wrongful homicide has not occurred. Is it the case that *before the fact* the one who mounts a lethal private defense does so as officially conscripted to serve the police force or the army?

Either (a) deputization is such that *every* single just case of lethal private defense is *necessarily* deputized state action (which, for St. Thomas, clearly involves judgments by individuals who represent the state); or else (b) deputization is purely a *contingent function of state permission* such that only state permission renders it just.

As to the former (a), it confuses the very nature of deputization. Deputization involves formal representation of the state by a private citizen, action in public rather than private *persona*. To say that every act of just private self-defense is deputized by the state seems to omit St. Thomas's requirement of authorization before the fact by competent state officials. More importantly, this account confuses any private action that serves the common good with the distinctive authority of the state to impose justice and to wage war. Every just act in some way serves the common good: but every just act is not an act of public authority, not "deputized." Already it has been noted that if this option holds, then there is no private defense, and so St. Thomas misdescribes his own putative position in *ST* II–II, q. 64, a. 7. More importantly, there do seem to be private acts of defense never commissioned or deputized by the state, whatever *post factum* approbation may later obtain. If every act approved after the fact by state authority is only rightly performed owing to state deputization, then are man and wife deputized to marry? Private acts may be just and yet not be deputized acts undertaken in public *persona*. Further, the justice of the act of private lethal defense is wholly independent of state permission: either some case of defense is just or it isn't quite apart from the judgment of the state (which may, after all, be incorrect). Of course, as has been indicated, such an explanation would remove the entire category of just private defense by rendering it essentially public: an anomalous conclusion for a reader of St. Thomas's article on the question (i.e., *ST* II–II, q. 64, a. 7) to draw inasmuch as he refers to just private defense in contradistinction from public defense.

As to the second (b), surely what makes lethal private defense to be just is not contingent permission by state authority, but the nature of the defense itself. If the defense is just, then the public authority has no business punishing or prohibiting such defense. Public authority ought inquire to be sure that no murder has been done, but this is not to say that one's rightful claim to defend oneself or others in one's care from unjust assault is wholly a function of empowerment by a state official. One does not possess being by virtue of state decree, and the tendency to persevere in being does not reasonably affect moral action solely through public deliverances of state authority.

To claim that a certain category of private acts must necessarily always occur as public acts would seem to require some evidence of the requisite delegating act. Yet nothing like such a delegating act is to be found, but only *post factum* inquiries aimed at assuring that no wrongful homicide has occurred.

Further, if private defenses are just only when expressly permitted by state authority, then what should one call those cases in which state authority *should* permit and *does not* permit? Are such cases instances of just private defense? If so, the justice does not derive from state authorization but is prior thereto and exists on other grounds. If the justice of such acts is not prior to state approval, then, howsoever useful it might be for the state to permit such acts, one has no ground for claiming that the state ever is obliged in justice to permit them, a conclusion that clearly is contrary to right reason (imagine telling parents that they acted wrongfully in saving the lives of their children from a deranged assailant because they lacked prior state permission).

Also, on such an account will stateless persons not have just claim to defend themselves when unjustly attacked? Granted that political society is natural to man, there are circumstances—men lost on a deserted isle—in which no state exists to authorize such defense. Surely one does not await official state deputization to defend oneself when assailed by a brigand in the outland wastes. Just as surely, if *all* acts of just private defense are instances of state deputization, then they are all *public*, and we then cope with the problem *by denying it exists: by denying the manifest truth that the private citizen as such and not merely as state minion rightly defends himself from wrongful assault.* This is precisely what St. Thomas Aquinas did not do, as the most casual reading of *ST* II–II, q. 64, a. 7 will manifest.

Granted that justice is a common good, and granted that just private defense serves it, it must be noted that many actions of private citizens serve the common good which are not acts undertaken only through special state deputization. Many acts of charity support the common good, but supernatural charity is insusceptible of merely terrestrial causation—although it does pertain not alone to the common good of beatitude but to all inferior common (and even particular) ends within the hierarchy of ends, inclusive of the common good of civil society.

Of course, *if* when we read *Summa theologiae* II–II, q. 64, a. 7 on private defense we possess the appropriate theoretic insight into moral object, end, and species, *then* we will not need to suggest implausible theses, unadvanced by St. Thomas, in order to obtain reasonable conclusions. For those conclusions are already to be found in *ST* II–II, q. 64, a. 7 itself, and only theoretic error regarding the teleological constitution of the object and species of the moral act obscures them. I have chosen to consider the argument for private defense as deputized by state authority both to illustrate the difficulty of coping with the issue of private defense in the absence of St. Thomas's proposed teleological grammar for the constitution of object and species of the moral act, and also because this hypothesis is not a bad attempt at redeeming a bad theoretical situation. Nonetheless it fails. And, of course, there are many even less successful attempts to retrieve the situation.

A Short Note on Intentional Killing by Public Authority

Often it is thought that the state has no more authority with respect to the infliction of pain, punishment, and death, than does the private individual, for surely both state and individual are subject to moral law. While it is true that both state and individual are subject to moral law, the state exists to serve not merely the individual but the common good. Hence it is not true that the state suffers the same moral limits as does the individual with respect to killing and punishing, for the simple reason that the political state is directly (and, one might add, *naturally* and *divinely*) ordered to the service of the common good of civil society, while indirectly being ordered to yet higher common goods in relation to which the political common good should be transparent (such as, for example, the common good of knowing the truth about God and the universe, or the even higher good of charity).

Common goods, ends which are more diffusive, communicable, and rationally participable than mere private goods, by their nature transcend such private goods. Hence for the sake of vindicating justice in civil society

the political state may under certain circumstances and with due proportion, coerce, punish, imprison, or kill either as penalty, or by way of warding
off assault, or by way of suppressing violent injustice by internal or external
foes of the commonweal. This authority the state *naturally possesses* from
God, because as naturally ordered to the service of the common good the
state possesses from God that which is implied and teleologically required by
this service. Thus in those circumstances wherein the commonweal requires
the killing of malefactors either in war, in quelling civil disturbance, or in
punishment,[9] *then* the *per se* ordering of such acts to vindicating a transcendent norm of justice and serving the common good of society gives the
determining moral species, and makes it licit for public authorities to *intend*
such acts. In such cases, the object includes the integral nature of the act.
Hence the moral object in such cases will, if it be just, be something akin to
"imposition of death as just penalty for the sake of the common good," or
perhaps in the case of resisting invasion or putting down rebellion "killing
for the sake of suppressing violence against the common good."

It is the state's obligation to vindicate justice upon the persons of those
who contemn it and harm or even war against the common good. The
political state does not serve justice as though this service were an act of
supererogation. Those acts that are *per se* ordered to the subjugation and
punishment of malefactors harming the common good and the vindication
of justice—either because by nature they tend toward these ends, or
because they are objectively required by these ends—are defined by the
most formal and containing moral species *derived from the end.* Hence they
are acts of justice, whether they be police acts, military acts, judicial acts,
applications of judicial sentence, *et alia.*

Insofar as the state serves justice, the state participates in divine
authority by its very nature—for, as St. Thomas always and definitively
insists, the natural moral law is *nothing other* than the rational participation of the eternal law[10]—indeed it is not other than the eternal law, but

---

[9] It is after all fairly clear that killing is *per se* ordered to suppressing violent enemies
either internal or external, and that it is also *per se* ordered to punishment (the
deprivation of a good of nature contrary of the will of the one punished for the
sake of vindicating a transcendent norm of justice) since life is a great good, its
deprivation tends to be contrary to the will of the person who is killed, and such
grave penalty is of its nature proportionate to grave crime.

[10] Cf. *ST* I–II, q. 91, a. 1, resp. & ad 1.

merely the limited and natural, rational participation of the same. Hence the state participates divine authority not by some "theocratic" *superadditum* of religiosity, but simply by its natural ordination toward securing justice: for just law is by its very nature and being a rational participation of eternal law. Just ordinances are so by virtue of conformity to the eternal law. *Hence the primal jurisdiction over life belongs to God alone, and all authority of the political state to execute, and even to punish, is delegated by God as a function of the participation of genuine human law in the eternal law: without which metaphysical participation, there is no authentic law.* That is to say, this reaches to the very being of law. *Mala lex, nulla lex.*

Hence as St. Thomas himself makes clear in his article on private defense:

> [I]t is unlawful to take a man's life, except for the public authority acting for the common good, as stated above, it is not lawful for a man to intend killing a man in self-defense, except for such as have public authority, who while intending to kill a man in self-defense, refer this to the public good, as in the case of a soldier fighting against the foe, and in the minister of the judge struggling with robbers, although even these sin if they be moved by private animosity.[11]

This is but to say that public officials can under certain circumstances justly intend death. St. Thomas made this point even clearer in his commentary on the Fifth Commandment, arguing that that the state serves as executor of divine providence in applying penalties:

> Some have held that the killing of man is prohibited altogether. They believe that judges in the civil courts are murderers, who condemn men to death according to the laws. Against this St. Augustine says that God by this Commandment does not take away from Himself the right to kill. Thus, we read: "I will kill and I will make to live." [Deut 32:39] It is, therefore, lawful for a judge to kill according to a mandate from God, since in this God operates, and every law is a command of God: "By Me kings reign, and lawgivers decree just things." [Prov 8:15] And again: "For if thou dost that which is evil, fear; for he beareth not the sword in vain. Because he is God's minister." [Rom 13:4] To Moses also it was said: "Wizards thou shalt not suffer to live." [Exod 22:18] And thus that

---

11 *ST* II–II, q. 64, a. 7, resp.

which is lawful to God is lawful for His ministers when they act by His mandate. It is evident that God who is the Author of laws, has every right to inflict death on account of sin. For "the wages of sin is death." [Rom 6:23] Neither does His minister sin in inflicting that punishment. The sense, therefore, of "Thou shalt not kill" is that one shall not kill by one's own authority.[12]

Of course, here one might note that all the Fathers and Doctors of the Church save Tertullian (who died outside the Church) and Lactantius allow for the justice of the death penalty, and Lactantius does not claim it to be a *per se malum* but only that Christians are called insofar as possible to something higher. One should also note the high theological note characterizing the profession required of the Waldensians in 1210 in order to re-establish ecclesial communion. The Waldensians were required to acknowledge, among other things, the essential justice of the death penalty for grave crime. This is a remarkable datum: the Church itself has insisted as a condition for ecclesial communion that the intrinsic justice of the death penalty be formally acknowledged and professed.[13]

St. Thomas actually articulates the nature of just penalty of death in the context of addressing charity toward felons:

> It is for this reason that both Divine and human laws command such like sinners to be put to death, because there is greater likelihood of their harming others than of their mending their ways. Nevertheless the judge puts this into effect, not out of hatred for the sinners, but out of the love of charity, by reason of which he prefers the public good to the life of the individual. Moreover the death inflicted by the judge profits the sinner, if he be converted, unto the expiation of his crime; and, if he be not converted, it profits so as to put an end to the sin, because the sinner is thus deprived of the power to sin any more.[14]

While the moral questions raised by war, capital punishment, and the lethal use of police power to quell civil disturbances transcend the scope of

---

[12] This commentary is reprinted in *The Catechetical Instructions of St. Thomas Aquinas*, trans. Joseph B. Collins (Manilla: Sing-Tala, 1939), 93–94.

[13] Cf. Henry Denzinger's *Enchiridion Symbolorum, The Sources of Catholic Dogma*, trans. Roy J. Deferrari (Fitzwilliam, NH: Loreto Publications, 1955), no. 425.

[14] *ST* II–II, q. 25, a. 6, ad 2.

this work, it is important to see that the state is, by reason of the good to whose service it is teleologically ordered, empowered to act beyond private individuals. Yet this empowerment is always one subject to charity and prudence, and bound to the minimal use of coercion consistent with lawfully sustaining and vindicating the order of justice.

As Charles De Koninck so effectually argued in his classic work on the subject,[15] it is the glory of the human person to be ordered (both naturally and supernaturally) toward an end which is not merely private but common and indeed transcendent. That this end is not a private good because of its superior radiance and ontological density does not cause it to cease to be good, nor is it by reason of not being a private good therefore alien to the person, who is ordered to the rational participation of the higher good.

Nor is there basis for the claim that the state's authority to marshal lethal force in behalf of the common good is in principle inconsistent with the Church's magisterium. For the Church does not teach, and never has taught, that the death penalty (or killing in just war) is of its nature a *malum in se*—howsoever much prudential conditions may and do limit its use.[16] This is *precisely because* this penalty may in principle and under some circumstances serve the *essentially nobler and transcendent end of the common good, a good superior to any private good of the same order prior to choice.* All of which implies an ethically pertinent ordering of ends prior to choice: the normative hierarchy of ends that defines the *ratio boni.* This datum tells us something about the popular but false thesis that ends are not naturally ordered in a morally pertinent way prior to choice. But our digression into general ethics and moral theology must end for the sake of the more proximate purpose of contemplating the object and species of the moral act.

---

[15] See Charles De Koninck's classic account of the common good, *On the Primacy of the Common Good: Against the Personalists,* ed. Ronald P. McArthur, trans. for *The Aquinas Review* 4 (1997).

[16] Of course, the overriding circumstance of the moral and juridic *culture of death* authoritatively treated by the encyclical *Evangelium Vitae* does indeed provide circumstantial reason for seeking to avoid the application of this penalty. For a treatment of the manner in which the culture of death undercuts the prime medicinal purpose of penalty generally but specifically of the death penalty; and also for an extended consideration of the relation of *Evangelium Vitae* and the tradition on the issue of the death penalty; see my work "*Evangelium Vitae,* St. Thomas Aquinas, and the Death Penalty," *The Thomist* 63 (1999).

SUMMING UP

This chapter has argued that *ST* II–II, q.64, a. 7 is the proving ground on which the defects of many accounts of the object and species of the moral act become manifest, and on which many serious attempts to break the code of St. Thomas's analysis of the nature of the moral act have foundered. *Moral philosophers who advert to the teaching of St. Thomas have come to sustain non-intersecting and indeed contradictory worlds: a general account of the moral object that cannot make sense of private defense (and other issues), and an account of private defense (and of other issues) that is either unrealistic, or further compromises the account of the moral object (by emptying it of its integral nature), or else amounts to a general flanking movement (the theory of private defense as deputized) with respect to the clear teaching of* ST *II–II, q. 64, a. 7.* Yet even the putative benefit represented by the theory of just private defense as deputized by state authority is achieved only by showcasing just how deficient such an interpretation makes Thomas's express account of private defense to be. It is thus a counsel of despair.

Rather than enlist the Common Doctor of the Church in behalf of such propositions, it is better to revisit his account of the moral act. This enables one to realize that his account of human action is wholly consistent with his account of private defense and when conjoined with it yields exemplarily reasonable conclusions.

CHAPTER THREE

■ ■ ■

The Principle of Double Effect

IS THOMAS'S ACCOUNT INCOMPLETE WITHOUT THE ADDITION OF A NEW SCHEMA OF DOUBLE EFFECT?

THERE IS, however, yet another objection to the account of private defense—flowing from the account of the object and species of the moral act—provided earlier. In his treatment of private defense, St. Thomas refers to "two effects" of one act, one of which is "intended" and the other of which is outside or beside the intention, *praeter intentionem*. This has often been taken precisely with respect to private defense as implying that the effect which is *praeter intentionem* is necessarily not included in the moral species derived from the intended end of defense. Hence, the genesis of the view—imposed from without upon St. Thomas's analysis, and at least strongly suggested by Cajetan's commentary[1]—that

---

[1] Cajetan's *Commentary on Summa theologiae (ST)* II–II, q. 64, a. 7 manifests his view of intention and of the matter of the act in private defense: "For the end and the means to the end fall under intention, as is clear with a doctor who intends health through a draught or diet. But that which as consequence follows from the necessity of the end does not fall under intention, but arises existing outside the intention, as is clear from the weakening of the body that follows from healing medicine. Likewise in two different ways it may be licit to kill, that of the public person and the private: for the public person, as for instance a soldier, orders the death of the enemy as a means to the end subordinated to the common good as is said in the text, but the private person does not intend to kill that he may be saved, but intends to save himself not depriving himself in defense—even though the death of the other should necessarily follow from this defense. And so in this way the latter [the private person] kills *per accidens*, while the former [the public officer] kills *per se.*" ("Nam & finis, & medium ad finem cadunt sub intentione, ut patet in medico,

the element of homicide cannot be materially included in the object of the defensive act.

We have implicitly dealt with this view above by providing a contrary account of the actual teaching of St. Thomas showing that the object is itself *praeter intentionem* in the most formal sense of *not being the end*, while not in the normative instance of the human act being *praeter intentionem*

---

qui intendit sanitatem per potionem, vel diaetam. Id autem, quod consequitur ex necessitate finis, non cadit sub intentione, sed praeter intentionem existens emergit, ut patet de debilitatione aegroti, quae sequitur ex medicina sanante. Et iuxta duos hos modos diversimode occidere potest licite persona publica, & privata: nam persona publica, ut miles, ordinat occisionem hostis, ut medium ad finem subordinatum bono communi, ut in litera dicitur, persona autem privata non intendit occidere, ut seipsum salvet, sed intendit salvare seipsum, non destitutus a sui defensione, etiam si alterius mortem ex sua defensione oporteat sequi. Et sic iste non occidit, nisi *per accidens*, ille autem *per se* occidit. Et propterea ad illud requiritur publica auctoritas, ad hoc non.") Clearly here "intention" is used univocally whereas it is analogical as between the end (whose intention is prior to and the condition of the choice of means) and the object (which is "intended" only because of this prior moving of the will toward the end which is that which is strictly speaking intended). Further, although there are occasions wherein lethality is purely accidental with respect to the particular act of defense, there are other occasions wherein the particular act of defense is deliberately chosen as lethal owing to the proportion between lethality and defense. Of course, in this latter case, the lethality is accidental to the end of defense as such, and if this is what Cajetan means by the killing following accidentally from the agent pursuing the end of saving himself "not depriving himself in defense" then the meaning can stand. Alas, it is more frequently read differently: as though lethality were not only accidental *vis-à-vis* the end of defense simply considered, but as though lethality were accidental to the *particular act* even when lethal means are chosen because they alone are sufficient for the end of defense. This latter reading—which it will be seen eviscerates the object of the moral act of the integral nature of the act itself, is, sadly, that which has been associated with Cajetan: although, on this point of the integral nature of the act being materially included in the object, a reading of Cajetan that is more congruous with the account given in this work is not impossible. There remains, however, the failure in this passage sufficiently to identify that what is at stake in just private defense is an instance of the *per se* case of the human act. That is, explication in terms of the *per se* ordering of object to intended end. Such identification of the *per se* case of the human act requires one to see that the object is only secondarily and analogically— by *pros hen* analogy—said to be intended. The very existence of the moral act and its object is testimony to the priority of the intention of the end as that without which no act or object ever comes to be. If we do not see that it is the end that is primarily intended, and that where the object is naturally ordered to the end that the most formal, defining species is derived from the end, then we are in danger of misconstruing the nature of the moral act.

with respect to species (for when an object is naturally ordered to the end, the most formal, defining, and containing species is derived from the end). Hence—since in a just deliberately lethal defense the lethal means is chosen only because of its essential proportion to defense and not because killing is independently sought as an end—there arises for St. Thomas the possibility of a "defensive homicide." Such defensive homicide is not merely the case of death following accidentally as *consequence* of defensive action, but of lethal means deliberately chosen as essentially ordained to defensive action.

St. Thomas distinguishes quite clearly between the act of self-defense and the end for the sake of which this act is performed. Thus we have no textual reason to adopt the wider and secondary sense of "intention" according to which intention extends analogically to the object, as distinct from the primary sense in which we speak (as *ST* II–II, q. 64, a. 7 speaks—"Actus igitur huiusmodi ex hoc quod intendatur conservatio propriae vitae. . . .") of intention as pertaining to the end.

Without doubt, this reading of *ST* II–II, q. 64, a. 7 is opposed to the view that St. Thomas intends to set out some general principle according to which what is *praeter intentionem* would not be included either in the end or in the object of the act. For the sense of intention in this article pertains strictly to the end in the normative case of human action wherein the object is *per se* ordained to the end and contained within the species derived from the end. Thus, what is apart from the end does not give species but is accidental with respect to the species (as indeed in the normative case of human action, the species derived from the object is an accidental specification vis-à-vis the species derived from the end) while yet contained within this species.

This analysis shows that the "two effects" of the one act do not require a fundamentally different schema—denominated the schema of "double effect"—to yield a coherent and morally reasonable account. Rather, the identical schema articulated by St. Thomas earlier in the *Summa theologiae* is more than sufficient to cope with the "two effects" in question, since only one is intended, whereas the other is either (a) merely an accidental consequence (in cases where the lethal effect is unforeseen and unforeseeable) or in the case upon which we have centrally focused, (b) is *chosen* rather than *intended* and is materially included in the object, which object is naturally ordered to the end of defense and therefore is contained in the species that derives from this end.

In short: the growth industry of a "principle" of double effect and of elaborate double effect schemas is stopped before it starts. And what stops it before it starts is recourse to the normative teleology at the fount of St. Thomas's teaching, without which there is no human action. Presuming that defense is just, then in that case wherein only lethal means hold the promise of successful defense and are thus chosen by a defender under the ratio of defense, the lethality is *contained within* the most formal and defining species which is derived from the end of defense. Where the object is *per se* ordered to the end, the most formal, containing, and defining species derives from the end, in relation to which species the species derived from the object is merely a further accidental specification. It is this *per se* order which is the foundation of the entire analysis.

Killing an assailant is to be avoided in general because it inflicts grave injury. But because killing the assailant naturally tends to stop the assailant's assault; because there are circumstances under which no other means will achieve the end of defense; and because killing is not an act under negative precept such that it is always and everywhere wrong, but only wrong in the absence of the form bestowed by just public authority or just defense—for all these reasons, killing the assailant is *per se* ordered to the end of defense. There simply is no need for the grand schema of double effect.

TWO TYPES OF POSSIBLE DOUBLE EFFECT CASES

Nonetheless, we are left with the question whether the idea of a "principle of double effect" might be of any use in any cases of significant difficulty, of the sort in which something is chosen which normally one would not choose. These are either:

1. cases wherein some foreseeable effect which we would never seek as an end in itself may nonetheless be deliberately chosen under the *ratio* of an end to which it may be essentially proportioned;

Or else:

2. cases in which some inadvertent consequence ensues upon an act which although not essentially caused by that act is yet in some fashion circumstantially inextricable therefrom or in relation to which the act constitutes a partial cause.

The First Type of Case

By virtue of the treatment given in the second chapter and reiterated above, it would seem that an answer to the first type of case has been given. For precisely what occurs in the case of justified lethal defense is that we choose under the *ratio* of defense that which we would never embrace simply as an end, and do so because of the essential proportion between the knowably lethal act and the end of defense. In this case the object is *per se* ordained to the end of defense and therefore the most defining and formal species is derived from the end of defense, and the species derived from the object is with respect to this species derived from the end an accidental specification (although of course it is not accidental with respect to *this act*—just as it is accidental to a trip as such that it be a car trip, although it is not accidental to this particular car trip that it be by car). It seems important, however, to provide further illustration of this analysis *apart* from the controverted and difficult case of lethal private defense.

As further illustration with respect to the first type of case that some have thought required a fundamentally new schema of "double effect" to account for, consider the case of one who takes an emetic drug precisely in order to vomit out poison that has accidentally been ingested. Normally the very effect of this drug—extreme physical nausea—would be avoided as harmful to bodily health. Indeed, deliberately causing oneself to be ill would seem to be contrary to divine commandment. Yet, precisely what causes this effect of extreme physical nausea is what makes the emetic helpful where no other means exists to counteract a poison accidentally ingested. What is not in any way a good which the agent should seek as an end—as no one in his right mind would desire to be sick and vomit for its own sake—is then sought as a means essentially ordered to the removal of poison from one's system. In the case where no other such means is available, the use of the emetic is indeed a *medical* use, because it is essentially ordered to remove a recently ingested and slower acting poison. Where the object is *per se* ordered to the end, the most formal, defining, containing species is derived from the end, in relation to which species the further species derived from the object is merely an accidental specification (although, again: not accidental vis-à-vis the particular act, but only *vis-à-vis* the species derived from the end).

Likewise, take the case of removing a gangrenous limb. No one reasonably desires to remove a limb simply for the sake of removing a limb—

indeed, to desire this simply, as an end, would be to seek bodily mutilation. But to seek to remove the limb because it is gangrenous and so poisoned in such a way as to threaten life and health, is perfectly reasonable. What we would not naturally seek as an end, we do indeed choose as a means; what we do not simply intend in the manner of an end, is nonetheless materially and integrally included in the object of the act. What is one doing who removes the limb to prevent gangrene from spreading? The answer is: removing a gangrenous limb for the purpose of protecting one's health from gangrene. The act is a medical act. Yet indeed, one who simply sought to remove a limb for the sake of removing a limb would be acting unreasonably and contrary to precept.

To move outside of the medical sphere, the seafaring merchant who casts his goods into the sea to avoid the sinking of his ship during a storm, is doing something that he would not reasonably seek simply as an end. Yet, given the storm, and the datum that losing ballast gives the ship greater survivability in the storm, it is clear that casting his goods into the sea is *per se* ordered to the end of stabilizing the ship during the storm. For there is such a *per se* order either when the object of itself naturally tends to the end, or where the end is such that it can in no other way be attained. Here both obtain, for by the nature of the case making the ship lighter enables it better to survive the storm, and also it may be that only this expedient can save the ship facing such a danger. Hence removing all that is not necessary to the sailing of the ship is of its nature ordered to making the ship lighter and more survivable—it is *per se* ordered to this end—and so its species is not unreasonable destruction of goods needed by others (and by oneself and one's own family), but rather, the species of protecting life—one's own and others'—and ship from imminent destruction.

The cases considered above are all instances of "mixed voluntary" acts, or acts wherein something normally repugnant to reason and which would never reasonably be sought for its own sake is done because of its natural proportion to an end which is reasonable. Note also that what is done is not under negative precept—it is not always wrong to take an emetic drug, or to cut off a limb, or to throw one's goods into the sea, or to be a partial cause of one's own death. One is not doing *moral evil* that good may come, but rather doing that which one normally couldn't do *as an end* without it being morally evil (contrary to one's health in the first two cases, to one's customers, workers, and family in the third) but which can be *per se* ordered to a good end and so partake of a good moral species (medical in the first two, life- and ship-saving in the third) and as such entailing only *physical rather than moral evil* (nausea and vomiting, a lost limb, or lost goods and fortune). But someone who simply enjoyed making himself vomit, or bodily mutilation, or destroying property, or who desired to kill himself, would have much to confess to his local parish priest—because these are not licit as ends, simply speaking. And—simply and *per se*—there is a difference between end and object, between the strict sense of intention and choice.

One should not be confused by the secondary usage of "intention" to include end and object, because clearly this is a secondary usage. The essentially prior sense of *intend* concerns the end in the strict sense, that without which there is no simple act, no placing of any act in its species, no complex act. In the *per se* or normative instance of human action which forms the unit of currency of St. Thomas's entire analysis of human action, the object is naturally ordered to end, and accordingly the species does indeed derive from the end intended and not from what is *praeter intentionem*, which is accidental with respect to the species derived from the end. This is true even while the species derived from the object is contained within the species derived from the end, because the object-species is an accidental further specification of the more fundamentally determining, defining, and containing end-species. A sign of this primacy of intention is indeed that one may intend the end prior to any determination of means.[2] The *per se* is prior to the *per accidens*; and since it is essential to the object that it bear always some relation to the end to which it is ordained, whether it be accidentally related or essentially related, the primary and *per se* sense of intention pertains to the end as such (without which there is no act and so no pertinent object). Further, there is a *per se* case of the human act—because the case where the object is only accidentally ordered to the end is actually, upon consideration, a case wherein one simple act with its own moral species is further ordered by the agent to another act with its own moral species, so that the latter is more defining than the former. But even to get to the level of such complex or composite acts, one must first have simple acts wherein object is ordered to end.

---

2 *ST* I–II, q. 12, a. 4, ad 3; see also *ST* I–II, q. 12, a. 1; *ST* I–II, q. 12, a. 3.

This *per se* or normative instance of action is that upon which all in St. Thomas's account of the moral act rests.

The Second Type of Case

So much, then, for the first type of case in which one might wish to deploy the principle of double effect: there is nothing for it to do, because the schema provided by the prior analysis of St. Thomas is more than adequate without introducing such anti-realist complications. This leaves only the case of the second possible use for a principle of double effect to be considered. One recollects that this is the case wherein *some inadvertent consequence ensues upon an act which although not essentially caused by that act is yet in some fashion circumstantially inextricable from it or in relation to which the act constitutes a partial cause.* These are the types of cases which literally *scream* "double effect" (and which yet are leagues removed from the case of private lethal defense).

For example: a mountaineer is hanging from a rope from the side of the Eiger Mountain, having fallen from near the top; his weight is in fact pulling the other members of his party down, as it is on the verge of dislodging the only remaining stay hammered into the side of the mountain from which all are hanging. If he cuts the rope, he will fall to his death; if he does not cut the rope, his weight will cause all his climbing troop to fall to their deaths with him. Now, making the load on the rope lighter is by its nature ordered to preserving the stay hammered into the mountain in its position and so saving the lives of the other climbers; but it is also ordered to his own fall and (short of a miracle) his death.

If the mountaineer cuts the rope, does he commit a sin of suicide? No: because his intended end is saving the lives of the other climbers, and where the object of the act is essentially ordered to the end, it takes on the defining species derived from the end. *Could* it be suicide? Yes, *if* he cut the rope *for the sake of killing himself.* But since he is cutting the rope for the sake of saving the lives of his fellow climbers, this is the end. But is not his ensuing death materially included in the object of the act? The answer is yes, *but being a partial cause of one's own death* is not under negative precept in every case, but only in that case wherein one's death is *intended* as the end or wherein being a partial cause of one's own death occurs owing to a failure to take ordinary care of one's own life. But the climber does not fail to use all ordinary means to sustain his life, nor does he intend his own death: indeed, if, at the moment of cutting the rope, he unexpectedly falls into a tree and survives, he will not then jump out in the hope of dying. *If,* however, being partial cause of one's own death were always under negative precept, then we would need to say, for example, that the last Tsar of Russia committed suicide by interposing his body to shield his children from bullet fire. But he did not seek his own death, but their protection, although this act was a partial cause of his own death.

Thus all such acts—leaping on grenades to save one's platoon, for example—are acts whose object is "saving the lives of others by heroically interposing one's own life." Indeed, this analysis could not work if the mountaineer cutting the rope or the soldier leaping upon the grenade were not as simple acts *per se* ordered to protect the lives of others even while also naturally harming the agent. Are there not two contradictory *per se* orders here? In moral terms, no, there is only *one,* with two effects: one of which is intended as an *end* and to which the object of the act is essentially ordered, and from which end is thus derived *the most containing, formal, and defining* moral species, which saturates and determines the act.

Only the datum that the object is naturally ordained to the end sought by such sacrificial action as that of the mountaineer or the soldier makes the defining and saturating species to derive from the end. *And while the permission of physical harm is included in the moral object materially speaking, this physical harm is not in this case (unlike that of lethal private defense) a* means: *for it is not one's death which lightens the load, or even one's death which absorbs the fragments of the grenade, one might live and have accomplished the end (because one fell into a tree and lived, or because the grenade didn't kill one, or perhaps didn't go off) without being disappointed.* One's death in such a case is not, contrary to that of deliberately lethal private defense, a means, but rather merely a likely and foreseen consequence.

Does this mean that one may kill oneself for the sake of idealistic purposes? No. The act of the mountaineer, or of the soldier, is not to kill himself, but to lighten the load on the line in a way that risks his death, or to shield others from harm in a way that risks his death. The agent in these cases is seeking the end of preserving others in life, and does so without neglecting any means of preserving his own. Indeed, in the case involved, all will die if no action is taken, but if action is taken then only the one acting dies. Clearly the agent knows that he is exposing himself to the greatest likelihood of death. Yet the end sought is one that the action is well-suited to: preserving lives under threat.

Per se teleological order is crucial. One could not, for instance, in order to "save lives"—by, for instance, gratifying a despot—kill oneself, as, for example, the German tank commander Erwin Rommel was offered the chance to kill himself to preserve his family from punishment of death. The reason is that this act is not *per se* ordered toward saving the life of one's family, but only *per accidens* so ordered. By contrast, making the load on the rope lighter so it does not break and send the other climbers to their deaths, or blocking the grenade shrapnel from the bodies of those it would otherwise kill, are *per se* ordered to saving lives. Indeed, killing oneself is only *per accidens* ordered even to gratifying the despot. There is nothing about suicide in itself that either tends of itself to gratify despots (it might infuriate them), or which is *necessary* for despots to find gratification (most seem to find gratification apart from imposing suicide).

Again, recollect that in the cases of heroic interposition treated above the agent's act does not in and of itself necessitate his death, nor is his death properly speaking the means to the end sought: he might somehow survive a fall into snowbank or tree, although that is unlikely; he might survive the grenade going off, or it might not go off; and the means is making the load on the rope lighter, or shielding others from grenade fragments by absorbing them oneself, and not properly speaking *dying*.

Two Objections

Objection 1. However, one might suppose that in the case of the grenade one would have reason to expect it to go off, and that this by its nature is ordered to kill. Let us suppose that this is so—or at least suppose that all that is necessary for it to *be* so is for the explosive device to be sufficiently powerful and knowably well-engineered. Then, at least in the case of the soldier shielding his fellows from such a device, since the integral nature of the act must enter into the object of the act, one would need to say that the object of this act is: shielding others from grenade fragments with one's own body, and at the cost of one's own life, for the sake of saving their lives.

This does indeed introduce a difference—for it is one thing to face likely death as *consequence*, yet another to embrace it *by the very nature of one's action.* Given this revision, do we now have a case of suicide? No. For one thing, it is not the action of the agent by itself which causes death, but only in conjunction with the working explosive. The explosive might not work, and if it does not the agent presumably will not seek out another opportunity to die. And *even if we posit that it is known to be uniformly effective by nature, it is not caused by the agent but is that to which the agent is responding (and which he is opposing so as to prevent its harming the higher good)* and which in the given example will in any case harm or kill the agent. That is, *it is not alone the agent's action which is the cause of death, but rather the agent's action is simply a partial cause of death.*

Further, as noted above, being a partial cause of one's own death is not universally under negative precept, but only when this includes careless-ness about the ordinary means to sustain one's life. But it is not careless-ness with respect to one's life to deliberately place it in hazard for the common good of justice, or truth, or for the lives of many others, but rather is this a noble honoring of the transcendence of the common good? As indicated in the first chapter, there is an essential hierarchy of human ends prior to choice. Some ends are objectively nobler than others. Life is desirable and good in itself, true; but it is not desirable and good merely *for* itself, but for the sake of objectively nobler goods, such as friendship, wisdom, holiness, justice, and truth. Hence for the service of these ends a good and just man will not hesitate to risk his life, even though the risk be of the highest order, or death even certain—because it is the service of these higher and common goods, goods which are more universal, diffu-sive, and irradiant, which define the good life. Such ends are not private goods—one may die to preserve justice—yet justice although not a private good is yet good for each and every person. It is not, as De Koninck mas-terfully taught, an alien good merely because it is *not a private good.* The common good is good for the person but not simply that person's private good—a more diffusive, rational, and universal good which the person owing to rational nature can participate in and serve.

Thus, even given the re-definition of the object of the act, it remains (a) that one's death is not precisely the means to the end even though willingness to be a partial cause of the sacrifice of one's life is included in the object of the act (because one is willing, in acting to save others from the explosive, to expose one-self to the explosive); and (b) that the species of this sacrifice is not suicide, but sacrifice for the sake of the common good, because where the object is naturally ordered to the intended end then the species derived from the end is most formal, defining, and containing. But physically shielding others from the explosive is naturally ordered to preserving them from it, and so the species derived from this intended end of preserving others is most defining and containing.

Of course, if one wishes to refer to the case of the mountaineer or soldier who interposes his life to save others as a case of "double effect" because one natural effect is sought *qua* end and the other is simply permitted, then one may do so. *But nothing in this requires the least alteration in the general action theory of St. Thomas. Rather, it is simply the application of one identical analysis to the most difficult of cases.*

Further, what gives the proper account to acts of sacrifice is indeed the transcendence of the common good, and not some form of logicist legerdemain. That is to say, that just as teleology is necessary to determine the species of a moral act, so likewise in the most difficult cases one finds that the transcendence of lower by nobler ends provides the essential *ratio* of just sacrificial acts. For although my life is good in itself, it is essentially ordered to higher goods, and in behalf of these goods it may be risked or, at hazard, sacrificed. Yet it will never be the case that the object of the act in such a case will be destroying one's life for any reason whatsoever, and this because in these cases the agent is but partial cause. Suicide remains *per se malum*, but interposing one's life in the service of the common good, even when that against which one interposes is knowably and lethally effective, is not the sole cause of death: for the agency against one interposes is part of the cause, and the one who interposes is not the cause of *that* agency but of its deflection from the innocent. Indeed, the one who interposes does not will this agency against which he interposes to be effective.

Objection 2. But does not this account then license something such as suicide bombing in a "just war" or good cause? No, because there is a distinction between interposing oneself to shield others from a threat—even though this be a partial cause of one's likely death—and authoring the agency which kills oneself. In the first case, wherein the agency that causes death is not authored by the one who interposes, we have one case; in the second, wherein it is authored by the agent, we have another.

Even the mountaineer is not author of the circumstance that has all pulling on the last stay in the mountain and will assuredly kill all; even the soldier who falls on the live grenade has not deliberately authored the grenade being present where it is with a view to harming himself. Nor does the mountaineer completely and directly choose his own death (because another agency is involved which he hopes will be deflected, as he hopes somehow his fall may be abated safely). Likewise, the soldier does not completely and directly choose his own death (because there is another agency present, and he indeed hopes that this agency is deflected short of his death, or fails altogether).

But the one who drives the suicide truck into the fortified installation is indeed choosing to be, not partial and indirect cause of his death, but complete and direct cause, for he devotedly contrives and sets in motion the agency which causes his death and indeed hopes it does that which will cause his death: he makes of himself, as it were, part of the mechanism of actuation of the bomb itself, which he seeks not to mitigate, redirect, or deflect so as to protect others, but to set in motion and actuate. Thus in the case of the suicide bomber, the object of the act includes materially that which is under negative precept and may never be done. Even this mere material inclusion is sufficient to bring the act under negative precept, since what is chosen and willed is a direct and complete cause of death *per se* ordered to the same, and planned so as to compass the same. This is the case even on the supposition that the agent wouldn't mind *per miraculem* accidentally surviving. The reason we say that a direct and complete cause of death is included in the object in this case, is that the agent has chosen his own death as materially implied in being part of the mechanism of delivery and actuation of the bomb itself: the loss of life is part of the essential causality *wholly designed by the agent.*

Neither the instance of the mountaineer, nor that of the soldier covering the grenade, involve the agent arranging, causing, and hoping for the completion of that which suffices to kill him. The mountaineer has not chosen to dispose the stay to be on the verge of failing along with the death this threatens, nor has the soldier disposed the grenade to explode; rather, each has only interposed himself, on the supposition of this other agency, to protect others from the effects of this other agency. *The suicide bomber has arranged it all, and cannot claim that the agency involved is not his own.*

Yet, were there not a difference in the object of the act between being willing to act for the sake of a higher end in such a way as to permit one to be a *partial cause of one's likely death, and being a proper and simple cause of one's own death, this difference could not obtain.* And then we would in fact have only suicide as one act ordained to various other ends, some of them noble but none justifying the evil of suicide. *But there is a difference in object—* indeed, the object of itself contains in each act a relation to the end. *In acts of sacrifice for the noble good the end is service to the common good; the means is an act whose object is per se ordered to this good but materially inclusive of a partial cause of one's (either likely or certain) death; and the object-species of this act is an accidental further specification vis-à-vis the species derived from the end.* By contrast in the case of the moral evil of suicide, the end sought naturally includes the termination of one's life* (likely as related to other deliverances, as from disappointment, humiliation, despair, imperial rule of another government, or unceasing physical torment); *the object is per se ordered to this end* (even when the unwitting agency of others is involved, as when someone thrusts himself into traffic on a highway, this agency of others is chosen by the one who attempts suicide precisely for the sake of achieving the extinction of his life); *and the object-species of the act is a further accidental specification vis-à-vis this suicidal intent.*

It is important here to see that an act is said to be suicidal not alone when this is the most formal aspect of the object, or in other words, not alone when this is principally what makes the suicidal object choiceworthy to the agent: not only when the agent principally *wants to die.* For example, in the case of the suicide bomber, what is most choiceworthy about the act may be its wreaking of destruction on an enemy. Nonetheless, an act is said to be suicidal not only when what is most choiceworthy about the act is the acquisition of one's own death, *but also when its generic nature is such as to materially and directly include the planned acquisition of one's own death, as for example when the end* (say, wreaking harm on enemies by blowing them up) *is sought by a total and deliberate arranging of means such as to include direct causation of one's death* (making of one's life an essential part of the mechanism of delivery and actuation of the bomb whereby havoc is wreaked). Surely, had the mountaineer been consulted, he never would have designed matters such that the lives of his party could be spared only by lightening the load on the line from which he is appended by cutting his own support. Rather, he opposes this situation by acting as forcefully as possible to defend the highest good he is capable of defending from it: by performing an act *per se* ordered to saving lives by removing the weight that elsewise will drag his company to its death. His own agency is only the partial cause of his own death, whether viewed as merely likely or as naturally certain, because he is not by acting as he does thereby the cause of the destructive circumstance against which his act interposes. The fall that carries him to the bottom of the ravine is an undesired consequence of an act *per se* ordered to spare as many of his party as feasible, and which, could he extend the interposing act to protect himself, he would.

But is not the act then evil in consequence, and so not integrally good and not to be performed? This is an erroneous conclusion, because an evil consequence is only such as to render the act immoral when it is no longer merely a circumstance, but when it forms a new object or else an essential condition of the act. But here, the circumstance though a physical evil does not introduce a new object, or form an essential condition, of the act in the requisite sense of rendering the object not to be *per se* ordained to a good end (saving the lives of his fellow mountaineers)—and so it is unlike the case of sacrilege, for example, which essentially conditions and adds a new object to what elsewise would be merely theft.

Further, when an act such as to be suicidal in its natural effect is chosen out of carelessness or omission of due consideration and action to sustain life, we say that the agent has omitted due care over the good of life and is seriously culpable of evil. Clearly a mountaineer who cut away at his rope for fun while hanging from the top of a mountain slope would rightly be judged sinfully careless of his life—whereas, a mountaineer who cuts away at his rope in service to the noble good of friendship and of the lives of those in his party is careless in an entirely different sense (for, in the example here intended, the agent acts to save the lives of those threatened by choosing an act naturally ordered to save those lives but materially inclusive of the likely cause of his own death). The agent's act of heroic sacrifice simply cannot be understood without grasping that man is ordained to the universal good even though it can be possessed only as universal and not as private good. The transcendence of the common good is conspicuous—it is good for me, though it be not merely *my* good and cannot be possessed as though it were merely my good. The good of saving the greatest number possible from evil circumstances remains a good even when it is not the case that the one saving is included in the number of those saved.

It is important to see that even were the agency that we have said to be "likely" to cause the agent's death were *apodictically* known to be a *certain* cause of death, that this agency is indeed *not proceeding principally from the agent*, and that *the agent is opposing this agency as fully as is possible by acting so as to prevent its harm to the higher good*. Again, that the mountaineer will die is given in the circumstance that the stay is coming loose, but what is not given is whether, before it does, he can lighten the load on it so as to save the lives of the rest of his party. Hence the mountaineer's choice is but a partial cause of his likely death, and indeed the choice is principally ordered to delimit the destructive circumstance and protect the party as fully as possible (were it possible to extend this protection to himself, he would happily do so). Thus what is encompassed in the object of the agent's act is merely *willingness to be a partial cause of his own death where this willingness is the condition of an act per se apt to oppose this destructive agency*. This is wholly other than *planned instigation of the destructive agency itself in a manner that causally encompasses one's death*. Heroic sacrifice, and suicide bombing, could not be more utterly diverse.

The Standard Conditions of Double Effect Applicable Only to the Second, and Not to the First, Type of Case

Yet it is also worthy of note that this second type of difficult case does in fact preserve what is often referred to as the structure of the principle of "double effect" for so long as this structure is interpreted according to sound philosophy. One might abbreviate the notion of double effect applicable in this second type of case—a notion which often is incorrectly thought to extend to the first type of case considered above in section II.a—in four conditions which must be met:

- first, that the action contemplated be in itself either morally good or morally indifferent;

- second, that the bad effect not be directly intended;

- third, that the good effect not be a direct causal effect of the bad effect; and

- fourth, that the good effect be "proportionate to" the bad effect.

Under these four conditions, on the standard account, the principle of double effect licenses performing an act with two effects, one good and one bad.[3] Even here the "bad" effect is *physical* and not *moral*, for one may not do evil that good may come.

It is also the case that often what is involved is not strictly "two effects" but rather one effect and one merely foreseeable *consequence* which may be to a greater or lesser degree predictable. But there are cases where literally two effects are involved (the first type of cases dealt with in section II.a above are such) and these are often those wherein the one effect is included within the object and is indeed a cause of the second effect or end. *These latter instances, while involving two effects, clearly do not fit the famed standard conditions of "double effect."*

Rather, only the second type of action (here taken up in section II.b above) *wherein the second effect is either mere consequence, or else the first effect (the end) is not literally the cause of the second even though it be a partial cause, strictly conforms to these conditions. To understand the application of these conditions properly requires the antecedent understanding of object and species articulated by St. Thomas Aquinas. For double effect is not a radically new schema of interpretation, but rather the one identical schema of interpretation developed continuously by St. Thomas as this applies to a certain sort of action.*

As has been shown, it is when the object is naturally ordained to the intended end that then the species derived from this intended end definitively saturates and morally determines the act, and only this truth renders the difficult cases of sacrificial action to be intelligible. This is why we speak of noble sacrifice in behalf of the common good in one fashion, and suicide in another. As Chesterton would have it, the martyr dies because he loves life too much, whereas the suicide dies because he loves it too little.

Even in the second type of case wherein the conditions for what is thought of as the double effect principle obtain, the intelligibility of these conditions wholly depends upon the earlier analysis of object and moral species. For example, a "bad effect" or "bad consequence" may be physically

---

3 For example, to quote Vernon Bourke's famed textbook *Ethics* (New York: Macmillan, 1951), 353, wherein he defines double effect as "where a moral action results in two consequences, one evil and the other good, the action *may be done morally*, if the good is in some reasonable proportion to the evil, if the good cannot be attained without the evil, if the two consequences are concomitant, and if the good is directly intended and the evil only permitted."

or morally evil, and this requires that we place the act in its species. But to place any act in its species involves normative teleology: we must know whether the object is *per se* ordered to the intended end, or not. If the object is *per se* ordered to the end, and the end is good, then the species derived from the object will be in comparison to this species derived from the end a mere accidental specification of the latter, contained within the latter, and fundamentally determined and defined by the latter. The diversity of object between heroically sacrificial and suicidal action has been set out above.

CONCLUSION

In short, one would do better to fathom the natural teleological grammar governing the constitution of object and species of the moral act than to dwell upon the standard conditions of the "principle of double effect." For the latter is merely a special case of the application of the former, and a special case which has been overextended to cases to which it does not apply, and which has been wrongly interpreted with respect even to the cases to which it *does* apply. Whereas, one may derive these standard conditions—appropriately understood—merely by correct application of the principles of Thomas's teaching (regarding the teleological constitution of object and species of the moral act) to the special and highly restricted category of actions to which the standard conditions of "double effect" may intelligibly apply. In this way, the unrealistic extension of these conditions where they do not obtain, and the misunderstanding of these conditions where they do obtain, in one fell swoop is corrected.

Of course—need one say it?—the richest irony of all is that St. Thomas never had the least intention, in *ST* II–II, q. 64, a. 7, of suggesting such conditions, much less of applying them where they do not pertain, that is, to the case of private lethal defense. But even where these conditions do pertain they cannot be properly understood outside the context of Thomas's account of the teleological grammar governing the constitution of the object and species of the moral act; whereas, these conditions can themselves be derived in their proper intelligibility by applying Thomas's account to the restricted category of actions to which the standard conditions of double effect apply. Accordingly, what is lost to the burgeoning industry of double effect reasoning is gained to the foundational realism of our understanding of the moral act.

CONCLUSION

▦ ▦ ▦

Summary Points
and Final Remarks

THIS BOOK has undertaken to present, in one dense theoretic reflection, St. Thomas's teaching regarding the natural teleological grammar governing the constitution of the object and species of the moral act. In the course of doing so, we have had occasion to stress the following salient points, which provide the key to any satisfactory treatment of the analysis of moral action.

1. Knowledge of the normative order of ends is necessary to the definition of virtuous action, because it defines the good life as an ordered whole to which virtuous action is ordered.

2. The object of the moral act is not merely formal in the sense of the form as a part, but rather is formal in the sense of the form of the whole. As such, the object of the moral act—what the act is about relative to reason—not only includes most formally that which renders it choiceworthy to the agent (the relation to reason, which is truly a relation to the end) but also and by the very nature of the case must materially include the act itself and its integral nature.

3. *The object may be treated merely generically and precisively, apart from any per accidens ordering to a further end;* or it may be treated with its full specification as ordered to the end sought by the agent in a particular act. *This is only possible because the object as such bears a relation and proportion to the end, such that we know the type of the end—otherwise there*

could be no object which falls by its nature, generically, under negative pre-cept. This again testifies to the truth that there is a per se, normative instance of the moral act for St. Thomas, namely the case wherein the object is per se ordered to the end. It is this which enables us to exclude from the object any natural order toward certain termini, as we for example exclude from "bodily mutilation and torture" any per se ordering to "repair of the heart." If the *per se* ordering of the object is such as to fall under negative precept, then it is impermissible irrespective of any *per accidens*, ordering in the mind of an agent to a further end. It is this which makes one realize that lethal defense is permissible, because while killing is generally to be avoided, it is not to be avoided as an absolute genus, because subsequent on the form of justice or of just defense it is permissible.

4. *When the object is naturally ordered to the end, then the most formal, containing, and defining moral species is derived from the end.* Of course, here the end is that sought by the agent, even should this be deprived in terms of the normative hierarchy of ends. Whether the end is deprived in relation to normative natural teleology (owing to appetites of the agent that are not rectified by reason), or is proper, objects of themselves bear a certain relation and order with respect to the end. When acts of themselves tend toward an end, they are said to be naturally or *per se* ordered to it; likewise, when attainment of an end *by the very nature of the end* requires a certain action, that action is also said to be naturally or *per se* ordered to the end. In cases wherein the object is *per se* ordered to the end sought by the agent, the moral species derived from the end sought is most formal, most defining, and most containing, and the species derived from the object is merely—in relation to the species derived from the end—an accidental specification of the latter.

5. Complex acts are simply cases wherein one simple act, whose object is *per se* ordered toward the end, is further ordered in the mind of the agent to some other act, whose end is more formal in the intention of the agent. Hence, even to distinguish complex from simple acts one must discover whether the object is *per se* ordered to the end or not. By complex acts, we refer to acts within multiple disjunct species; and by simple acts, to acts all of whose objects are essentially contained within the species deriving from the intended end, whether there is

only one such object or many. Thus "simple" and "complex" are not to be taken merely materially, but formally.[1]

6. Further, because when the object is *per se* ordered to the end the most formal, defining, and containing moral species is derived from the end, it is also true that to determine the species of an act one must refer to natural teleology.

7. It follows that natural teleology provides the grammar for the constitution of the species of the moral act, and also for the constitution of the object of the moral act. For the object is either *per se* (i.e., naturally) or *per accidens* ordained to the end, and in the latter (*per accidens*) case one is dealing not with any normal object but with an entire simple act with its own moral species, which is in the mind of the agent further ordered (*per accidens*) to the end of a distinct act with its own distinct moral species. And so, whether one deals with an object *simpliciter* or with an object which is in reality an *entire simple act with its own moral species* can be discerned *only with reference to natural teleology*.

8. The fundamental *unit of currency* of St. Thomas's entire treatment of the moral act is the *per se* instance of the human act: namely, the instance wherein the object is *per se* ordained to the end. For all other cases of human action depend upon this case and are related to it.

9. Intention is spoken analogously of the means or object of the act, but principally and properly of the end, for the end may be intended even prior to the determination of means, and the very reason for the going out of the will toward the means is indeed the prior intention of the end. Intention is not indifferently to be used, then, of end and means, and the more proper term is "choice" with respect to means. This is all the clearer when it is recognized that there is a *per se* case of the human act, the case where the object is *per se* ordered to the end, and so there is a case wherein this discrimination of object and end is most formal, howsoever much it is true that in a secondary sense the object is intended, or that in complex act the end of the first simple act serving as a quasi-object is intended.

---

[1] These observations are added in the second edition to clarify a point that has confused some.

10. Hence there are five capital errors to be avoided: (1) to deny the perti-
    nence of, or overly abstract from, the naturally normative hierarchy of
    ends prior to choice, in relation to which virtues and vices are defined
    in terms of the ordered whole of a good life; (2) to suppose that the
    object of the moral act is entirely formal after the manner of a part
    rather than as *the form of the whole*, so that the object would then
    exclude the act itself and the integral nature of the act: this would
    transform the object into a purely ideational reality, a "proposal"
    which can be changed merely by *redescribing it*, and also rule out the
    generic intelligibility of certain objects considered apart from further
    specification in concrete acts with respect to the end; (3) to suppose
    that natural teleology is irrelevant to complete understanding of the
    object and species of the moral act as such and in the concrete,
    whereas it clearly is essential: for where the object is *per se* ordered to
    the end, the most formal, defining, and containing species is derived
    from the end. This is crucial both for knowledge of the moral species
    and for distinguishing simple and complex acts, as well as being the
    condition of possibility for generic knowledge of certain moral
    objects; (4) to lose sight of the truth that the fundamental unit of cur-
    rency of St. Thomas's analysis of human action is the *per se* case of the
    human act, namely that case wherein the object is *per se* ordered to the
    end; and (5) to suppose that intention is univocal as taken of the
    means or object and as taken strictly of the end, whereas it is properly
    analogous, with the principal and proper sense of intention pertaining
    to the end.

11. Grasping these antecedent truths will spare one the regnant counter-
    intuitive readings of St. Thomas's express teaching regarding private
    lethal defense, which he nowhere indicates is contrary to moderation
    in defense, and which he only says cannot be *intended*—as an *end*—
    by the private citizen, and not that it may never be *chosen* as a *means*
    because of the proportion it bears to moderate defense in some case.
    In short this instance is not necessarily one to which the classical
    schema of double effect applies, since the lethal effect may be either
    the result of deliberate deployment of lethal means under the *ratio* of
    defense (in which case it does not apply) or the lethal effect may be a

purely accidental consequence of defense (in which case it may apply if it is foreseen but only partially caused by the agent).

12. Grasping these antecedent truths is sufficient to indicate that the principle of double effect properly pertains only to those cases wherein some inadvertent consequence ensues upon an act which although not essentially caused by that act is yet in some fashion circumstantially inextricable therefrom or in relation to which the act constitutes a partial cause. Even so, care must be taken to be sure that what is a circumstance in relation to one object does not add species either by (1) introducing a new principle condition of the object, or (2) constituting an entirely new object.[2]

13. Even where double effect replies, it is not a radically new schema for the interpretation of human acts. Rather the standard conditions for the application of the "principle of double effect" are simply the result of applying the natural teleological analysis of the human act to a particular restricted category of cases, namely those indicated in twelve above.

14. The applications of this analysis follow.

These considerations all point to the primacy of *nature* and of *teleology* in the theory of moral action. Any account which overabstracts from nature and from teleology is in danger of losing the cognitive gaze on the real that makes possible genuine moral analysis. In any case, clearly St. Thomas's analysis of the nature of the moral object whether taken generically, or as the object of the concrete specific act as such, is dependent upon his analysis of the teleological grammar governing the constitution of the object and species of the moral act—and this analysis is of perennial validity. It is eminently defensible in speculative terms, and the insight which it offers into the nature of human moral action is unsurpassed. Contemporary moral philosophers unwittingly bereft themselves of crucial resources when they too quickly, under the impetus either of Humean or of continental rationalist tendencies, renounce the foundational import of natural teleology in the analysis of human action. And so, for the sake of right reason in moral philosophy, it is important to advert to the foundational role

---

2 These observations are added in the second edition to clarify a pont that has confused some.

of nature and of natural teleology in moral analysis, and to acknowledge the teleological grammar governing the constitution of the object and species of the moral act.

Yet, at the end of this brief work, it is important to introduce a cautionary observation with respect to the teleological *place* of St. Thomas's luminary account of moral action. For the purpose of this account is ordered not alone to insight into the nature and moral species of human actions, but to the *complete* contemplation of the good life as a whole, inclusive of the perfection of teleology in virtuous action within both the philosophic and theological orders. That is to say that argumentation regarding the character of certain actions, while important both to systematic rigor and to the informing of conscience, points to the perfection of natural teleology in acts of virtue. It would be wrong, then, to end a volume whose purpose has been to point out the ineluctable saturation of moral action theory by teleology, without indicating that the teleological order is made effective not chiefly through deductive argument, but through the development of virtuous dispositions both moral and intellectual. Only a very small part of the moral life—as we all know—can be summed up by the "difficult" cases (considered under the *ratio* of double effect above, and also in the appendix below). But the case which is truly difficult is otherwise: it is that of the ordinary need to develop the spiritual ascesis requisite to the natural knowledge of the ordering of ends and the application of this knowledge in the light of prudence so as to develop acquired virtue under the orchestrating suavity of infused virtue and the theological virtues and gifts of the Holy Spirit. Hence in this book we have tried to consider something of vital importance both for the moral life and for moral and speculative wisdom. But important as it is, it is part of the narrative of law, grace, and virtue perfected by St. Thomas in the later chapters of the *prima secundae* and in the *secunda secundae* of the *Summa theologiae*. And it is to this wider horizon of the good—aided powerfully throughout by St. Thomas's unified teleology—that one turns for the completion of moral philosophy and theology. To that end this book is offered, in the hope that a realistic account of the nature of human moral action, and of the teleological grammar governing the constitution of the object and species of the moral act, may provide means for the wayfarer to move onward in appreciation of the natural and supernatural good.

APPENDIX 1

■■■

Particular Applications
to Difficult Cases

The cases that follow are illustrative of the extreme difficulty that practical cir-
cumstances may afford to moral analysis. There is no attempt here to provide
anything like a comprehensive treatment of typical cases, but only to afford a
glimpse into the application of natural teleology to some of the most difficult
and objectively complicated of moral questions.

INTRODUCTION

OFTENTIMES difficult issues for moral analysis are treated today in a free-standing manner, quite apart from any prior insight into the foundational truths of moral teleology. This treatment of difficult cases is also virtually presented as though the prime test of moral theory is the facility with which this relatively small body of cases may be treated. Yet while it is of course a test for moral theory that it be capable of extending to the more complicated problems, any such extension is in fact a derivative function of the antecedent teleological analysis of the ordinary moral case—involving our generic knowledge of the *per se* teleological ordering of objects to ends (whereby we can indeed see that certain types of actions are simply and generically incompatible with the structure of a good life). Hence the cases considered below are treated under the separate rubric of an appendix, indicating both the derivation from prior analysis of the principles pertinent to their solution (dealt with in the text above) and the fact that the relatively confined category of such complicated cases does require distinctive attention. One can, without engaging the sorts of objectively trying difficulties considered below, gain great moral leverage in the treatment of the bulk of moral cases simply through understanding the body of the text, above. The philosophical hypotheses and casuistry involved in contemplating the more objectively trying cases here considered are not of the essence for achieving a general understanding of the moral life. Yet as St. Thomas taught, the further out we extend the application of moral principle, the more objective complication of reasoning we find (and the more ways of going wrong!). Thus, there is room for the secondary and derivative analysis of difficult cases. Secondary and derivative with respect to what?—With respect to the primary teleological considerations unfolded in the main text, and the life of virtue specified thereby.

About some of the analyses below there is widespread agreement (for example, that the principle of double effect obtains in removing a gravid cancerous uterus). About others, there is widespread disagreement (for example, the case of, Mary and Jodie, the congenitally joined twins which will be discussed further in the Appendix). But the same principles extend to all.

Of course, many other cases might have been included, but the purpose here is the illustrative application of St. Thomas's account of the nature of the moral act. It should be noted that the purpose here is to show that teleological analysis does provide traction for the analysis of these sorts of cases—cases that commonly are treated in the literature. But no claim is made for infallibility in the application of teleological analysis, and of course the judgments regarding every case here considered are subject to the further discriminations and authoritative teaching of the Holy See. Nonetheless, the purpose is to provide illustration of the extension of teleological analysis to more difficult cases. While neither the sole nor the sufficient test of the probity of a theory of moral action, it is nonetheless important that such a theory be capable of providing guidance regarding such cases. Hence it would be my hope not that every aspect of the analysis below be received whole cloth, but that it be taken as pointing toward the types of considerations that are pertinent—in the light of the teleological grammar constituting the object and species of the moral act—in the handling of difficult cases.

This is perhaps the occasion to note that certain cases included below manifestly are more straightforward than others. The case of craniotomy, and of the proposed use of condoms by married couples in order to avert AIDS, do not to this author appear objectively complicated. Yet, by reason of confusion about the nature of the object and species of the moral act, they have come to be viewed as difficult. For this reason they are included here, although perhaps strictly speaking they may be said to be "difficult" only by analogy of attribution.

MORE WITH RESPECT TO DOUBLE EFFECT

It seems fitting to provide three more vintage illustrations of the super-fluity of any radically new schema of "double effect" before turning in earnest to a few central applications of St. Thomas's teaching with respect to contemporary moral controversies regarding difficult cases. And, for this purpose, it is worth noting that what makes these two prime illustra-tions of double effect reasoning intelligible is the standard teleological analysis of the constitution of the object and species of the moral act.

The Case of the Gravid Cancerous Uterus

By now, the case of a mother suffering with a cancerous uterus has become famous, and virtually all concur that it is licit to remove the uterus, even though this will predictably entail the death of the child. Why? Double effect of the second category which we considered in the preceding chap-ter, which on the account here given is the only category wherein there seems to be even a minor difficulty confronting the basic teleological analysis. And, as also seen earlier, even this minor difficulty dissolves if one patiently works through the analysis on the basis of St. Thomas's funda-mental teleological approach to the object and species of the moral act. Let us proceed to consider this case in exactly that light.

In this case, the child will die in any case if the child remains *in situ*. Fur-ther, in this case one is not directly acting against the bodily integrity of the child as such, but altering its circumstance of place albeit in a manner known to involve predictable death. Why is one acting in this way, and toward what end? One acts in this way to shield the mother from the effect of cancer, and toward the end of such a shielding. For this purpose, the uterus would need to be removed whether there were a child in it or not. The acts taken are *per se* proportioned to the removal of the uterus, and not *per se* directed to the harming of the child. It is a knowable consequence of this action that pre-dictable harm will accrue to the child. But the harm accruing will accrue in any event, and more crucially the action is only a partial cause of that harm. The fundamental harm is a function of the cancer, to whose threat the action is responding by preserving the good as fully as this may be preserved. The object of the act is then removing the uterus for the sake of shielding the life of the mother from cancer in a way that involves being willing to be a partial cause of the death of the child, but not a direct cause. Since the act is *per se* ordered toward removing the uterus so as to shield from cancer, and involves no direct infliction of harm on the child, the species that is derived from this end is the most formal, defining, and containing species. Hence the act is a medical act. Further, it follows the pattern of interposing against an agency or threat of which one is not the cause, and it is only because the good can be served effectively only by being willing to permit a foreseen evil (physical evil rather than moral evil) consequence that the consequence is permitted. There are two effects, but one is the *per se* end of the act, and the other is merely a consequence of which the agent is not the total cause. The agent would be the total cause of the effect if the nature of the act directly were such as *per se* to bring about death to a child in every such case (but it isn't) or if the killing of the innocent child were indeed in some way a *means* to the end of aiding the mother. But it is not by killing the child that the mother is aided, but by removing the uterus, which would be done in any case whether the woman were pregnant or not. The famed standard conditions of "double effect" here apply, but indeed only because the basic teleological analysis presented by St. Thomas does, when applied to the case, indicate that they are warranted. The act is in itself good (interposing against the threat of cancer to medically aid the woman suffering with cancer); the evil effect is not the end sought by the agent, but only permitted, and the act is only a partial and not proper and complete cause of the death of the child, which is to say, *simpliciter*, it is not the cause of the death of the child; the good effect which is indeed the end of the act is not achieved through the evil effect as a means (it is not through the death of the child that the uterus is removed, there is no direct action against the child as such, if the child lived the uterus would *still* have been removed, and the definition of removing the uterus does not involve killing a child); and there is indeed a proportion between the good and evil effect such that the evil consequence is not so great as to make the act unworthy of choice (the child is dying in any case, but the mother will die too in the absence of an interposing act).

Here we have nothing else than the systematic application of St. Thomas's basic analysis to that category of cases in which a consequence follows from a *per se* good act which is such that one would generally wish to avoid it. The consequence knowably follows from the act in such a way that the agent is a partial cause, but not the cause *simpliciter*, of the consequence. And the good end sought is such as to outweigh the evil which ensues. The standard conditions of double effect apply here, provided that we understand them through the lens of St. Thomas's basic analysis.

The Submerging Submarine

A submarine during WW II has surfaced to take on oxygen and to make certain repairs at sea. Enemy fighter planes spot the submarine, and undertake a strafing run to destroy it. As the crew scrambles below, one tardy crew member does not make it back inside the submarine, but is left on deck. If the captain of the submarine orders the submergence of the submarine to save the submarine and its crew from death (and its mission from defeat), then the crew member on deck will predictably die. If, on the other hand, the captain of the submarine does not order the submergence of the submarine, but orders the hatch opened and awaits the return of the crew member, the submarine and all its crew will be destroyed, and the mission will end in defeat. When the captain orders the submergence of the submarine, does he commit murder?

No. Once again, the same analysis applies. The submarine commander is interposing by his act to ward off the threat posed by the enemy planes. The action taken, the submergence of the submarine, is *per se* ordered to save crew, submarine, and mission from destruction by taking all out of the reach of the attack. Where the act is *per se* ordered to the end, then the most formal, defining, and containing moral species is derived from the end. This is, accordingly, an act of defense for the sake of saving all from destruction. Given the circumstance that a crew member remains on deck, the submergence of the submarine is a partial cause of that crew member's death (as he may be sucked down by the descent of the submarine, or else drown in the ocean in the absence of any help). But though this be a predictable consequence, the end sought is not his death, and the choice to submerge the submarine involves only a willingness to be a partial cause, and not the cause *simpliciter*, of his death. No direct action is taken against his person, and the action itself is interposing against a threat which would in any case kill him.

The famed standard conditions of "double effect" once again apply, and for the same reason that they will always apply when they do apply, namely only because the basic teleological analysis does when applied to the case indicate that they are warranted. The act is in itself good (interposing against the threat to slay all on board, destroy the submarine, and defeat the mission); the evil effect is not the end sought by the agent, but is only permitted, and the act chosen is only a partial and not the proper and complete cause of the death of the crew member, which is to say, *simpliciter*, it is not the cause of the death of the crew member. Of course, if another vessel, or even floating debris, is nearby, he could live—but even if one considers his death to follow with predictable necessity, nonetheless the submergence of the submarine is not *per se* ordered to his death; nothing in its definition requires his death—it would indeed be submerged in this circumstance even if he did not exist; and the crew member's death is but a consequence of a good act of interposition against another's agency for the sake of the safety of others, an act whose efficacy sadly does not extend to the crew member who is equally attacked. The good effect which is the end of the act is not achieved *through the evil effect or consequence as a means* (it is not through the death of the crew member that the submarine is submerged and taken out of harm's way, there is no direct action against the crew member as such, and if the crew member lived the submarine would *still* have been submerged: the definition of submerging a submarine does not involve killing a crew member). Further, there is indeed a proportion between the good and evil effect such that the evil consequence is not so great as to make the act unworthy of choice (the crew member will die in any case, but the whole crew will die too in the absence of an interposing act). It is, as always, important to see that the most formal, defining, and containing species is derived from the end when the object is *per se* ordered to the end, and the submergence of the submarine is *per se* ordered to its escape, an escape whose nature only *per accidens* and in the way of consequence involves the death of the crew member. The commander must, it is true, be willing to choose an act which entails being a *partial cause* of the death of the crew member, but not the cause *simpliciter*, because it is the circumstantial causality—inclusive of the attack—and not mere submergence of the submarine which is involved in the sailor's death. Why must the submarine be submerged *now*? Because the crew must be shielded from attack. Does submergence of its nature *per se* threaten anyone? No, but only under a circumstance. And what *causes* that circumstance? Not merely the captain (who did not order the crew member to remain on deck beyond the time available to get below), but the attack (maximal speed was *required* by crew members to leave the deck in order to avoid the attack, and he could not muster that speed). See, again, the distance that separates this and the case of the suicide bomber considered in chapter 3, for the suicide bomber arranges the circumstances in detail so that he himself forms part of the mechanism of the bomb's delivery and explosion. The captain does not here arrange the circumstance which is the critical element in the sailor's death, namely his being on deck beyond the time when the submarine must, to save lives, submerge. It is the accidental slowness of the sailor, and the extreme speed with which submergence must occur in order to spare lives, which forms this causal narrative.

What makes all these cases difficult is that one can predict the evil consequence, and that the agent must be willing to be partial cause—but not cause *simplicter*—of the evil consequence as part of an act that is *per se* ordered to a good end. But the analysis of each of these cases will, on reflection, be found to be the same.

Salpingectomy

The third additional illustration is that of the surgical procedure known as salpingectomy, a procedure often performed when the fallopian tube is infected and must be removed. However, the concern here is with salpingectomy which occurs when a woman suffers an ectopic pregnancy, that is, a pregnancy in which the *conceptus* lodges in the fallopian tube. In this position, the child will predictably die upon the bursting of the tube, while the mother will suffer a severe and possibly fatal loss of blood. It has been thought by some that a salpingectomy procedure would not constitute a direct action against the child, but rather simply removal of a part of the fallopian tube that is swollen and inflamed and so needs to be removed anyway. In this way, salpingectomy is often presented as superior to simply and putatively directly acting against the child by removing the child (but removing is not the same as spearing or poisoning, a distinction that some skirt in use of the term "remove").

This, of course, like the other cases above, is a difficult matter. But if it is true that a section of fallopian tube must in any case be removed for the sake of the mother's health, owing to its radical swelling and inflammation, then this is the end sought, and the means are *per se* ordered to it. Where the object is *per se* ordered to the end, as we have seen, the most formal, defining, and containing species is derived from the end. And thus the moral species of this act is that of a medical procedure for the sake of the mother's health.

Here again the standard conditions of "double effect" apply solely because the basic teleological analysis as applied to the case indicates that they are warranted. The act is in itself good (interposing against the threat of a burst fallopian tube to medically aid the woman); the evil effect is not the end sought by the agent, but only permitted, and the act is only a partial and not proper and complete cause of the death of the child, which is to say, *simpliciter*, it is not the cause of the death of the child (removal of inflamed fallopian tube does not by its nature have anything to do with the *conceptus*, save by circumstance); the good effect which is indeed the end of the act is not achieved through the evil effect as a means (it is not through the death of the child that the fallopian tube is removed, and there is no direct action against the child as such; if the child could be kept alive the fallopian tube would *still* have been removed, and the definition of removing the fallopian tube does not include the killing of a child); and there is indeed a proportion between the good and evil effect such that the evil consequence is not so great as to make the act unworthy of choice (the child is dying in any case, but the mother will die or suffer grievous harm as well in the absence of an interposing act).

One notes again how remote this is from the case of the suicide bomber who arranges the circumstances in detail so that he himself forms part of the mechanism of the bomb's delivery and explosion. The mother does not here arrange the circumstance central to the child's death, namely its being in the fallopian tube where it cannot live and where it also is causing the tube to become inflamed and to move toward rupture and hemorrhage. It is the accidental position of the child and the harm that this causes both mother and child which occasions the need for a medical act with respect to the woman's fallopian tube, an act which if the woman suffered the same pathology without an ectopic pregnancy could be dealt with in the same way.

But in the case of an ectopic pregnancy could not the child be directly removed from the fallopian tube? We must first know what "remove" *means*. If it literally means a change of local position with no direct harm inflicted upon the *conceptus*, then it would seem to be permissible. This, it will be argued, attrites the lifespan of the child, doing it direct harm. Of course this identical objection might be aimed at salpingectomy in the case of ectopic pregnancy, that is, that it attrites the life of the child and does direct harm. But the act that has harm as a consequence is not aimed directly at harming the child in either case. Note again, however, that we refer to a purely hypothetical case in which the *conceptus* is simply *moved* but is not scraped, lacerated, crushed, or chemically destroyed. Hence, for example, this hypothesis directly excludes the use of methotrexate and other drugs whose natural effect is the destruction of tissue essential to the life of the *conceptus*. It also excludes procedures that essentially would "spear" and remove the *conceptus* like a mere growth of tissue. These procedures seem to be indistinguishable from therapeutic abortion, and so to be morally impermissible. The hypothesis we forward here is that of simply *moving* the *conceptus*, albeit in a circumstantial *context* wherein this will knowably hasten its death. While it is unclear that such simple removal of the *conceptus* is now technically possible, it may one day be so. In any case, consideration of the hypothesis of mere removal enables one to contemplate the difference between acts terminating in the crushing, poisoning, spearing, or lacerating of the *conceptus*, and acts that move it, albeit to a place where its lifespan is attrited.

In the case of the use of salpingectomy in ectopic pregnancy, the act is aimed at removing an inflamed fallopian tube in danger of rupture. In the second case where the child is, and the tube is not, removed, one is directly *moving* the child. But this motion does not terminate in *death* but in a new locale for the child. It may even be a locale wherein the dying child may stay alive for a shorter period than if it were left in the fallopian tube, for so long as (a) the action is taken because the position of the child causes serious harm to the mother's health, and (b) no action which *per se* terminates in the child's bodily damage or death is undertaken.

That the dying child has an even shorter lifespan apart from the fallopian tube than it does in it does not make the movement of the child from where it does not belong and where it harms the mother to be an evil act. For such an act is only a *partial* cause of the death of the *conceptus*. Nor do we mean by this merely that the logical definition of movement does not involve death, but rather that by its very nature merely to move it is not to cause death, save owing to some other circumstance. Recall that the *conceptus* draws nothing from the mother at this stage—there is no need for oxygenation of blood at this stage (there are no blood vessels), nor is the *conceptus* nourished by the mother. The hastening of its death is either (a) a function of our hypothesis not obtaining, that is, of it being impossible to remove it without directly damaging it; or (b) the hastening of its death is a function of not being able to provide laboratory conditions that would permit it to live for an equivalent period of time. The former (a) seems to be the case with many techniques proposed today, and such techniques are indistinguishable from therapeutic abortion. It is the latter case that the current hypothesis under consideration concerns. And the latter case does offer comparison with *the rejection of extraordinary means* in terminal cases. That is, one might say that it is an extraordinary means to provide a life-sustaining treatment for a person who is suffering terminal disease, when that life-sustaining treatment *of its nature* involves serious harm and/or threat of death to another person.

For example, suppose there is a terminal disease suffered by a few, whose effects can with high probability of success be mitigated and slowed—but not stopped—only if two kidneys from the same host (identical DNA) are donated. Now, this is purely fictive—there isn't such a case. But if there were, it would be tantamount to the death sentence for the donor, and we would judge such an organ donation under the aspect of therapy for the sake of treating a patient suffering with the terminal disease in question to be supererogatory and possibly even suicidal—even if the donor were a mother and the patient her young child. In this case, the question would be, is such donation permissible? Even were it judged to be permissible, one would be inclined to think it could not (at least where no question of the transcendence of the common good enters the picture) be obligatory. Now, under the current hypothesis, the *conceptus* is where it ought not to be, and suffers in its development accordingly—there is no place where it can properly develop so as to live even to be a baby. It is unwell, and it is dying, and there is no place where it can receive adequate treatment to heal it. And the fallopian tube is not *per se* ordered to sustain it—it can provide nothing to aid the development of the *conceptus*. The situation, then, is very similar, because the mother temporarily mitigates the disease suffered by the *conceptus*, but cannot cure it, and the cost of providing this extraordinary aid is likely harm or death to the mother.

Likewise, under the terms of the present hypothesis, the *conceptus* may be removed without crushing, chemically poisoning, lethally lacerating, or otherwise terminating one's motion in it in a way that immediately inflicts any other injury than the local motion which (because the conditions in the fallopian tube cannot be adequately paralleled in the lab) predictably hastens its death. It is being removed from receiving an extraordinary assistance which the mother does not owe the child insofar as the child cannot be adequately assisted by it, and the aid given will in fact either grievously harm or injure the mother. Under this circumstance, one might think that to remove the minimal aid of the fallopian tube from the *conceptus*, not to provide the extraordinary means—even though this hastened the death of the *conceptus*—is not the complete and proper cause of the death of the *conceptus*. For there is no environment on earth, and no extant means, whereby the *conceptus* could live—not even in the way that a brain-dead person on a respirator can live. If it may be licit to refuse the extraordinary means of the respirator to a brain-dead patient—and how many persons are there in the world who have died because such means are, *de facto* and by circumstance of economics, withheld?—then cannot the mother withhold the extraordinary means of harboring the terminal *conceptus* in her fallopian tube at the cost of her own hemorrhage and possible death?

If this circumstance is truly out of one's control, and the need to move the person is grave and justified as the only act to preserve good from a circumstance that otherwise threatens death to mother and child, then—for so long as the action as such is not inflicting harm or death, but these follow only by way of foreseen consequence, the act seems arguably permissible.

Need one say that yet again the conditions of "double effect" apply solely because the basic teleological analysis as applied to the case indicates that they are warranted? The act is in itself good (interposing against the threat of a burst fallopian tube to medically aid the woman by relocating the being that ought not to be there and which is causing the harm to the mother); the evil effect is not the end sought by the agent, but is only permitted, and the act is only a partial and not proper and complete cause of the death of the child, which is to say, *simpliciter*, it is not the cause of the death of the child (relocation of the child out of the fallopian tube attrites the lifespan of the child, but the child dies for precisely the same reason it would die if left in the fallopian tube, namely because it is not in the womb of its mother: which has been true from the start); the good effect which is indeed the end of the act is not achieved through the evil effect as a means (in the hypothetical case it is not through the death of the child that the child is relocated, and there is in the hypothetical case no direct action against the child as such; if the child could be kept alive he would *still* have been removed from where he ought not to have been, namely in the fallopian tube where his presence was harming his mother.

Further, the nature of "removing the child from the fallopian tube" is not what causes the child's death, but rather the incapacity—for technical reasons—of any artificial environment to sustain its life. In the latter respect, the example of life-support is again condign, because in the example above, if the mother does not donate both her kidneys to sustain her child's life, her child perishes sooner not because of this "non-donation" but because no adequate technical substitute exists. To continue regarding double effect, there is indeed a proportion between the good and evil effect such that the evil consequence is not so great as to make the act unworthy of choice (the child is dying in any case, but the mother will die or suffer grievous harm as well in the absence of an interposing act). Moreover the death is not the *cause* of the *conceptus being moved*—the good effect (removing the *conceptus* from being a proximate cause of harm to the mother) is not *caused* by the foreseen and partially caused evil consequence of moving the *conceptus.*

Of course, this implies that the child is only relocated and *not directly killed.* It must be noted that one cannot abstract from the datum that the child is *not where it should be,* that this datum and even its own growth *harms not alone the mother but even itself by way of moving toward the rupturing of the tube and its own death,* and that hence *it ought to be moved.* If it becomes feasible to keep the child alive within an artificial womb, this would be the ideal solution.

Granted that under these circumstances to move the child will result in the child's death, the reason for this is the one and the same original reason of its death and none other—namely that it is not where it should be, within the womb of its mother, but where it should not be and cannot survive. This constitutes an *illness* on the part of the child, who is in exactly the condition of a terminal patient receiving the aid of extraordinary means which are then withdrawn because of their undue cost, their inefficacy, and of course in this case their extreme hazard. One notes also that the act whereby the child would, if possible, be merely relocated, is an act interposing between the threat to the health of the mother and the mother. The end of this act—to remove the cause of harm to the health of the mother for the sake of her health—is good. The means of removal are *per se* ordered to this effect, and do not cause the disease from which the *conceptus* suffers nor its lethality. It is, then, difficult to see how the act can be other than a good act unless either the harm threatened to the mother by the burst tube is slight (but it is not) or the *conceptus* is where it belongs (but it isn't), or the *conceptus* were not dying in any case (which would roil the analysis but not necessarily alter it if what were involved were giving therapy to the mother, as is the case, say, with radiation therapy to save the patient from cancer: but in any case, this isn't true, either). For so long as the child is being moved *from where it does not belong*—from where it will in any case not only die but also hurt the mother—and inasmuch as this does not entail directly killing the child—for example, by scraping or crushing it with a medical knife or killing it with chemicals—the simple removal of the child from the fallopian tube appears licit.

But suppose we press further: by removing the child from where it ought not to be, we *hasten* its death. And this *hastening* is another, and an avoidable, evil. Ergo it should not be done, since to *hasten* the death of an innocent is wrong. We may agree that normally it would be wrong to hasten the death of an innocent. Indeed, here one might also think that the act involved is a "direct" hastening of death, whereas with salpingectomy the act is an "indirect" hastening of death, inasmuch as there the act aims to remove part of the damaged fallopian tube and only accidentally also moves the *conceptus*. For this reason, there would seem to be a reason for preferring salpingectomy over direct removal of the *conceptus*, if only because the former is clearly a more indirect and accidental though foreseeable hastening of the death of the *conceptus*.

But here, the innocent is indeed where he ought not to be, and how can it be wrong to remove an innocent from where that innocent ought not to be, especially when the innocent person *being* there is itself *a cause of dire harm* both to himself and another? Neither party is *responsible* for the anomaly of the child *being in the wrong place*. But this does not change the fact that it *is* in the wrong place. To move it from the wrong place, given the threat of serious harm, is, just so far, licit, especially since the definition of its *being moved* does not *of its nature* kill, and the death of the child is accordingly *a foreseen consequence* but is *only partially caused* by the mother (for the circumstance that *moving* it is no more friendly to its survival than its *staying in place*, and also the circumstance that *moving it* does knowably and *per accidens hasten* its otherwise ineluctable death, are alike *not caused by either mother or child*). However, in section IV below, we shall have more to say accentuating the natural dimensions of this particular type of "being where it does not belong," both for its own sake, and also as prelude to a brief consideration of so-called embryonic "rescue."[1] *And so, the final note needed for the proper completion of this analysis is to be found only in section IV below.*

The preceding three cases are simply three of many difficult cases following the same pattern: wherein some inadvertent consequence ensues upon an act which although not essentially caused by that act is yet in some fashion circumstantially inextricable therefrom or in relation to which the act constitutes a partial cause. In such cases, the application of the teleological grammar for the constitution of object and species of the moral act suffice for analysis, but exhibits the standard "conditions" for what has come to be known as "the principle of double effect." Yet, it isn't so much a separate and distinct principle, as it is merely a distinctive type of case nonetheless subject to the same matrix of analysis as is every other moral action.

CASES OF THE FALSE DIAGNOSES OF DOUBLE EFFECT

Of course, as has also been seen, there are false cases of double effect. Let us consider two: craniotomy, and the use of condoms by marital spouses to avoid the transmission of AIDS one to another.

---

[1] Even given these reasons, however, this consideration remains troubling, precisely because although the child is dying where it is in the womb, it is not yet dead, and as noted above clearly its death can be hastened. Further, a circumstance can be a principal condition of the object and so change species. Even given the datum that the child is not where it ought to be, there seem to be limits to what one may reasonably "hasten" for an innocent being by one's actions. It now (circa 2015) seems to the author that only if genuine efforts are made to help the child to survive outside the womb would such movement of the child be reasonable. There should at least be sustained efforts, which may perhaps help to spark progress in medical technology. Medical institutes should try to do what they can to help these children—it is arresting that such effort, or at least the popular awareness of it, seems to have fallen into abeyance.

Craniotomy

Craniotomy is, of course, the direct crushing of the skull of the *conceptus*, so as to remove it from the birth canal and save the life of the mother in whom the child had become lodged. This procedure is scarcely undertaken today, given the availability of Cesarean section. But the issue remains to some degree alive in parts of the world wherein this latter procedure is not readily available. It might be thought that this procedure is permissible because it need involve no intention other than that of aiding the mother by decreasing the size of the skull of the child. Yet this language is deceptive. One must ask *in what* does the action terminate? The answer is that the act performed does not terminate in any way in the body of the mother, but directly terminates in the person of the *conceptus*. And *how* does the action terminate in the *conceptus*? The answer is by *harming the skull in a manner per se sufficient to inflict death*. Hence this is not a mere *consequence* of an act otherwise good—indeed, it is the *per se* terminus of the action undertaken, an action which terminates directly in harming and killing the *conceptus*. The end sought would seem to be to reduce the size of the child's skull, for the sake of the further *per accidens* end of freeing the child from the birth canal without harming the mother. Yet the *per accidens* ordering of crushing one person's skull toward the bodily benefit of another cannot make this act essentially medical, for the person whose skull is crushed, in whose person the action terminates, is not receiving medical treatment, that is, treatment *per se* ordered to heal or to improve health. Crushing one's skull is not plausibly ordered toward improving the health of the *conceptus* on whose person the surgeon is operating. And what is done is not merely *reducing the size of the child's skull* but rather *harming the child's skull*.

It is no more a medical act *performed on the mother* to crush the child's skull, than it is a medical act performed on the mother to *shoot the next of kin with a shotgun*. Both are acts that directly[2] terminate in harm to another, and

---

2 But what does "directly" mean? It refers to the *per se* terminus of the action taken: in what does this action stop? In the case of the mountaineer, the action terminates in *cutting a rope*, which effect is a *partial cause* of his likely death, a likely death which is merely partially and permissively willed because of the higher call to serve the common good of the climbing troop by limiting the destructive situation of the weight pulling all to their deaths so as to save as many of the troop as possible. In the case of the craniotomy the action terminates in harming, by crushing, the skull

so the very *means whereby* the desired aim of freeing the child from the birth canal is achieved, is *by the evil means of directly harming the child lodged in the birth canal.* To be clear, this act has the same structure as that of private lethal defense with one significant difference: to harm or kill one who is unjustly assailing an innocent is not an act under negative precept; whereas directly and deliberately to harm or kill an innocent child is under negative precept. One may not do evil that good may come. So: the end is shrinking the cranium of the child so as to free the child from the birth canal; the object is crushing the skull of the child, thus harming and indeed killing the child, for the sake of freeing it from the birth canal. The end of freeing the child from the birth canal is good, but the object—crushing its skull and so harming and indeed killing the child—is not good, nor is it even a medical act.

The AIDS Couple and Condom Use

It is, of course, to be doubted that there are many AIDS-infected couples simply waiting for the flag from Rome to use condoms. But, putting all difficulties in the suspension of disbelief to one side, there remains the moral analysis of the case. If a married couple should choose to use a condom so as to be able to perform the conjugal act without spreading AIDS (which already involves a certain imprudent expectation placed upon the

---

of an innocent child, who is not capable even of performing *inculpable* conduct (and so there is no question of "defending" against the assailing conduct of the child, although by its location the child does naturally menace the mother). It is one thing *to move* the child if possible without directly harming the child (i.e., without performing an act whose *per se* effect is to damage the child physically), even if this has as a further consequence the child's likely death. In such a case, if the damage being averted is grave, this only partially and permissively willed consequence of death owing to the moving of the child is permissible under double effect. It is another thing to perform an action whose *per se* terminus is harm to the innocent child. Bear in mind that an act is *per se* ordained to the end either (a) if by the nature of the end *the only way to move toward the end in any case* is by the act in question; or (b) if, even though there are many different acts that might by their natures tend toward the end, nonetheless a certain type of act *does by its very nature* tend toward the end. Now, crushing the skull of the child is ordained *per se* to the physical harm, and likely death, of the child. An act which is *per se* ordained to harm the innocent (and here we mean by "innocent" someone *both morally and performatively innocent*—i.e., either someone who is a morally responsible agent guiltless of any wrongful assault, or someone not morally responsible but still free of generating any conduct which constitutes a wrongful assault) is thus *directly ordered to harm the innocent.* Such an act ought not to be performed.

impermeability, unbreakability, incapacity to slip, of the condom), would this be morally permissible?

The argument for it might be as follows: the couple wills only to prevent transmission of the virus, and not to prevent the transmission of procreative matter. It is an accident that the only means to achieve the former is one that also achieves the latter. Therefore, all the couple *intends* is the former, whereas the latter is merely a consequence of limited technology. Why then cannot the couple use a condom without standing guilty of contraceptive intention?

First, it must be noted that intention of the end is insufficient to make for a good act: it must also be good in its object, it must also be choice-worthy, and not merely done for the sake of a noble end. But irrespective of what the couple might do in a different circumstance wherein they could sieve out the virus but not prevent transmission of procreative matter, in this circumstance they would be choosing to prevent the transmission of procreative matter. That is to say, they are both planning a venereal act, and with respect to this very act choosing to act so as to prevent the transmission of procreative matter. Their end cannot make this choice to be licit, because the choice is to use means which are such by their nature as to be contraceptive.

But is this not the error of "physicalism"? And does not *Veritatis Splendor* no. 78 state that:

> By the object of a given moral act, then, one cannot mean a process or an event of the merely physical order, to be assessed on the basis of its ability to bring about a given state of affairs in the outside world. Rather, that object is the proximate end of a deliberate decision which determines the act of willing on the part of the acting person.

These words refer to something wholly outside the order of choice: for example, someone who is hit by a car and then becomes infecund is not thereby acting contraceptively in the conjugal act. *Veritatis Splendor* precisely does not mean to affirm that the physical order is *excluded* from the moral object, but only that the object is *not merely* physical. The difference is immense. Likewise, to point out that one may not deliberately and directly choose to impede the procreative character of the conjugal act is not "physicalism" in any sense which would imply error. What kind of act, after all, is it? Ethereal? Merely logical? If someone strangles a person for the sake of art, is pointing out that the physical character of one's chosen act is such as to cause death immaterial to distinguishing that this is an act of homicide (wrongful) rather than of artistic creation?

Oftentimes in arguing for the conclusion that a married couple should be permitted to use condoms to avoid the spread of HIV infection, the historical example is forwarded of the Holy Office's (today known as the Congregation of the Doctrine of the Faith) permission for religious women in the Belgian Congo to use contraceptives as a defense against rape. For example, Redemptorist Fr. Brian Johnstone, a leading moral theologian at Rome's Alphonsian Academy, said in an April 25, 2006 interview with the *National Catholic Reporter* that this example highlights the truth that it is not the "physical character" of the act, but the "intention behind" the act, which is pertinent. Yet the historical example of the Holy Office's permission to the sisters in the Belgian Congo was given on the basis of a principle *diametrically opposed* to the principle alleged to be the "anti-physicalist" reason for the decision.

In order for an act to fall under the moral species of contraceptive sin, *one must first intend a venereal act.* That is, *contraception is a species of venereal sin*, and so in order to commit a contraceptive sin *one must first intend a venereal act.* Since the sisters *neither intended nor chose any venereal act whatsoever, and in fact intended and chose to resist the forcing of such an act upon their persons, it was accordingly impossible for them to be guilty of contraceptive sin on the classical analysis.* But note carefully that *the very reason of this impossibility* was the datum that under no conditions did they intend to perform a venereal act. Accordingly one might question the prudential reasonability of the permission ceded them to use contraceptives on other grounds (perhaps of proportionality, for example, inasmuch as the contraceptive permitted was abortifacient), but one could not properly say that the sisters were guilty of contraceptive sin. In short, it is because *the nature of the act intended* by the sisters *was not a venereal act at all*, that the sisters *could not* have been guilty of specifically *contraceptive* sin: if one neither chooses nor intends X it is *impossible* to choose or intend X as Y. One who neither chooses nor intends a venereal act, cannot choose or intend a venereal act as contraceptive.[3] Thus, far

---

3 With respect to this point, the lines of St. Thomas from *Summa theologiae* I–II, question 18, article 6, are often cited by proponents of the permissibility of condom use

from the putatively "merely physical" character of action being excluded from the object of the moral act, the fact that the sisters intended an act whose "merely physical" character *was not venereal* is the decisive point that made it impossible for them to be guilty of any sin in the genus of venereal acts. This is crucial: the sisters intended no venereal act, and hence could commit no venereal sin while holding firm in that intention. *By contrast,* in the case of the married couple suffering with AIDS and proposing to use a condom in order to prevent the spread of disease, the couple proposes to use the contraceptive *precisely in relation to a venereal act that they intend and which they freely choose to perform.*

The couple intends a conjugal act, and chooses to impede its procreativity. Whether they would choose to do so under other circumstances or not, they are choosing a means which is directly contrary to what *Humanae Vitae* no. 12 refers to as "the inseparable connection, established by God, which man on his own initiative may not break, between the unitive significance and the procreative significance which are both inherent to the marriage act." One notes the language: *inherent to the marriage act* are the unitive and procreative significance whose *inseparable connection is established by God* and which *man on his own initiative may not break.* If this is true, then—given that the proposition is *not* that *man on his own initiative may not break the inseparable connection between the unitive and procreative significance inherent to the marriage act unless he or his spouse suffer with AIDS*—it would seem that deliberately choosing to use a contraceptive means in relation to some given conjugal act (for whatsoever reason) is excluded from the licit moral options.

The essential point, however, is simple: that the fundamental teleological analysis of object and species in the moral act does not discriminate the use

---

by a married couple suffering with AIDS for the sake of preventing the spread of infection. St. Thomas there writes of external acts, "nor have external acts any measure of morality, save insofar as they are voluntary." It is thought that this shows that the mere physical character of contraception is insufficient to place an act within the species of contraceptive sin. *This is true;* but it is *not true* that the physical character of the act performed is not materially included within the moral object of a voluntarily chosen act. The reason is simple: an act of contraception may occur because a venereal act is forced upon someone who wholly refuses it, and in that case the whole moral culpability for the contraception and any consequent evil falls upon the person forcing the act. *But, if one voluntarily chooses to perform an act, then the integral nature of the act voluntarily chosen is always materially included in the moral object of the act.*

of the condom and the condom's contraceptive character within the venereal act as a mere "consequence" of seeking a good end through an object *per se* ordered to that end. For the object of such an act is "uniting conjugally in the procreative act while using a means that is objectively contraceptive for the sake of avoiding the transmission of AIDS." This object is not *per se* ordered to the end of procreation. The introduction of contraceptive means severs the order of the act performed toward procreation. It is precisely this which falls under negative precept and may never be done. Further, the object of the moral act—"what the act is about relative to reason"—always materially includes *the act itself and the integral nature of the act*, which accordingly constitutes one—only one, but certainly one—cause of the moral species of the act. To refuse to acknowledge that the physical structure of the act materially enters into the moral object of an act is pure *angelism*, a residue of Cartesian error. It is cognate with logicism in treating that which is natural as reducible to a cognitive entity. Whereas, to the contrary, acts and their natures are not mere snakeskins to be shed by an agent whose acts are confused with Pure Geist.

If it is said that on this analysis those who are accidentally infecund may not procreate, the entire nature of normative teleology has been misunderstood. For those who through purely physical accident are unable to procreate are not the cause of this impediment to the conjugal act, whereas those who seek to perform venereal acts and choose, in relation to these very acts, to alter their nature so as to cause them to be infertile, *are* guilty of contraceptive evil. Likewise, it is no sin for a man either wholly or partially blind to try to see; but deliberately to choose to mutilate oneself and make oneself blind is, all other things being equal, wrongful conduct. There are not two teleologies, one for those with poor vision and one for those who see clearly; there is one normative teleology, which can suffer deprivation which is merely physical, or deprivation through the intellect and will of an agent who culpably chooses to deprive the act of its due order (as the due order to sight of the eyes is deprived by a man who willfully damages his own eyes). And it is this last which is at stake when a married couple deliberately deprives their venereal acts of procreativity through using a contraceptive means for whatsoever end. For one may not do evil that good may come.

It helps to see how different this case is from those cases in which a woman would be prescribed contraceptives to help regulate her cycle. In such cases, there is no reference to any specific conjugal act whatsoever—she may indeed not even have the remote intention of engaging in the marital act. Whereas in the present case, in particular reference to a specific conjugal act, the couple elects to use a contraceptive means for the sake of avoiding the transmission of AIDS. The means they select is a means which achieves this end of avoiding the transmission of AIDS only by blocking the transmission of procreative matter. To put this in the language of the standard conditions for the application of double effect, the good effect is achieved only through the evil means. But this is precisely what is ruled out by the standard conditions of double effect, and for good reason: for it suffices to establish that the evil done is not merely a *consequence* that is *partially caused* but rather a *means embraced by choice* whose *integral nature thus must be included within the object of the moral act*. What type of act shall we say that this is, then? It is a *contraceptive* act of intercourse, wherein the couple deliberately deploys a contraceptive means because by its contraceptive agency (blocking the seminal matter) they hope to avoid the transmission of AIDS. If this intention automatically exculpates one of any moral responsibility for the object of one's action, then if the husband decides to mutilate himself to prevent the transmission of AIDS, is this merely to be morally taxonomized as "AIDS prevention"? Is it not instead a sin of self-mutilation, whose object would be something like "mutilating one's procreative organs for the sake of making it impossible to transmit AIDS through genital intercourse"? *The object of the moral act is not a mere proposal: the act has being, a nature, and a natural order, such that the act itself and its integral nature are always materially included within the moral object.*

It also must be seen, of course, that the couple's choice is not between violating the moral law and using one another for sexual release at the risk of harming one another through transmitting deadly disease. The dignity of marriage is slurred by those who suppose that ever-ready copulation is the source and summit of the marital life. For grave reasons, out of charity and prudence, the couple may reasonably withhold themselves from the act of conjugal union. But as our focus here is on analysis of the structure of the act, we digress.

As has been argued above, the only category of acts to which the standard conditions for double effect apply are those cases in which some inadvertent consequence ensues upon an act which although not essentially caused by that act is yet in some fashion circumstantially inextricable there-from or in relation to which the act constitutes a partial cause. But the con-traceptive character of the condom use in relation to the venereal act is not merely an inadvertent *consequence* because it is *directly chosen*—it is materially included in the object. The standard conditions of "double effect" *do not* here apply precisely because the basic teleological analysis presented by St. Thomas *does not*, when applied to the case, indicate that they are warranted. One can-not reasonably choose—in relation to a specific conjugal act—to deploy means whose very nature is such as to deprive the conjugal act of its procre-ative character and then protest that this deprivation is a mere *consequence* of an act good in its species. To the contrary, it is an act which may be done from good motives (desiring not to spread AIDS) but whose objective char-acter is bad because essentially inclusive of what is contrary to reason (inas-much as it is contrary to the natural teleology of the act itself).

The act is in itself bad (deliberately and by choice introducing means to render a particular and intended conjugal act to be infecund); the evil effect is sought by the agent and not only permitted, especially clear since (a) the agent could either not perform the conjugal act at all, or (b) could choose to perform it without deliberately rendering it infertile, while in any case (c) it is *through* the contraceptive character of the chosen means that the effect sought is actually obtained. Thus the act is a proper and complete cause of contraception because the contraceptive element is deliberately chosen in relation to this conjugal act;[4] the good effect of preventing the transmission of AIDS is achieved *through* an evil means of deliberately performing a con-jugal act while choosing to impede its procreativity (it is *through* obstructing

---

4 This is, for example, much different from the case which once obtained, wherein contraceptives might be given to a woman for purposes of regulating her cycle. Note that this latter instance does not involve *any reference to a planned conjugal act whatsoever*, and so does not by its nature generically partake of contraceptive evil: for contraceptive evil presupposes intention to perform a venereal act. The person who poisons another's oatmeal with contraceptives is doing something wrong, but what it is that is being done is not a contraceptive sin. Rather, it is a sin of doing bodily harm to the couple—doubtless *for the sake* of interfering with procreation. But what the poisoner is doing is not just what makes it attractive to him, but the act itself and its integral nature—poisoning oatmeal with a contraceptive for the sake of doing material harm to the couple if they choose to embrace as a spousal couple. Nor is the couple guilty of contraception if they join in the conjugal embrace in this circumstance, since they do not know and are not responsible for the impeding of their act consequent on the harm inflicted by the poisoner.

the transmission of procreative matter that one seeks to prevent the transmission of AIDS). Such an act is directly contrary to the procreative good, and indeed if the procreative material were transmitted, AIDS also might be.

Finally, even were we to cede for argument's sake that this were a case of double effect—which clearly it is *not*—there exists no *proportion* between the effects such that it could be permitted. The proportion necessary would be: a bad *physical* effect is permitted for the sake of a more profound *moral* good; but the proportion that obtains in this case, were we contrary to fact to view it as a "double effect" case, is: a morally evil act is permitted for the sake of avoiding a physical evil. For in the deliberate embrace of contraceptive means there is not merely physical evil but rather also moral evil.

The failure to meet the standard conditions for double effect is merely the indication that the act itself and its integral nature are not mere *consequences* but necessarily enter materially into the object of the act. Thus it is folly to suppose that one may simultaneously (a) deliberately choose to physically contracept in some given conjugal act, while nonetheless (b) not being morally guilty of contraception. Such a view requires a completely disembodied account of the human person and of the object of the moral act: a ghostly action theory. This is like saying that I may deliberately choose to strangle my innocent friend to death while not being guilty of murder—perhaps what I really want is to exercise my muscles in a certain way, and I can't quite find a suitable duplicate such that my purely intelligible proposal for action *per accidens* involves strangulation. It is utter nonsense: for the object of the act *always* materially includes the act itself and its integral nature. Hence, one may not deliberately perform acts of certain types, because they are generically defective—their *per se* ordering is such that it is definitively incompatible with the nature of the moral good.

How, on the view of the object as merely an intelligible proposal which excludes the act performed itself and its intelligible nature, is one to make sense of the prohibition of murder? Bear in mind that murder is not equivalent with killing: it is *wrongful* homicide, and hence includes a judgment as to the nature of the killing in question. Nonetheless, inasmuch as the killing is wrongful, it will not matter to what further end one proposes it be appended as a means: for no matter how noble the end, one may not do evil that good may come. So: deliberate and direct slaying of the innocent (where this is understood both *morally*—the slain person is not morally guilty of any offense for which slaying constitutes the legal penalty and *per-formatively*—the slain person is undertaking no conduct that wrongly assails another and against which that other could hence reasonably *defend*), slaying by a citizen acting on his own recognizance, is wrongful homicide. Having achieved this generic insight, we do not then need to know the full specifics of the end sought by the agent, because whatever that end is, his action is gravely unjust. If the spouses agreed that one should kill the other so that they thus made sure never to spread AIDS, would we say: "The end of AIDS prevention is their intention: the fact that this intention is realized only by killing an innocent person is immaterial to the object of their action?" No, the object would be wrongfully killing one's spouse to fulfill a joint plan of the couple to prevent themselves from spreading AIDS. Wrongful killing would indeed be included within the object.

But is not the *circumstance* that the couple suffers with AIDS sufficient to render the couple only a *partial* cause of contraception, as is the case with the undesirable effect in other instances wherein the standard conditions for double effect obtain? No. For the means they deploy is *of itself and by its nature, and in the context of the very venereal act that they intend, contraceptive.* That it has two different effects, and that there be unfortunate circumstances, does not make the standard conditions of double effect automatically apply. Thus, stranded sailors on a boat may not, if they are hungry, rightly kill and then eat one of their own number to stay alive on the grounds that they intend only to "obtain nutrition" and do not intend wrongful homicide, which is somehow forced on them by circumstance. For the very nature of their act is such as to include wrongful homicide, and nothing in their circumstance can ever require them to *choose* to perform wrongful homicide. Likewise, nothing in their circumstance can ever force upon the couple *the choice* of contraception as a means of deliverance from whatsoever evil.

Compare this with the case of the mountaineer in the last chapter: he is not committing suicide, because he does not ignore a means available to spare his life (in any case he is going to fall, and the issue is only: shall he take others with him?), nor does he seek death as an end, and death is only accidentally involved and owing to circumstance (the circumstance that he is in any case falling and has only one option to limit the destructiveness of the fall). Now compare this with the couple one of whom has AIDS: is it necessary that this couple perform the conjugal act, irrespective of the harm threatened? No. Nor is matrimony merely an institution licensing unlimited copulation irrespective of the prospective harm: the view that it is such an institution is a direct besmirching of the dignity of the married couple, whose life of union as man and wife should indwell charity and be regulated by prudence. Since this act is not necessary and is gravely dangerous, it should be avoided through abstinence. The alternatives are not to perform an act which may cause harm to one's spouse, or to use a contraceptive which is contrary to the good of marriage. Secondly, the nature of the act performed is in and of itself contraceptive, whereas the nature of the act of the mountaineer is indeed sacrificial but not directly suicidal (it is the circumstance of his falling that is in any event deadly, and not his *limitation* of the fall to his own person).

One might suppose that the circumstance of having AIDS is one whose destructiveness is likewise limited to his own person by the husband who uses a condom. But, whereas the fall against whose destructiveness the mountaineer acts by delimiting it to himself will elsewise kill his whole party, there is nothing about the circumstance of having AIDS that in and of itself requires one to perform the conjugal act. That is to say, it is not as though the circumstance, "having AIDS," is such that it will ineluctably cause the death of one's spouse unless one uses a condom for the couple need not engage in the conjugal act. The view that they must reduces their temperance and self-governance to those of mollusks. The act of conjugal union is not a *circumstance* into which one is propelled by fate, and in the light of which one must limit some otherwise ineradicable harm. Nor is the purpose of the conjugal act that of impeding the spread of AIDS: its purpose is unitive and procreative, or procreative through being unitive. Hence what the couple designs to do in this case is to obstruct the proper motion to the end by performing an act under negative precept, because otherwise *on the supposition of performing the conjugal act* they might transmit AIDS.[5]

---

[5] The question arises as to the use of condoms by sterile couples seeking to avoid the transmission of AIDS. But, first, this is contrary to the one flesh union of the couple, which requires penetration and the vaginal deposit of semen, even if lacking sperm. Further, one might hold—paradoxically—that even given sterility that the use of the condom were, moreover, contraceptive, since the act is yet a deprived act of a *species* normatively ordered toward procreation. The volitional adding of an impediment is not the act of someone who respects the normative ordering of the act, which is an ordering still obvious in many facets of the act such that we can say that the conjugal

To which the response is: do not perform the conjugal act, exercise absti-nence for the sake of the common good and in cognizance of the dignity of the spouse and of the marital union as such.

If the AIDS couple is licitly permitted to use contraceptives on the ground that what they intend is only to avoid transmission of AIDS and not to avoid the transmission of procreative matter, then the one who sets a smoker afire when using a flamethrower to light the person's cigarette might equally be permitted to do so on the ground that, after all, the aim was only to achieve with maximal certainty the lighting of the cigarette and not the smoker (whose ignition is merely supposed to be a likely con-sequence) because the part of the flame that ignites the cigarette is distinct from the part that ignites the smoker. After all, according to some it is only the agent's intelligible proposal, and in no way his action or its inte-gral nature, which enters into the moral object. This is, indeed, worse than secondhand smoke. It is a failure to consider the actual nature of the act deliberately chosen and performed on the supposition that the delineation of one's purely intelligible proposal is sufficient to constitute the object of the moral act. Whereas, to the contrary, the object of the moral act always materially includes the act itself and its integral nature (and when these of themselves fall under negative precept, the further delineations become indifferent: one may not do evil that good may come).

---

act performed by sterile spouses is an involuntarily deprived act that nonetheless is of a unitive-procreative nature. This is to say that the one flesh union is such that it is the whole act, and not only the ejaculate containing sperm, that is ordered toward pro-creation—and so, when this absence of sperm is involuntary, it is still possible for the spouses to honor the original purpose of the act. But when an additional voluntary impediment is placed, the original purpose of the act is no longer regarded. Why else must the deposit be made vaginally, save that it is normatively ordered toward procre-ation even in the presence of defect? Indeed, the contrary view might end by suggest-ing that condomitic intercourse is only truly contraceptive on but a few days of the month—whereas, it is the normative teleology that defines it as contraceptive, inas-much as it is the conjugal act as such, and also the entire feminine cycle, which really are ordered toward and for the sake of procreation. Further, many acts which are deprived such that they cannot attain the end are still defined by the end sought; for example, students who are not blessed with great intelligence may yet study, although the end of the study—mastery of the subject—may not be possible to them short of a miracle. There is a danger of scientistic reduction of the essential procreative dynamism of the conjugal act to a mere issue of fertile semen, whereas this last is but one crucial element in a whole that is defined by procreative ordering, a procreative ordering that hence remains even in the presence of involuntary accidental defect.

A DIFFICULT CASE: SEPARATING
CONJOINED SIAMESE TWINS

Of course, there are many difficult cases, including those considered above. But some clearly are maximally challenging, not to say heartrending. Among such cases is the famous case of the congenitally joined (Siamese) twins who were born on August 8, 2000, in Manchester, England, sharing one heart and one set of lungs. The first, whose name was Mary, had non-functional heart and lungs. Joined at the lower abdomen with her sister Jodie, both she and Jodie depended entirely on Jodie's heart and lungs. As is well-known, the English legal system became involved, and commanded—contrary to their parents' wishes, and to the guidance of their local priest and of Archbishop Cormac Murphy-O'Connor—that Mary be surgically separated from Jodie, although this would knowably cause her death. The court founded its judgment on the medical estimation that it was highly probable that if Mary were not separated from Jodie, both would die. Nonetheless, it must be noted that medical authorities have frequently been wrong in estimating the lifespans of children with abnormalities, and that this estimation was rather short of the parting of the heavens to reveal apodictic truth. In any case, the surgical separation occurred, and Mary died. Although this is what transpired, below I will largely treat of this case in the present tense, as though it were wholly contemporaneous, the point being to gain some principled leverage of insight into the matter.

Putting aside the court's intervention, and its reasonableness or lack thereof, the question that I would like here to focus upon is narrowly restricted: if we grant the maximal weight to all the predictions that both twins would die in the absence of separation, would it be *permissible* to separate these twins knowing that doing so would lead to the immediate death of Mary? Mary is an innocent human being, and it might be thought that the act directly causes the death of Mary inasmuch as it severs her from heart and lungs. On what ground could such an act be permissible?

Assuming, as has been said, the worst case scenario with respect to the non-survivability of both twins if they were not severed from one another; and assuming, also, that no organ transplant could be successful in helping Mary to survive once she were separated (an option which, as far as I can tell, the British court did not so much as investigate), is it plausible that this case should fall under the *ratio* of double effect? Or is it not rather the case that this act involves direct killing of an innocent and so falls under negative precept, whatever the motivation for the sake of which the action is done?

Here we must proceed carefully. First, we must ask a question which some might consider physicalist: namely, upon *whose* heart are we operating when we operate on the heart? In the case of craniotomy we saw that although the *motive* was to help the mother, that the *act performed* terminated in the person of the *conceptus*, crushing its skull. Hence, in the case of the craniotomy, the act cannot be designated a *medical act* designed to *help the mother* because it terminates not in any act of healing, but in *directly inflicted harm to the conceptus*. It is then a classic example of doing evil that good may come, directly killing the child by crushing its skull because this may have good effect for the mother. That is simply a wrongful homicide, clear and simple.

Now, take the case of the twins. The surgical act does indeed intrusively affect Mary in removing her direct physical attachment to the heart and lungs of her sister, this is true. Yet what the surgical act directly affects is tissue which contrary to the normative teleological ordering of human nature connects one human person who lacks working heart and lungs with the body of a person whose heart and lungs work. Why "contrary to the normative teleological ordering of human nature"? Because one human person's heart and lungs are by nature ordered to circulate and oxygenate that person's blood (of course, we are not here speaking of *the case of the bond of the mother and child in the womb, which is also and per se natural, and which includes a natural dependence of the human* conceptus *upon her mother, via the umbilical cord and the placenta, for the oxygenation of its blood*). This is the teleological pattern always or for the most part discerned in human beings.

Hence it is not merely an undue physicalism to ask *whose heart and lungs* are at stake, because we need to know upon whom we are acting and how. If we say that the heart and lungs belong to Jodie, *then* we can proceed further to inquire as to the character of the obligation of any human person to share lungs and heart with another. But, it will be objected, this is not a case of *establishing* such a sharing by surgery where it has not before existed, but rather one in which this sharing antecedently exists owing to an anomaly of nature. It seems then to bear certain similarities with the case of persons who are placed on artificial life support: with respect to whom the issue must arise as to under what conditions, if any, such artificial life support may be ended.

Such a comparison of the situation of Mary with that of a patient on artificial life support could be challenged, it would seem, only if one could establish that the heart and lungs of Jodie by nature belonged to both, or by nature belonged, contrary to appearances, solely to Mary. The latter seems to be ruled out by the medical evidence, and it is not clear what it would mean to say of such a case that Jodie's heart and lungs "by nature" belong to others beside Jodie. Clearly, in the normative case, one person's heart and lungs do not "belong" to another. All the more, then, might it seem that one person's heart and lungs do not belong to another when the use of them by that other involves the likelihood, or certitude, of imminent death either for Jodie or for Jodie and Mary.

The question here is whether this case has any likeness to that of salpingectomy in the instance of an ectopic pregnancy, wherein an inflamed section of fallopian tube containing a child is removed. One recalls that in this case, inasmuch as the inflamed tube would in any case need to be removed to safeguard the mother from serious harm consequent on rupture and hemorrhage, that the choice of removal is only a partial cause of the death of the *conceptus*. For the conceived child would indeed die in any case in the fallopian tube, where in addition the child hurts the mother. All that surgery affords is to prevent the additional harm to the mother that accrues from the child being where it cannot live and where it can do no other than hurt the mother. Once again, harm which is already being caused is limited, but is not originated, by the agent. Rather, the agent merely opposes and limits the harmful extension of the destructive circumstance as fully as possible without directly willing or properly causing harm to the child.

Likewise, in the case of the twins, *if* no possibility of organ transplant exists, and *if* the twins will certainly die if the twin lacking working heart and lungs continues to use the heart and lungs of the other twin, then to remove the external strain on heart and lungs would be indicated no matter what its cause were. One cannot wholly refrain from noting again the enormity of the court's omission to consider whether organ transplant were at all feasible, or whether Mary could have survived on an artificial lung and with a heart transplant. Also, one may well observe that the certainty that the twins could not continue to live was not apodictic.

We are simplifying the actual historical case in order to determine whether, *if* the worse case scenario obtained, the severing of such twins could be reasonable. So simplified, the following answer seems forthcoming: since the heart and lungs belong to Jodie, and since they are needed by Jodie to live, and no other being has a naturally just claim on their use, the confinement of their use to Jodie and no one else need involve no positive choice to harm another. Indeed, were organ transplant actually available, then clearly severing Mary from Jodie would have involved no harm to Mary. It is clear, then, that what threatens harm to Mary is her lack of working heart and lungs, and her lack of any substitute for working heart and lungs. Would we require that someone else other than Jodie permit the use of heart and lungs by Mary to the point of that person's death? Probably not, although such a person could always volunteer to undertake extreme risk in the effort to keep her alive. But is the undertaking of such a risk *obligatory*, that is to say, is it morally incumbent upon Jodie that she share her lungs and heart with her sister until both perish?

In severing Mary from Jodie, the purpose is not to harm Mary, but to remove a life-threatening strain upon the heart and lungs of Jodie. Such strain would need to be removed, whatever its source. In the absence of any plan for a substitute for the lungs and heart Mary lacks, this act will cause Mary's death. But her death is caused by her lack of her own heart and lungs—and this lack is not caused by protecting Jodie's heart and lungs, but is antecedent to anything done by surgeons. Ideally, the surgeons would have tried to hook Mary up to some artificial lungs or heart when preserving Jodie's heart and lungs from the putatively lethal strain of Mary's use (we assume it to be so for purposes of argument, but this is an intrinsically questionable judgment). The good act of preserving Jodie's heart and lungs from lethal strain is not accomplished by killing Mary, because in principle the lack of heart and lungs by Mary is antecedent, and is the cause of her death insofar as it ensues. Further, the severation might have taken place together with the application of substitute means (organ donations or artificial means) for Mary (although this is not in fact what took place): which makes it clear that the separation of Mary from the cardiovascular system of Jodie is not in and of itself the cause of Jodie's death. The root cause is the *naturally anomalous circumstance* that Mary has no heart and lungs, and this becomes clear when sustaining the life of someone (Jodie) with heart and lungs requires protecting these from the strain of Mary's use and consequently detaching Mary from Jodie's heart and lungs. It is only the fiction that Jodie's heart and lungs are either, like atmosphere, such as to belong to everyone, or that indeed that they naturally belong to both Jodie and Mary, that can make preserving Jodie's heart and lungs seem to constitute an aggressive stance toward Mary.

But what of our earlier claim, from the first chapter, that "If we choose to perform an act whose integral nature is *per se* ordered to be directly lethal to the patient, whatever else is in our minds, we have chosen a homicidal act." Is not unhooking Mary from Jodie's working heart and lungs *per se* ordered to be directly lethal to Mary? The answer in strict teleological terms needs to be that unhooking Mary from Jodie's working heart and lungs is such as to be *per se* ordered to her death *only on the supposition of natural anomaly such that Jodie's heart and lungs are inoperative, that is, only if we include in the per se definition something that is an anomaly. But no per se definition is constructed around anomaly.* For were the *per se* and the *anomalous* identical what is always or for the most part would need also to be simultaneously freakish, accidental, and unusual. This is just to say that the *complete cause* of Mary's death entails non-working lungs and heart of her own, which is a circumstance caused by no one: a fact that also indicates that the harm to Mary here is *indirect.* For it is not alone helping Jodie's cardiovascular system, but doing so in a context wherein Mary lacks working lungs and heart, that brings about the bad effect of Mary's death. Hence an act naturally and *per se* ordered, *absolutely speaking,* to the health of Jodie is, by circumstance, now an act that will be a partial cause of Mary's death. But it is not the complete cause, and it is clear that it is only the causality of circumstance that makes the *per se* ordering of an act preservative of Jodie's health to be harmful to Mary.

That the relation is *per accidens* does not mean that this is not a grave matter: it is. Accordingly, there must be a proportionate reason for deliberately performing an act whose predictable if *per accidens* outcome will be harm or death to another. But it is not *per se* defined by harm to Mary, because by nature, always or for the most part, keeping Jodie's heart and lungs from failing due to undue strain owing to the compromise of her physical integrity is an act *per se* ordered to Jodie's health. Recall that an act is *per se* ordered toward X either when the attainment of X by nature uniquely and exclusively requires that act, or when many different acts might attain X but the act in question tends of itself toward X. Now removing unnatural and anomalous strains to heart and lungs is *per se* ordered to the well-being of a person by preserving that person's heart and lungs from harm, and any other entailment is accidental.

Yet these observations are likely to be received as vexatious. One imagines a critic arguing as follows: granted, the act of removing strain from Jodie's lungs is not in the physical realm *per se* ordered to harm Mary, but in the moral order, given the constellation of circumstance, it is such that it will. Likewise, if a man is on a ledge on a high building, we can say: he isn't there by nature. If we push him, we can say: it is only accidental that he is moved from a place where he is safe to one where he is endangered: there is nothing *per se* about pushing that makes the pushing harmful. Ergo pushing isn't *per se* harmful, and therefore when we push the man off the Empire State Building this act isn't *per se* harmful.

But in response to such criticism, one cedes that a *physically per accidens* entailment may be as lethal, and as morally serious, as a *physically per se* entailment: that is why there must be a proportionate good in order *even merely to permit the per accidens* harm. Further, "pushing" is as such under-defined as an object, being merely a physical type of action, whereas preserving heart and lungs from undue external anomalous strain for the sake of one's health is by virtue of the essential proportion of the act to health a medical act: That is, we are in a position here generically to cognize the object of the moral act. Medical acts aren't *per se* harmful to others because they are *per se* ordered to health; "pushing" isn't *per se* ordered to harm because, absent more information, we have no way of putting it in a moral species or determining the moral object of the pushing, that is, no way of saying that the pushing is ordered to anything in particular. "Pushing" like "movement" is not determinate enough to provide a basis for moral evaluation. For we need answers to questions such as: pushing what? How? Where? For what reason? With whom? Why?

If someone attempted to aid Jodie by cannibalizing Mary's body parts, or by drawing out all her blood, this clearly would be a direct assault on Mary's person by its physical nature. But while harm is circumstantially certain to accrue to Mary as a result of preserving Jodie's heart and lungs from external strain, preserving these from external strain is something that is owing in the normal and natural course of things for the sake of Jodie's health. The object of the act is to preserve Jodie's health by preserving her heart and lungs from potentially lethal external anomalous strain, by separating the cause of that strain—who is Mary—from her heart and lungs.

If a man is hanging for dear life onto my windpipe to avoid falling over a cliff, and is about to kill me by crushing my windpipe, am I obliged not to move his hand from my throat so I can breathe because of his highly probable ensuing fall and death? No, I am not so obliged, because one has no brief for suicide, and one is (all things being equal—although one might have a special divine call to sacrifice one's life in some cases) obliged *to breathe*, which is *per se* ordered to health and only *per accidens* a cause of the other's harm. Of course, I should try to clasp his hand. But if one tries and fails to clasp hands in such a circumstance, and the other person falls to his death, it is not true that murder has been done.

It becomes clear, then, that in the case of Mary and Jodie we are coping with a *natural anomaly*, and natural anomalies do not define *per se* teleology. The dependence of Mary upon Jodie is a serious matter, and it is a dependence for her life; but that dependence is anomalous and cannot make what befits the health of Jodie's heart and lungs to be *per se* directed toward harming her. For it predictably harms her only because of *circumstance*—although even this would be sufficient reason not to act were there not a *proportionate good* which Jodie seeks, that is, her life.

Suppose the case of a *Fantastic Voyage* scenario, conceived on the model of the well-known film of that name, wherein miniaturized human beings are inserted into a human body to achieve a microsurgical repair of tissue. The idea is impossible. But were it to be so, and were it a fatal injury to such miniaturized human beings for the host to *breathe*—the equivalent of a killer tornado in the lungs—surely we would not say that the host had the duty to suffocate himself. The reason is simple: the *per se* order of the lungs is to oxygenate that person's blood, and as a living being that host cannot be compelled to suicide. Now, the case with Jodie is similar: she cannot be compelled to suffer an anomalous compromise of her cardiovascular system that will kill her, even though *per accidens* harm will predictably ensue to a person lacking working heart and lungs and benefiting from that anomalous compromise of Jodie's health.

The conclusion here is that if it were knowably true that non-severation would cause the imminent death of both twins, that then severation is certainly reasonable, but that ideally such severation should have included efforts at saving Mary's life by providing either organ transplants or artificial means to circulate and oxygenate her blood. But simply to take steps to see that external strain not utterly destroy the heart and lung function of a child does not in and of itself imply death to another, even if that other is the cause of the strain: because this prescinds from the effort to supply other means to sustain Mary's life. In the absence of such means, it must be seen that the death of Mary ensues *not* because of the *life* of Jodie—indeed, it is only the life of Jodie which kept Mary alive beyond her life expectancy—but *because Mary lacks heart and lungs, an anomalous defect of nature for which no human choice is responsible.*

The choice to sever the connection between Mary and Jodie is an act *per se* apt to preserve Jodie's heart and lung function; it is only *permitted* to be a partial cause of Mary's death (where the real cause is the circumstance of her lacking either natural heart and lungs or any substitute that can keep her alive: recollect that, under the hypothesis with which we are working, both twins die if they stay connected, so this does not answer to Mary's need for working heart and lungs any more than does her death when separated from Jodie). If other means are supplied, it becomes clear that preserving Jodie's heart and lung function is not Mary's cause of death. If not, surely this severation is a partial cause, but only a partial cause, since this *presupposes* the natural circumstance of her deprivation of her own heart and lungs, a deprivation which is the true cause of her death. That the death of Mary is not the cause of Jodie's heart and lung function being preserved is clear, because the test of these functions being preserved is in no way sufficiently provided by the answer to the question as to whether Mary is or is not alive. Rather, the answer is provided by the answer to the question whether unnatural strain to the heart and lung function of Jodie has been avoided.

So, to go through the standard conditions of double effect: the act is in itself good (interposing against the threat of cardiovascular collapse in an innocent child—Jodie—brought on by unnatural external strain); the evil effect (harm to Mary) is not the end sought by the agent, but only permitted, and the act is only a partial and not proper and complete cause of Mary's death, which is to say, *simpliciter*, it is not the cause of the death of Mary (for if organ transplants, or artificial means, were available, or if her own heart and lungs could be made to operate properly, there would be no harm to her whatsoever, whereas removal of the external strain would still preserve the life of Jodie); the good effect which is indeed the end of the act is not achieved through the evil effect as a means—it is solely the removal of the strain on Jodie's heart and lungs, and not the death of Mary, which defines the preserving of Jodie's heart and lungs, and this is consistent with Mary's own heart and lungs being made operative, or with her using organ transplants, or using artificial means. Indeed, were the strain something else, it would be removed as well. There is no direct action against Mary as such, and the definition of removing the strain on Jodie's heart and lungs only *per accidens* involves Mary's death. Further, there is here indeed a proportion between the good and evil effect such that the evil consequence is not so great as to make the act unworthy of choice (Mary is judged to be dying in any case, but Jodie too will die if the harmful impact of the evil circumstance is not delimited).

But if the act itself, and its integral nature, always are included in the object of the act, how can the direct effect of the death of Mary not be included in the object of the act? The answer is that the act itself is only a partial cause of Mary's death, and that Mary's death is not sufficiently caused by that act. To preserve the integrity of Jodie's heart and lungs from external strain—even where Mary is indeed that strain—is not directly to act against the life of Mary. Were it to be so, then it would be absolutely impossible to dissever the twins and then even *attempt* an organ transplant for Mary, or her connection to artificial means of circulation and oxygenation of her blood. But this is not the case. If what were needed, to make the act effective, were an act which terminates directly on her person—as the crushing of the skull in craniotomy terminates directly in the person of the *conceptus*—then there would be an argument. Suppose that what is required to "save" Jodie the external strain is to *dismember* Mary. If this were true, it would be directly contrary to the moral law and could not be done, any more than the *conceptus* may have its head crushed for the ulterior purpose of helping the mother to survive. But this is not the case.

I have attempted only to indicate that in this case the causality of the circumstance killing both twins is such that the will to *limit* the destructiveness of this circumstance by preserving the one child's cardiovascular system cannot be taxed with being the complete and proper cause of death of the other child. The act is aimed at *limiting* the destructiveness of the circumstance by preserving the integrity of bodily function of a child from unnatural strain, and in no way does it *directly* impose harm on the innocent child who lacks heart and lungs, who will in any case (on the hypothesis under which we are operating) die. Rather the mortal harm threatened by the circumstance suffered by both twins is, by the action taken, *limited,* and the act itself is only a *partial* cause of the likely death of one of the twins, and this is *permitted* but not directly caused. (The definition of removing Mary from the heart and lungs of Jodie is not, in and of itself, the cause of the death of Mary— the well-being of Jodie's cardiovascular system is not defined by her death, and were Mary's death averted that would not alter the good done to Jodie's cardiovascular system by removing the unnatural strain from Jodie's heart and lungs.)

Compare this to the simplest of cases: one person is falling off a cliff, and another tries to save the first by clasping hands with him and keeping him from falling. However, the first ineluctably draws the second down, until it is clear that if their hands stay clasped, both will fall to their deaths. Is it wrongful homicide for the person who sought to save the endangered party to disengage from that party when it is clear that otherwise both will fall and die? No. The second had done all in his power to save the first, but is not obliged to die with him. Likewise, we might say, that Jodie has done all in her power to save Mary, but cannot be obliged to die with Mary by being required to suffer for Mary's deprivation of heart and lungs, any more than the second agent can be required to suffer for the first's deprivation of a good handhold or footing and to fall and die.

But is not saying that Mary's death is not part of the definition of preserving Jodie's cardiovascular integrity rather too neat and logical? Granted that in some other age there may be technical means to aid Mary to survive, in this world, at this time, there aren't such means, and to sever Mary from Jodie's heart is to assure her death. If, however, her death is otherwise equally assured, we have some reason to endeavor to save one of the two, for so long as we are not required directly to harm or kill Mary. But the fact that harm *knowably* will ensue to Mary from being severed from Jodie's heart and lungs does not make this severation the *per se* cause of that harm. Indeed, no harm would be involved whatsoever, could Mary's heart and lungs be gotten to work. It is clear that the cause of the harm is Mary's lack of heart and lungs, and for this no human agent is responsible, much less Jodie.

However, it is at this point that we conclude, as we began, with the caveat that this whole stretch of reasoning presupposes the adequacy of the diagnosis that elsewise both will die. Insofar as there is any significant reason to doubt this diagnosis, there is just so far reason to attempt to keep both, and not only one, alive. If, however, at the end of the day, there is not merely a highly speculative diagnosis but one that is judged so probable as to be virtually ineluctable, then just so far does it become reasonable to seek to limit the destructiveness of the natural anomaly of Mary's deprivation of heart and lungs. The tragedy is that there is not now a way to limit this destructiveness so as to preserve both children from harm. But there should be no doubt that the prime cause of harm is the deprivation suffered by one of the twins, which imposes on the second an undue strain and threatens the death of both. Since the nature of the act—its very essence, which is not merely something logical and ethereal, but to be blunt quite physical—does not include Mary's death but only the removal of the strain on Jodie's heart and lungs, the likely death of Mary is a grave circumstance. It can be justified to perform such an act only because otherwise both will die, and only given that preserving the bodily integrity of Jodie *per accidens* includes only a partial, and not the *per se* and complete, cause of Mary's death.

Could it ever be obligatory to separate such twins surgically? If one could know with *certainty* that both would die, and if the analysis given thus far is correct (to the effect that preserving the bodily integrity of Jodie does not by its nature require or presuppose the death of Mary), then under that circumstance one might argue that because it is obligatory on the parents so far as possible to preserve their children from death they are bound to preserve Jodie's life even though this entails the grave circumstance of the death of Mary. Hence, on the supposition of such certain knowledge that otherwise both will die—certain knowledge which in truth no one possessed at the time this event historically occurred, and which in all probability would not be available in any similar case—it would seem that such an obligation could obtain.

Yet in the absence of such certain knowledge, to coerce the parents in such a matter is a decision so wantonly speculative and so violative of ordinary parental discretion as to constitute a violation of the rule of law. For no law in Great Britain establishes the court as infallible assessor of unverifiable or inherently questionable medical prognoses—as this prognosis was, and indeed would be today, questionable. For there is a long history of medical experts issuing gravely mistaken prognoses regarding children suffering anomalous illnesses and defects. The experience of such cases as that of Mary and Jodie was simply insufficiently common to make the judgment of "high" probability of death so certain as to be obligatory on any rational agent. That the court undertook to rule in such a matter with no more cognitive resources than those possessed by the parents for the requisite judgment must stand as a monument to the impunity with which contemporary legal regimes in the first world seek to supplant the ordinary jurisdiction of parental authority with their own.

Nonetheless, putting at one side the wrongful usurpation of authority represented by the court, and the dubiety of the prognosis on which its decision was based, that which the court decided is not intrinsically and on its merits necessarily wrongful. Even if in the informed judgment of those concerned there is but a high probability that both twins will perish if they are not severed, such a decision is in principle defensible under the *ratio* of double effect, although it is clearest and most unequivocal when this probability is tantamount to natural certainty. Yet the reasonability of trying to save both twins rises *pari passu* with the degree to which such a prognosis is unclear or subject to reasonable dispute, as likewise it rises with any medical feasibility of organ transplant or the use of artificial means to sustain Mary. Nonetheless, the unequivocal fact that the working heart and lungs *are Jodie's* and that another is using them *to Jodie's harm* seems to imply that removal of that harm is licit, even though Mary intends no harm (as Jodie, and the surgeons, wish no harm to Mary, and would if they could provide her with working substitutes for the non-working organs which are the reason for her plight, and indeed for Jodie's plight too).

By the nature of the case, there is no analysis which can relieve one of the sadness of the natural anomaly that causes such dangers and difficulties. But although these matters are both tortuous and torturous, the natural teleological grammar governing the constitution of the object and species of the moral act remains the key to their understanding.

FURTHER THOUGHTS ON ECTOPIC PREGNANCY: WHY NO DIRECT ACTION AGAINST THE *CONCEPTUS* IS ETHICALLY WARRANTED

It might be thought that just as one may, in the extreme case, reasonably use lethal force against a morally guiltless assailant who is not responsible for his conduct (by reason, say, of a brain tumor or of dementia), that so one may rightly use lethal force directly against the *conceptus* in ectopic pregnancy. For, does not the *conceptus* being where only grave harm will be caused to the mother as well as to itself warrant *stopping* this menace by direct and lethal force? Yet, this inference does not follow. The reasons are as given below.

Whereas the morally inculpable assailant is still *performing conduct*, albeit morally inculpable conduct—conduct which wrongfully assails and threatens death or grave harm—the *conceptus* is only, by virtue of its mal-positioning through anomaly of nature, a *natural menace*. Now, one may indeed seek to avert natural menace, but not by such means as will be directly and of its very nature lethal to innocent persons. Suppose that there is only enough oxygen left in a room for one person to live, but there are two persons. One of these cannot licitly kill the other so as to survive longer in the hope of rescue. The reason is clear: while the other person's drawing of air away from oneself is indeed naturally menacing to one's life, it is not a wrongful activity, not even a wrongful activity that is inculpa-ble—rather it is a bad *situation* the whole burden of which may not in jus-tice be wholly borne by only one (who is to be killed) when in fact *two* lives are at stake. This is likewise true of ectopic pregnancy, although in this case it is true that the *conceptus* is where it does not naturally belong.

Hence one may remove the *conceptus*—who, unlike the person in the chamber with limited oxygen supply, is where naturally speaking *he ought not to be*. One may do so because while the *conceptus* will die owing to being where it does not belong and also harm or kill the mother unless removed, the mother will live if the *conceptus* is removed. *Moreover, it is not the act of removing which causes death*—rather, it is the lack of any habitat in which the *conceptus* may survive that is the cause of death (for otherwise the child could be placed in a survival-friendly environment).

This circumstance does indeed constitute for the *conceptus* a terminal disease. *No human person is responsible either for the child being where it cannot survive in the fallopian tube, or for the lack of any better place where the child could be moved in order to survive.* Since if the child remains in the fallopian tube the mother will be harmed or die as well as the child, and there is no reason why the mother should die because the child is not where it belongs, removing the child would be—*if it did not involve chem-ical poisoning or direct killing of the conceptus*—reasonable.

Not being in a position to save the child from its having been placed by natural anomaly where it cannot live, is quite different from performing an act whose very definition is such as to include the child's death—such as poisoning or crushing it. Poisoning a child or crushing a child are not medical acts: they are defined by their per se order to inflict harm on the child, and this harm is in no way medically aiding the person toward whom it is directed. It is, accordingly, no more medical than is shooting someone because otherwise that person will take the last dosage of a medicine of which one has urgent need oneself. Nor is there arbitrariness in definition here, as though if one defines the removal of the *conceptus* as including the circumstance of there being no survival-friendly environment that therefore the action of removing the *conceptus* is defined by this circumstance. It is indeed a grave circumstance, and one that is morally significant: if there were any way to save the life of the *conceptus* this would be morally pertinent. *But that there is not any way to save the life of the* conceptus *is a circumstance that is not caused by removing the* conceptus *from where it harms the mother.*

The circumstance responsible for the death of the *conceptus* is that there is no place, following the natural anomaly of being implanted in the fallopian tube, where it can avoid untimely death (unless and until an artificial womb should be available): and *this is not a circumstance caused by anyone.* Hence when removing the *conceptus* one is a *partial cause* of its death: but its death is only completely and properly caused by the fact that by natural anomaly there is no place where it can survive. To perform an action which is simply to *move the conceptus* is not to *cause the circumstance that there is nowhere that the conceptus* can survive, a fact which obtains in any case. It is not by dying that the *conceptus* moves, nor is it because of the *moving* of the *conceptus* that there is *no place where it can survive*: and so *moving the conceptus* does not directly kill or harm, although it is knowably an indirect and partial cause of death for whose permission there must be a proportionately grave reason.

The difference between "direct" and "nondirect" is teleological: upon what does the action bear, and what defines its completion. If the removal of the *conceptus* is defined by a change of local place, this does not in and of itself constitute killing, but only owing to the *circumstance* that, owing to no one's choice, there is absolutely no safe environment for the *conceptus*, including the place from which the *conceptus* is being removed: *and of course, even this alone is not sufficient to justify the action.* It is not as though one could, in the case of two persons with limited oxygen in a space capsule, justify one pushing the other out a hatch to the outside, on the grounds that after all that person would in any case die inside too: for in such a case, each is as much *where he is supposed to be* as the other. It is only because owing to natural anomaly the *conceptus* is where it naturally and in teleological terms *does not belong*, and so—for the sake of the protection of an innocent, that is, the mother—*the conceptus* must be removed, that the action is justified. Without natural anomaly incurring serious harm to the innocent there is no reason for the action.

Thus to directly harm the innocent to avert natural menace is far different than to do so indirectly and by way of consequence, although even this requires *sufficient reason*. The extent to which this is so is perhaps insufficiently clear from what already has been said. It will require further clarification to make it so.

First Example

Suppose in the case of the space capsule that one of the two persons will die in any case, because he suffers a deathly but slowly unfolding allergy to an antiviral agent uniquely included in the oxygen supply for one chamber in that capsule; suppose, also, that this same person *was not supposed to be in that chamber at all*, but is present owing solely to a fluke failure of the computer program which will not open the door to the other chamber of the capsule (a door that cannot be forced). Suppose also that there is a way out of the spaceship, but not back into any other part of the ship. Now we have what *initially appears* to be a situation partially similar to ectopic pregnancy.

That is, we have the case of a person who is dying *in situ* in any case, together with a circumstance caused by no one, namely that, short of a miracle, this person *cannot survive* anyplace he can be moved. This person dying in place also is where he does not belong. Given the fact that his presence will in fact also cause another to die by using up the available oxygen (oxygen which does not even help him to live, since he is allergic to the point of death to the antiviral agent in it, although the death takes awhile), we must say that *simply to move him* is only a partial cause of his death. The real causes seem quite similar, initially, to the causes in the case of the removal of the *conceptus* in the ectopic pregnancy. (1) He is allergic to the point of death to an antiviral agent present in that chamber where he is trapped (the *conceptus* will cause the fallopian tube to burst and so will die itself at that point, if not far sooner owing to malnutrition while nonetheless irritating and bursting the tube to the harm of the mother). (2) Outside the chamber there is no atmosphere for the astronaut to breathe, so he can't survive there (the *conceptus* cannot survive outside the mother because the environment is even less apt there than in the fallopian tube). (3) There is no other place to move him (*ditto* for the *conceptus*, unless and until a workable artificial womb is designed and microsurgical techniques further perfected). And finally, (4) his presence in the chamber causes deadly menace to a person who *will* survive longer—perhaps long enough to return to earth from shallow orbit—if he leaves (the mother *will* survive longer apart from the menace represented by the *conceptus* being where it ought not to be). Local motion, it would seem, is the least of this person's worry—although his motion is pertinent to the other person in the capsule.

Nonetheless, it is precisely here that we see how utterly different this case is from that of removing the child in an ectopic pregnancy. For how is moving this person outside the capsule different from simply killing him? It has the knowable effect of killing him—as does leaving him in the chamber. Either approach will have the same effect. That there is no place this person can live is already factually given, it is a circumstance that one cannot avoid. (Although one should make sure! That is, if there is doubt about the allergic reaction, for example, the entire analysis is materially different.) So, given that no matter what the person's local position is that he will die, should his position be such as to make it likelier that other innocents live, or not? Obviously it seems that the answer is that his position should be such as to make it likelier that other innocents live. And this seems quite different from, let us say, wounding him to death with a knife, or poisoning him.

But, there is a salient and crucial objection: by moving him, do we not in fact hasten his death? If we deliberately hasten the death of another—and let us suppose we do so against his will—do we not then commit murder?

Second Example

Suppose the same case, not in a spaceship but in a submarine trapped on the ocean floor, and with two feet of water in the compartment. Let us suppose that there is the same antiviral in the oxygen, and that the same deadly allergic reaction has ensued in one of two persons in a closed chamber. But let us say there is no question of getting out.

If it is licit to ask the person in the spaceship to *leave the ship* rather than to stay and die of allergic reaction, or even licit to *force* the person to leave the ship, *then* is it not likewise licit to make the person in the submarine *put his head in the water and drown*? Isn't *drowning someone* the same as *killing that person*? *That the person may die anyway a little later does not justify directly murdering him, does it?* If it does, is active euthanasia now implicitly permitted? Further, isn't the person asphyxiated *in exactly the same way,* namely by putting him where he cannot access breathable oxygen? It seems we have run into an impasse: indeed, an impasse that might make us wish to rethink, and alter, the view that removing the child from the fallopian tube in an ectopic pregnancy is morally permissible.

But while this example may move us to rethink our conclusion regarding ectopic pregnancy, it should not move us to alter it, and for one very excellent reason: the body of the mother is not a spaceship, nor is it a submarine, and the malplacement of the child is a disease for both mother and child. For an innocent to be *where he does not belong* when that "where" is *within the body of another* is utterly different from being *where he does not belong* when that is, as it were, "neutral space." For the *conceptus* to be where it does not belong, is for it to suffer illness itself—not to be implanted where it can be adequately nourished and develop appropriately, but instead merely to consume its small stock of native nutrients and grow toward rupturing the tube and dying while simultaneously harming the mother. Also, for the *conceptus* to be where it does not belong is for it to usurp the body of the mother, every bit as much as a cancer, or an infectious illness. Nor does this warrant *abortion* which is homicidal.

For the child to be in the mother's body *but where it does not belong* is a cause of its own sickness and death, and also puts it outside of the *integral order of procreation* according to which it is ordered to be but in one place in the mother, namely the mother's womb. Naturally speaking, the *conceptus* has no more business being implanted in the mother's fallopian tube than it has being in the mother's brain. In this case its *being where it ought not* places it quite literally in the status not only of suffering disease itself—and certainly not of being a disease inasmuch as it is a *person*—but in the status of being a constituent part of a disease for the mother.

The malpositioning of the conceptus *constitutes a terminal disease for the child and both a disease and a grave threat of bodily harm or death to the mother.*

For this reason it is paradoxically the case that when the mother withholds further use of the extraordinary means of her fallopian tube—thus hastening the naturally ineluctable death of the child—she is freed from the cognate effects of disease and disproportionate harm to her own health caused by the child's malpositioning. Note how even here it is teleology that makes matters intelligible. When a person's local position where he does not belong in the body of another enters into the sickness or harm of the other, then the person becomes a constituent cause of a disease. As such, that person may then be moved from the wrongful place in which place alone is that person a constitutent factor in the disease—*moved,* not poisoned, not crushed, not speared, not lacerated.

Whether we look at the matter (1) from the vantage point of the *conceptus* as suffering a disease for the amelioration of which the slight help offered by the mother's fallopian tube is an extraordinary means; or (2) from the vantage point of the *conceptus* being a constituent factor in a disease affecting the mother by reason of the *conceptus* being where it does not belong and cannot live; *in either case* there is reason for the mother to remove the *conceptus* from the fallopian tube. And this is true solely because of the *nature of the body and of bodily teleology.* Of course, the *gravity of the harm* of its being where it ought not to be is pertinent: for (a) this enters into the *ratio* of the judgment that for the mother to retain the child in the fallopian tube is an extraordinary means; and (b) if the disease caused to the mother by the *conceptus* being where it did not belong were not seriously dangerous, then to cure a slight disease by being the partial cause of the death of a human being would be morally unbalanced. But here the harm is not slight.

One is not obligated to provide extraordinary means for the temporary amelioration of a deadly disease, especially when this aid by its nature threatens one with harm or death (which is yet another index of its being an extraordinary means). But the mother who provides the use of her fallopian tube as an extraordinary and quite temporary partial means of treatment is threatened with harm and death by this provision, and for the sake of what is only a very slight help to the child. Clearly the mother is not obliged to provide such aid.

Hence, when we say that it is *not alone* the circumstance that there is no place where the person can survive which justifies moving the person so as to hasten his death—even in a case wherein the person is *where he does not belong* and is by that fact *jeopardizing others* (e.g., the spaceship or submarine illustrations)—this is *crucial*. It is the difference between rationalizing *drowning someone* in the submarine, and merely permitting the hastening of the death of a child as the result of treating a disease of which the child is both victim and by natural anomaly a constituent factor (by reason of its being radically misplaced *within the mother's body*). It seems fitting to add that insofar as it one day becomes possible to move the *conceptus* in ectopic pregnancy without poisoning or spearing or crushing it, *then* it will be necessary that medical personnel treat it differently than as *discarded tissue*.[6]

So we conclude this return-consideration of ectopic pregnancy by observing that the mother's body is not a submarine or spaceship. One might think that this is *per se nota*. But so great is our distance from natural teleology that all of us today easily think of our bodies as merely neutral space, different from Rick's Café in Casablanca only by accidental grid markings. But our final illustration will further address the sad fact of this remotion from natural teleology with respect to our bodiliness as it pertains to the so-called "rescue" of frozen embryos. For this "rescue" wrongfully embraces *surrogate motherhood* for the lofty cause of saving embryonic human beings wrongfully alienated from their mothers' wombs, unnaturally frozen, and left to die.

EMBRYONIC "RESCUE"

What is true "naturally speaking" is not simply a function of *techne*—rather, what technology effectuates is always *relative* to nature. We consider natural teleology in determining whether medical means are suitable or not. For example, our natural knowledge of what health is determines the reasonability of seeking medical aid in overcoming disease. But we do not first define health technologically: rather, medical technology exists to promote health and impede disease. Since, in precision from technology, the mother carrying the child is a condition of the spouses enjoying the delivery of a live rather than a dead child, and naturally speaking she alone can carry the child, it is clear that this capacity is integral to the procreative purpose of delivering a live rather than dead child. To repeat, the other and more remote ends of the nourishment of the child outside the womb, its breastfeeding and housing and clothing and education, all may in the paradigmatic natural case yet be

---

[6] See footnote 1 on page 168 above.

performed by others should the parents perish. But in the paradigmatic natural case, only the mother can bear her child so that the integral end of procreation—a live baby rather than a dead one—is achieved.

The carrying of a conceived child thus is at the heart of the procreative purpose of marriage. Since its whole *raison d'être* is to serve the integral procreative purpose of marriage, to which it is naturally necessary, it necessarily follows that childbearing falls within the scope of that which belongs to the spouses as spouses, and which is not rightfully transferable to others even if this may technically be possible. All the other acts which marital spouses perform in caring for children can at need, naturally speaking, be performed by others, from wet-nursing to feeding and housing to educating. But naturally speaking, the mother alone can bear the child.

That is, just as the acts leading up to and including conception are rightfully those of the spouses as spouses, so the bearing of the child, which is integrally necessary to the procreative purpose, belongs rightfully only to the spouses as spouses and to no one else. *The bearing of the child in the womb by the mother is naturally and normatively necessary to the end of a live child, and so that which generically pertains to the procreative good belongs to it insofar as it is integrally necessary to the procreative good. The other further ends to which parents are also ordered may, naturally speaking, be fulfilled by others; but naturally and normatively the maternity of the mother in her bearing of the child in her womb is necessary to the procreative purpose of the delivery of a live child.* Integrally procreative faculties, then, extend beyond the mere geometric point of conception, for the normative natural purpose of procreation is the delivery of a live rather than of a dead child.

It is also true that either all that is necessary to the integral procreative good is bestowed uniquely by the spouses upon one another, or not. If not, then marriage does not involve the unique gift of integral procreativity, and it necessarily follows that marriage is not essentially but only accidentally ordered to procreation. But this latter the Church has always denied.

It is not solely *surrogate motherhood* for the sake of ministering to emotional imbalance, or to get money, which is wrongful. It is true that *Donum Vitae* chiefly had these in mind, together with immoral means of *conception* that violate the natural bond between the unitive and procreative good of the spouses. But it is the *nature* of surrogate motherhood which is contrary to reason and to the natural order, according to which the bearing of children is ordered to flow from a distinct act of conjugal union of man and wife. The integral procreative good includes that which is *per se* requisite to the generation and transmission of human life, and this transmission is of course a reference to the bearing of the child in the mother's womb. Further, if it is said that the wife may bear her husband's children, and those of others as well, then it may as well be said by the husband that he can enjoy the unitive good with his first wife, and also with his second and his third. That is to say, that what belongs to the couple as couple for the sake of generating and transmitting human life does not belong to others, because the standard is a function not merely of pragmatic possibility, but of natural teleology.

Theologically, just as the one flesh of sacramental marriage witnesses the oneness of Christ with his Church, so the wife's spousal donation of her childbearing to her husband bears witness to the unique fruitfulness of the Church. *Naturally,* childbearing is *per se* ordained to flow from specific acts of conjugal union between man and wife. To dissever this natural bond by promoting surrogacy for the sake of humanitarian relief is to treat the *sacramentum* of marriage as though it were merely a collection of public services.

So, even for so sublime an end as *saving* frozen embryonic human beings no one can justify violating marital intimacy, or the chastity of the unwed, or simple religious chastity. Because *carrying such children* who are not conceived with one's husband in a specific act of conjugal union is wholly to supplant the *natural teleological order* which defines what is rightful and what is morally illicit, and according to which certain things should not be sought out except in the context of marriage. Just as the womb is not a spaceship, or a submarine, so too we may with a certain wryness observe that *it is not a hospitality suite*, like an extra bedroom in which friends may stay.

What is the *end* of surrogacy undertaken for the sake of saving frozen embryonic human beings? It is a humanitarian end of saving life. What is the *object* of the moral act in the case of surrogacy to save frozen embryonic human beings? It is *having a child not conceived within one's marriage with one's own husband and implanted in one's womb for the sake of saving its life. But this is exactly what surrogacy means—to carry in one's womb a child who is not the fruit of conjugal intimacy with one's husband.* The integral procreative capacity is what the spouses donate to one another solely for the use of the spouses as spouses, if marriage is essentially ordered to procreation.

But marriage is essentially ordered to procreation—and so not only the geometric point of conception belongs to the spousal couple as couple, but the integral procreative faculty of childbearing. Without grasping this essentially teleological datum regarding human marriage, one will not know *what the act is that is being performed* in surrogate motherhood, for surrogate motherhood *violates* this spousal gift.

Surrogate motherhood is under negative precept, and it is indeed definitory of the object of the moral act of choosing to carry the child of another, even for humanitarian reasons. This alone suffices to indicate that it ought not to be done. The act itself, and the integral nature of the act, are always to be included in the object of the moral act. Here the integral nature of the act performed is surrogacy, and this is illicit. It is illicit for the teleological reasons, and the spiritual reasons, noted above.

Further, it should be noted just how crucial the teleological analysis is to the comprehension of the spousal donation in marriage. For that which belongs to the spousal couple as couple is known in relation to the ends of marital society, which are essentially unitive and procreative; and the procreative end is achieved not merely with conception but, integrally and naturally speaking, with the delivery of a live rather than a dead child, which, in the natural and paradigmatic case, only the mother can perform. This gift is, then, *at the very heart* of marriage. The error regarding this matter is, then, cognate with that of those who reject *Humanae Vitae*, although in this case the idealism of saving those in jeopardy of death offers some significant explanation.

Lacking teleological analysis, the grammar governing the constitution of object and species of the moral act will not be understood, and our understanding of the morality of human actions will be seriously impeded. In this way, even those *defending* a teaching whose thoroughly teleological nature is manifest—*Humanae Vitae*—are liable, in the very next breath, to undercut its conclusions. Of course, there is also the need to observe that analysis of such difficult issues as we have considered in this chapter is not the primary application of natural teleology: rather, that honor belongs to the role of teleology in the development of virtue for the sake of achieving the ordered whole of a good life. Nonetheless the correct understanding of the object and species of the moral act—which is necessary for judging the moral act rightly—depends wholly on natural teleology.

But it is here that our illustrative application to cases of St. Thomas's doctrine of the teleological constitution of the object and species of the moral act must rest: not for lack of further illustrative and clarifying analyses, but because our purpose has been to vindicate the power of St. Thomas's teaching rather than to apply it everywhere it may be well applied.

APPENDIX 2

■ ■ ■

A Brief Word Regarding
Two Difficult Cases

This appendix seeks briefly to address two difficult cases. The first difficult case regards the nature of formal and material cooperation, and the assessment of the "conscience waivers" that the Obama Administration requires Catholic institutions (those it will acknowledge) to sign with respect to the provision of insurance for vicious actions such as the use of contraceptives, sterilization procedures, and so on.[1] The second concerns the use of contraceptives by married women regulating the cycle, and considers whether it is preponderantly better for married couples to abstain during such therapy. While much more could be written, it seems appropriate to summarize certain considerations and conclusions here, which perhaps on some suitable future occasion may be more fully developed.

AUTHOR'S NOTE ON THE HHS MANDATE

In the time since this analysis was first written, legal facts have changed, yet the basic concerns remain. The need for this type of analysis clearly is growing rather than diminishing given not only continued harassment regarding the "health insurance" mandate, but also the SCOTUS radical redefinition of marriage. As for the legal changes regarding the health

---

[1] Of course, by the time this edition goes to press, the legal cases may be decided— one hopes in such a way as legally to end the effort to subdue conscience through coercion and to force Catholic institutions and men and women generally to promote financial aid for vice. In any case, one hopes that the reasoning of this chapter may be of assistance in understanding this and similar cases.

insurance mandate, the Hobby Lobby decision seems to have voided the requirement with respect to EBSA Form 700 for at least some institutions. Thus this particular pressure to command institutions to direct their third party providers or insurers to cooperate with evil has, for at least some institutions, been stopped. Whether this decision will be justly applied to Catholic institutions of higher learning remains unclear, and so the analysis below may yet be of proximate practical pertinence. While freed of the constraint of EBSA Form 700, the Little Sisters of the Poor have as of this writing been directed by a federal court to provide the government with contact information for their insurers. While this is not the same thing as being required to authorize their third party provider to release contact information to promote the distribution of funds for vice, it is nonetheless a variation on the same theme. The state wishes to command Catholic institutions to provide what the state requires in order to do evil. If all the government sought from the Little Sisters of the Poor were a statement of conscience, they could have this in triplicate any time they desired. However, the state wants more. It wants the institution to "grease the sleds" for its evil action by providing either direction to others to cooperate or—after the Hobby Lobby decision stopped this at least for some institutions—it wishes to be given the contact information for the insurers that is necessary to aid the government's plan to distribute funds for vice. But what one may not do oneself, one may not authorize or direct others to do as was protected in the victorious Hobby Lobby decision, which one hopes will be legally applied to Catholic institutions of higher learning. Nor may one supply essential aid to another to do the wrong as in the present case of the Little Sisters of the Poor, who are intrepidly continuing their just legal opposition. Just as one does not reload the weapons of genocidal exterminators killing innocents in front of one, even when under threat; so likewise one does not provide essential aid to a state attempting to supply funds for vice. In any case, I hope that the moral analysis below highlights the continuing centrality of the intelligible judgment that essential complicity in regard to the object of a wicked external act is not justified merely because one does not share the malefactor's intention with respect to the end.

A further analysis is worth providing here. It might be argued that a normal insurance company (rather than third party provider) is already under an imposition of positive law (howsoever unjust) to supply the necessary information to the government. On this view, the institution (let us say, a university) that informs its insurer of its refusal to cooperate, is not "authorizing" anything but merely "de-coupling" itself from the putatively legal "obligation". But to the contrary, although the general legal origination of the coercive pressure on the insurance company derives from the government, the notice of refusal to cooperate delivered to the insurer does "trigger" the application of this government mandate. This triggering is moral and existential, not merely legal, since the government could unjustly bully the insurance company in a different way without altering the statutes. Thus imagine the comparable case of trying to get someone to command an execution of an innocent person without the person commanding being morally guilty of ordering the execution. So, one tells someone on Christmas day, go to the firing line, and when the (innocent) prisoner has his hands up, say to the soldiers "I refuse to command you to shoot." And that is the signal to shoot. But since the man saying "I refuse to command . . ." doesn't know they will shoot, he has no moral complicity. Now, suppose that the same man knows that when he goes to the line and shouts to the soldiers, "I will not command you to shoot" they have been ordered to shoot; in fact, he is being coerced to go to the line and shout "I will not command you to shoot" for the express purpose of executing the innocent. Of course, the soldiers being under orders to respond this way or that is not the fault of the person being co-opted to be complicit, and the soldiers could be ordered by someone else. The originating orders do not come from the person being co-opted into complicity. But this is irrelevant. The person enjoined to say "I will not command you to shoot" cannot do it if he knows that those he addresses are under orders to execute innocents when he speaks. He is not the originator of the order to the soldiers. But he is essentially contributing to the evil by knowingly triggering the act, even though others might also be able to trigger it. Similarly, the fact that the insurers are under (wrongful) legal constraint to act makes it worse (irrespective whether other "triggers" are possible) like the soldiers ordered to fire when they hear the words "I will not command you to shoot" (who could of course be ordered in some other way). An institution's communication of its "non-cooperation" to the insurance company itself triggers the evil actions of the company given the government's coercive command to the company—not by its logical content, but by the circumstance of state coercion of the insurance company to perform evil at the reception of such notice, which changes the species of the act. The notification is commanded by the state explicitly for this precise purpose. Knowing that one must provide the "notification" because the government commands this for the sake of triggering the malum, such "noncooperation" in fact becomes a direct and essential contribution to evil-doing (the fact that the state could order things differently—as the soldiers could be ordered to execute in a different way—does not make the actual "triggering" to be reasonable and good).

Practically speaking, institutions will find the state's broad attempt to rope them into complicity difficult to avoid, precisely because they do not wish to abandon their employees. Clearly the mammoth pressures involved, and overt state coercion, drastically reduce culpability. Nonetheless, the honor of Catholic institutions as such in refusing complicity with evil is imperative. This is the true reason why the heroic stance of the Little Sisters of the Poor has been more effective in catalyzing opposition to the mandate's tyranny than almost any other factor. In a situation so desperate, it is nonetheless true that the Sisters merit emulation. Institutional fidelity to the truth of this matter is unlikely to be either easy or pain free: and one wishes this were not so. Institutional complicity with evil is something more to be feared, and to be avoided, than even that most horrible evil of the unjust suffering of families. No university is under divine precept to offer health insurance: but individuals are under divine precept to care for their health, and can morally undertake what institutions cannot, because they can guarantee that they will not use immoral options (but no institution can absolutely guarantee this with respect to all its individual members). Catholic integrity should not easily be sacrificed even to the noble good of helping families with their medical needs.

The objective facets of this question remain pertinent, and so the analysis of a slightly earlier state of the question (but of course postdating the original text of the first edition of this book), is offered below.

I. FORMAL AND MATERIAL COOPERATION, AND THE CASE OF THE HHS MANDATE

A SEPARATE BOOK could be written on the subject of formal and material cooperation with evil. But for our purposes, it is sufficient to note that the analysis of co-operation necessarily follows upon the analysis of *operation*. This work has argued that the object of the external act includes the act itself, its integral nature, and *per se* effects, as well as the *ratio of appetibility* for the act chosen. Thus, one chooses not alone *what one proposes* to do through the act, *not* only that which is desirable to the agent in the act, but rather in choice one's will goes out to the act itself, its integral nature, and *per se* effects (granted that the agent's reason for preferring or accepting the act itself is the more formal part of the object), and so these are contained in the essential character of the act and should be good.

Likewise, this work has argued that, while the object of the external act is something formal, it is formal with a formality of essence considered as a whole, which includes a more formal part (the *ratio of appetibility*) and a more material part (the act itself, its integral nature, and *per se effects*). Just as the essential nature of man is on the one hand something formal (but with the formality of a whole and not merely as a part—not merely as the rational soul is formal vis-à-vis the matter of the human composite), but nonetheless includes matter (the matter of the composite—or, in the definition, the genus "animal" taken as material vis-à-vis "rational" as formal), so similarly the object of the external act is formal while having nonetheless a material dimension. And so, with respect to *operation*, neither the intention of the end nor the *ratio of appetibility* whereby an act is either *preferred over others* or minimally judged *acceptable* (where it is the only way to move to the end, its unique modality must still be accepted by the agent) wholly constitutes the object of the external act. We choose not merely the *aspect* under which an action is attractive to us; we choose the act itself.

One may *prefer* an act for a reason that is quite valid, while nonetheless the act itself preferred is vicious. The man waiting in line for life-saving therapy who realizes his prognosis will run out before the line ahead of him will, and who accordingly *shortens* that line in order to obtain life-saving therapy by killing those ahead of him in line, cannot rightly characterize his action as "merely removing impediments to life-saving therapy." The married couple that decides to use a condom in order to prevent the communication of AIDS cannot rightly characterize their action as "merely preventing the communication of AIDS" inasmuch as the chosen means by its very nature contracepts by suppressing the procreative character of the act (it only prevents communication of AIDS by suppressing the procreative matter). Not only is the couple not performing a marital act in this case, but the couple is also by the very nature of the chosen action culpable of the wrong of contraception.[2]

What is true of *operation* pertains also to co-operation. It is not the case that the only way to cooperate with evil is to share the intention of the agent (unless we include in "intention" direct and essential aid with respect to the evil voluntary operation specified by the object of the external act). This is certainly true of the teaching of St. Thomas Aquinas, who does not deploy the language of "formal" versus "material" cooperation with evil, but who speaks only of grave wrongdoing proceeding from defective intention or choice.

If one were to insist upon using language similar to the terms we have received from St. Alphonsus Liguori, for St. Thomas the categories would

---

[2] To the risible delight of some, it must be observed that even for a sterile couple there is a morally significant sense in which the use of a condom is contraceptive. Just as someone who says he wishes to drive to Cleveland in his car but cannot do so because of a flat tire would be shown insincere if, in addition to the flat tire, he set out to destroy the engine and the chassis—since injuring these too is contrary to driving the car to Cleveland (even though it is presently impossible to make the drive with a flat tire)—likewise, the sterile couple who adds further impediment by using a condom acts against the natural procreative order, an order that suffers accidental impediment in them but to which as human persons they are normatively subject and with respect to which, moreover, they may introduce even further deliberate impediment and deprivation. And this is arguably in a certain respect not only a sexual sin but a sin against piety. Of course, in an obvious respect, such a choice is not immediately contraceptive if we mean that it blocks the act proximate to procreation, because in the sterile couple there is not an act that is in every respect proximate to procreation. But it is not only the fertility of the seed or the ovum but the entire procreative act as a whole that is ordered toward procreation. And that order can suffer further harm. Likewise, if there were no water to drink on the earth, it would remain the case that human persons were naturally ordered to drinking water; the normative ordering of human nature is not merely the empirical status of a particular human being, and it is the former that defines rectitude regarding powers, act, object, and end. The eye does not have two different teleologies—seeing and not-seeing—as between those who see and those who are blind; rather, there is one natural teleology, which is susceptible of deprivation and defect. And in this light, adding further deprivation or defect taken in itself is something to be avoided. The question is more reasonable in the case of the sterile because of the seeming connection with medical necessity. But it remains an impiety with respect to the ordering of nature; the conjugal act ought not be performed unless the couple is not actively opposed to conception, whereas use of the condom by a sterile couple is such that, were God to heal the couple, they would contracept.

appear to be "more (or even most) formal" (sharing the malefactor's inten-tion of the end), "formal" (direct and essential aid bestowed by the coop-erator with respect to the object of the agent's act), and "material" (purely circumstantial).[3]

Of course, as has been commented in the introduction, such language perplexes many today even with respect to *operation* because of failure to understand the manner in which the object of the external act is either essentially or accidentally related to the intended end, whose causality is pri-mary with respect to the act. The language of Thomas with respect to the species of the end in the case of *per se* order of object to end as "more for-mal," and his general insistence that even in the case of *per accidens* ordering that the intention of the end exerts the greatest causality with respect to the act totally and with respect to the character of the agent, indicates the pre-cise senses in which one may rightly judge the intention of the end to con-stitute the most formal element in the human act. But this causality of the end occurs by way of our being moved to deliberate and choose actions that are either through themselves or accidentally helpful in achieving what is intended—actions that are indeed specified not only by the end but by what they proximately bear upon (because we achieve the end by means of some-thing else than the end). Due to a certain degree of confusion regarding St. Thomas's analysis of *operation*, it is not surprising that there should also be confusion regarding his analysis of co-operation.

Some have thought that St. Alphonsus Liguori gives support to the idea that formal cooperation with evil occurs only when we share the inten-tion of the wrongdoer. But in a brilliant paper,[4] Fr. Kevin Flannery, SJ, shows that St. Alphonsus's language regarding the nature of formal cooper-ation with evil—namely, that such cooperation involves contributing to the

---

3 Of course, what initially appears as a circumstance may in fact constitute the prin-cipal condition of an object, which directly bears upon the morality of action; and, likewise, what in relation to one consideration regarding an action may be a cir-cumstance may, in fact, represent in relation to another consideration the intro-duction of a distinct object to an action. But inasmuch as these can change the species of an action, they are not "pure" circumstances, since a pure circumstance precisely as such is an accident of a human act.

4 Fr. Kevin Flannery, "Two Factors in the Analysis of Cooperation with Evil," to my knowledge as yet unpublished, but given as a paper at Thomas Aquinas College in 2014, and used as the foundation for remarks delivered to the Ave Maria University graduate program in theology in 2014. Hereafter cited as "Cooperation with Evil."

evil will of the wrongdoer—does not for Alphonsus himself mean simply "sharing the intention" of the wrongdoer but extends to direct and essential contribution with respect to the object of the wrongdoer's action. Or, at least, this is how I read the paper.

Fr. Flannery notes the example given by St. Alphonsus, wherein Alphonsus considers whether the secretary who out of grave fear of punishment writes or conveys amorous correspondence to his master's lover acts licitly or sins. Alphonsus says that the servant cooperates formally with evil in doing so. Fr. Flannery notes that St. Alphonsus likewise gives the example of a lookout for a thief or assassin, observing that such cooperation is intrinsically evil and can never be licit, even if done only under the fear of death.[5] It is noteworthy that the case of the secretary expressly concerns either writing or merely conveying such correspondence, although Fr. Flannery notes that the sources that St. Alphonsus engages do seem by "writing" to intend not merely copying the words of the master but rather the secretary composing the letter himself. But nothing of this alters the datum that St. Alphonsus also considers simple delivery of such wrongfully amorous letters to constitute formal cooperation on the part of the secretary. In other words, it appears that what is in question is essential and direct aid with respect to the object of the wrongdoer's external act. A lengthy quotation from Fr. Flannery follows that dusts away the intentionalist cobwebs with which the actual teaching of St. Alphonsus has been covered by those who seemingly have read him with insufficient care:

> And so, especially in recent writings on cooperation, one often comes across the passage in which, most prominently, Alphonsus sets out the distinction as he understands it. (In what follows, I shall refer to this distinction as "the Central Distinction"; it appears in the second book of his most important theoretical work: his *Theologia moralis*.) Having first mentioned the way in which certain others had distinguished formal from material cooperation, Alphonsus writes:
>
> > But it is better, with others, to say that that cooperation is *formal* which contributes to the bad will of the other and cannot be without sin, but that cooperation is *material* which contributes only to the bad action of the other, beside the intention of the cooperator.

---

[5] Flannery, "Cooperation with Evil," footnote 3.

This certainly sounds as if Alphonsus were saying that one cooperates formally with a malefactor only when one shares his intention, and that otherwise one cooperates only materially. Thus, to use a contemporary example, a pro-life nurse who is forced to participate in an abortion since otherwise she will lose her job, cooperates in the abortion but only materially since her intention is only to keep her job. Some of those scholars and pastors who would call the nurse's cooperation material would also say that it is "immediate material cooperation" and, for that reason, immoral. But they will also have placed the nurse's action into a category of actions that could be moral, depending on their closeness to the act of the malefactor.

This understanding—and use—of Alphonsus's Central Distinction is, however, incorrect, for it fails to appreciate the difference, presumed by Alphonsus, between the will of the malefactor and his intention. Alphonsus says that formal cooperation "contributes to the bad will [*voluntas*] of the other" and that material cooperation does not share the same intention [*intentio*] with him. But this does not eliminate the possibility that a person cooperating formally might not have the same intention as the malefactor. Indeed, in the very section of his *Theologia moralis* we have been considering, Alphonsus gives examples of formal cooperation in which this is clearly the case. He speaks of a servant who writes or conveys amorous letters to his master's lover: even though he does these things out of "grave fear" that he will be punished, says Alphonsus, such a servant cooperates formally. In a work that appeared a few years after his *Theologia moralis*, Alphonsus gives a couple of other examples, including that of someone who acts as a lookout for a thief or an assassin. Such cooperation, he says, is intrinsically evil and can never be licit, no matter what the reason for cooperating, be it even the threat of death.

This understanding of the distinction between intention and the will (or the voluntary) is set out by Thomas Aquinas, and shared by the large majority of moralists who contributed to the Church's teaching at least up until the Second Vatican Council. When analyzing a particular human act, the most distant point in the "scenario" under consideration is called the agent's intention: what he intends.[6]

It is remarkable to what a degree such a view is in stark opposition to the way in which this Doctor of the Church's teaching is portrayed in

---

[6] Ibid., pp. 2–3.

contemporary conversations. One might hope that consideration of the two Doctors of the Church whose influence on the moral magisterium has arguably been the greatest—St. Alphonsus Liguori and St. Thomas Aquinas—would exert more traction on contemporary conversations. St. Thomas's teaching is of particular importance because of the great systematic clarity that he brings to the analysis of moral action. Yet, his account often is subjected to the logicist reduction that is adverted to in the text above, the insistence that only the *ratio of appetibility* or the most formal part of the object in relation to intention is morally definitive of action.

This is conspicuous in the arguments formally proffered by Professor Therese Lysaught defending the abortion at what used to be St. Joseph's Hospital in Phoenix, Arizona, over which that hospital lost its Catholic status. The hospital requested her to author a brief defending its action. In that argument (regarding *operation* rather than *co-operation*), the thought of Fr. Martin Rhonheimer, Professor William Murphy, and Professor Germain Grisez was adduced to argue that for so long as what was *intended* was help to the mother, it was *impossible* that the act performed be an abortion, even though the action performed had the causally direct effect of destroying the body of the fetus.[7] It is remarkable that Lysaught argues that her account of the object of the moral act, taken from Rhonheimer, Murphy, and Grisez, does not exclude the physical character of the act, while at the same time she affirms:

> A proper description of the moral object, then, certainly includes the "exterior act"—since it is a necessary part of the moral action as a whole—but it derives its properly moral content first and foremost from the proximate end deliberately chosen by the will.[8]

Absolutely lacking here is any recognition that the physical causality of an action may be morally pertinent to its choiceworthiness *irrespective* of the end that is sought—or that such physical causality may constitute "moral content."

---

[7] Therese Lysaught's defense of the hospital, "Moral Analysis of a Procedure at Phoenix Hospital," citing Rhonheimer, Grisez, and Murphy to the exclusion of the consensus of the Thomistic commentorial tradition, and reducing the morally significant content of the object of the external act merely to the *ratio of appetibility* or to what is most formal in the object, may be found online at http://epublications.marquette.edu/cgi/viewcontent.cgi?article=1372&context=theo_fac. It has been published in *Origins* 40, no. 33 (January 2011): 537–48.

[8] Cf. "Procedure at Phoenix," 542.

It is this type of utterly erroneous intentionalism that—never having displaced the tradition of the Church regarding the analysis of *operation*—now threatens to be introduced into the analysis of *co*-operation. Political pressures—both on the Roman Catholic Church and on Roman Catholic institutions that have some analogical share in the sacred mission of the Church through their charitable works and doctrinal commitments—make the actual temptation to accede to such accounts under political and legal threat to be significant. This is most manifest in the case within the United States of America of the Health and Human Services mandate regarding the health initiative of President Obama. This mandate requires Catholic institutions that do not wish to provide insurance for vicious activities such as sterilization, contraception, and abortion to sign "conscience waivers" whose state-mandated function is to serve as requisition forms that enable those seeking financial help for such purposes to obtain this help.

The question is whether such aid is formal cooperation with evil or merely material cooperation. There are accounts that would hold that it is proximate material cooperation that is gravely wrongful and may not be performed, and this approach is certainly superior to the view that the cooperation is material and yet might be possible.[9] Nonetheless, such analysis follows the teaching neither of Aquinas nor of Liguori regarding the nature of the moral act inasmuch as it blurs categories (the pure circumstance versus circumstance that becomes a principal condition of the object and so is of *formal* pertinence) in a way that is unsustainable. The analysis of this type of argument, which finally is an attempt to hold an "excluded middle" between the systematic rigor of the tradition and the new (and extremely widespread) intentionalist exegeses of the tradition, could itself fill a small book. This is not the place fully to engage it. Rather, bringing to bear the teaching both of St. Thomas Aquinas and St. Alphonsus Liguori on the analysis of the HHS mandate, this analysis will simply consider the requirement of the mandate with respect to its moral admissibility, and with respect to whether such cooperation with evil is formal or material.

---

[9] Cf. "Options for Non-Exempt Employers under PPACA," *Ethics and Medics*, Special Issue 2012. Note the account of formal and material cooperation on p. 2 at note 10 in the text, which when followed to the footnote matter indicates that the analysis derives from John A. McHugh and Charles J. Callan in their work *Moral Theology: A Complete Course*, vol. 1 (New York: Wagner, 1958), 616.

Let us take a fictional case by way of comparison. Suppose a political state wishes to compel various institutions to provide abortion "services," and the institutions refuse. The state then mandates that such institutions will be permitted not to provide such services, if they sign a conscience waiver that signals to another party that it must provide the abortion "services," or perhaps alternately may be taken by those seeking such "services" to those who will provide them. Or, suppose the state expressly wishes one class of persons to have the right legally to commit wrongful homicide on members of another class of persons (which, after all, is what abortion "rights" are), and wishes to compel institutions to help them to do so. Those institutions that do not wish to do so are compelled to sign a "conscience waiver," which similarly aids those seeking help to commit wrongful homicide by being "redeemable" for the homicidal help they seek in exterminating members of the officially designated class of persons who may be murdered. Or, take a different case. The state wishes institutions to provide aid for those seeking access to prostitution "services." Those institutions that do not wish to provide such aid may sign a "conscience waiver" that will then trigger release of funds by a third party enabling those who wish to obtain the services of prostitutes.

All these examples above are of the same form as one finds in the case of the "conscience waiver" whose signature is now forced upon Catholic institutions by the US federal government in the case where persons wish to obtain funds for abortifacient contraceptives, sterilization procedures, and so on. Two questions arise regarding such cases: (1) What is the moral nature of the act of signing such a waiver? (2) What kind of cooperation with evil does it represent?

The courts, of course, focus only on what is *stated* in the waiver. The fact that the entire purpose behind coercing such a signature is to function as a requisition form for obtaining morally illicit things is not yet officially noticed by the courts, which simply cannot imagine that it is not merely the words one writes but the use that one knows these words are directed to that matters. But, *sed contra*: if one knows that holding up a sign that says "Jesus loves you" is the cue for an assassination attempt on an innocent, then following Aquinas and Liguori, one must conclude that, even if one is threatened with death for not holding up the sign, one may not proceed. Even if the one holding up the sign knows that the assassination may not occur (perhaps there are other steps in the "assassination check-list," and holding up the sign is only the first), holding up the sign has the character of an essential contribution for the assassination attempt. That the one threatened to hold up the sign at the given moment does not share the intention of the assassins is not enough; that person may not willingly, directly, and essentially contribute to the action undertaken. It is immoral deliberately, voluntarily, and directly to contribute to the object of the external act of achieving a gravely evil action; and to provide the essential means for the performance of an evil act cannot be done. "Direct" here does not mean merely "part of a proposal for action." To the contrary, it refers to the nature of the action embraced voluntarily, which is more than merely that aspect of the action that makes it appetible to the agent. Someone may kill those ahead of him in the queue for life-saving therapy merely because otherwise he will not live long enough to receive the therapy; but this does not make the wrongful homicide of those ahead of him in line merely to be "removing impediments to life-saving therapy." Rather, the act is "murder."

Accordingly, to sign the perversely and almost diabolically named "conscience waiver" when this is the essential cue and the required means for someone to acquire assistance for an essentially and gravely evil act is—like the secretary's knowingly delivering the evil salacious correspondence of his fornicating master in Liguori's example—formal cooperation in evil. What the "waiver" certificate *says* does not alter the essential purpose for which it is coercively mandated. Like the nature of the act of the person under dire threat giving the cue for an assassination by holding up at the required moment the sign saying "Jesus loves you," the nature of the act of signing the conscience waiver is to trigger action that is gravely morally wrong. How wrong? Those who perform such deeds with full deliberation and consent invite their eternal loss of heaven, and even without full deliberation or consent such deeds are destructive. To co-operate with such deeds by directly, essentially aiding them is gravely evil. This is formal cooperation with evil.

The signing of the waiver certificate is not needed so that persons will know that the Catholic institution does not approve of providing money for vice; the institution could signal this merely by not providing any such monies and stating why. The signing of the waiver certificate is coercively mandated by the state for the purpose of having a signed "ticket" or "coupon" specifically triggering or authorizing the distribution of funds for vice. *While the triggering role of the waiver is already clear, further and distinct indication is provided by the fact that, not only is the institution required to sign the waiver, but it is also required to direct its insurance provider or third-party administrator to provide contact information* (the institution is commanded to inform either its third-party administrator or insurance company of its contractual obligation to provide the monies).

Suppose we take a case in which the non-Catholic world, and even much (not all) of the anti-Catholic world, might agree about the wrongfulness of the act in question. Let us take the case of a local police force unwilling actively to aid in the extermination of Jews. Imagine now that the state provides the same option of signing a conscience waiver against including the contact information of those to be exterminated. The state provides "recourse" to those troubled by their consciences; it indicates that if the local police do not wish to help kill particular persons, or even to provide records identifying them for execution, all they need to do is to sign a conscience waiver, and give it to the record office indicating that it must provide contact information for any such persons to be exterminated, including addresses and known associates. After this, the Gestapo or SS will be happy to take care of such persons. Clearly, if a morally reasonable person were asked whether an institution could sign such a waiver and direct others to provide such contact information, the answer would be a resounding no. The same is true for the case of the HHS mandate: Catholic institutions cannot provide what is essentially a form aiding and directing bad action.

Lest it be thought that the enormity of the example renders it otiose for purposes of comparison, it must be observed that the comparison is quite precise; in each case, there is direct essential aid given to the state in the execution of a *malum*: in one case, simple murder, in the other, provision of monies for vice.

Further, if it is said that what may be done with the conscience waiver is a mere circumstance and that the expression of conscience is a separate matter, *sed contra*. Species are an essential difference *in relation to reason*. What is with respect to one term in the process of reason a mere circumstance may in relation to a further term in the process of reason constitute a principal condition of the object (and so it is not a "mere circumstance" at all). Thus, *Summa theologiae* I–II, q. 18, art. 10, resp. states: "But the process of reason is not determined to one thing, but is able at whatsoever point to proceed further. And thus that which in one act is taken as a circumstance superadded to the object that determines the species of the act, can again be taken by the ordering reason as the principal condition of the object determining the species of the act."[10]

The man returning the borrowed shotgun to his neighbor notes many pure circumstances. However, when his neighbor demands the shotgun abusively, swearing and angrily intimating his proximate intent to shoot his other neighbor, who is likewise in her front yard cursing him, the borrower is no longer merely returning borrowed property, but if he proceeds, he is being an accomplice to wrongful homicide. What is in relation to one consideration of reason a circumstance may be, in relation to another, a principal condition of the object of an act, or arguably even a new object (wrongful homicide has a definition different from returning borrowed property, and is more than merely a manner of returning borrowed property).

To ignore the fact that for the state the conscience waiver is merely a means to communicate monies for vice—using the conscience waiver and a set of contact information connected to it for this purpose—and so to focus only on what the conscience waiver *states*, is very much like the borrower of the shotgun ignoring the fact that the man reclaiming his shotgun intends to kill his neighbor, and focusing instead only on his duty to return borrowed property. In relation to the latter, the clearly expressed homicidal intent is a mere circumstance; yet, it is in itself something that is indeed morally essential to the prospective act, changing its species. In the case of the mandate, the state has no interest in the conscientious judgment of the institution; it wishes to use the waiver as a means to disseminate aid for vice. Since the institution is, from the state's point of view, "queasy" about disseminating the aid itself, it offers the opportunity for the institution to simply sign a waiver, which can be extended to a group of people as giving them the right to obtain aid for vice (that is why

---

[10] *"Sed processus rationis non est determinatus ad aliquid unum, sed quolibet dato, potest ulterius procedere. Et ideo quod in uno actu accipitur ut circumstantia superaddita obiecto quod determinat speciem actus, potest iterum accipi a ratione ordinante ut principalis conditio obiecti determinantis speciem actus."*

contact information is required, and why Catholic universities, for example, are commanded to give a copy of the "waiver" or "certification" to third-party administrators and health insurance companies, indicating that they must supply information enabling distribution of monies for vice). But since the waiver is that which is the essential requisite to the aid for vice being disseminated—and which exists for that purpose—to sign it is not possible. Again, if the state wishes to know what the conscience of the institution mandates, it could purchase a copy of the *Catechism of the Catholic Church* and begin to learn. That is decidedly not its intent, which from the start is to disseminate aid for vice and to command Catholic institutions to join in this evil enterprise.[11]

Using the threefold schema we have suggested above as that of St. Thomas, such cooperation with the HHS mandate clearly does not consti-

---

[11] Of course, in his January 11, 1998, letter to the German bishops, Pope John Paul II communicated his decision regarding a more difficult case than that of the HHS mandate. On the following website, http://www.priestsforlife.org/magisterium/98-01-11germancounseling.html, his decision is described as follows: "In a letter dated January 11, 1998, the Holy Father sent to the German bishops his decision in a matter that he had discussed with them and other Vatican officials for some time. German law requires that a woman seeking abortion present a certificate, obtained from a state-approved social services center, showing she has received counseling. This puts counseling centers in the dilemma that while such women need our assistance and should be counseled, the issuing of the certificate becomes a necessary step in the procuring of an abortion. The Holy Father's direction was therefore sought regarding whether Catholic counseling centers should be allowed to issue such certificates.

The text of the Pope's decision follows. He has asked that Catholic counseling agencies not issue the certificates, but at the same time find ways to continue, and in fact increase, their outreach to women tempted to have abortions."

As for the text, allow me to quote two passages (#7): "After careful consideration of all the arguments, I cannot avoid the conclusion that there is an ambiguity here which obscures the clear and uncompromising witness of the Church and her counseling centres. I would therefore urgently ask you, dear Brothers, to find a way so that a certificate of this kind will no longer be issued at Church counseling centres or those connected with the Church." In fact, he also stated (#7) that the certificate "certifies that counseling has taken place, but it is also a necessary document for an unpunishable abortion during the first 12 weeks of pregnancy." Thus, he noted that the legally required counseling certificate "has in fact acquired a key role in carrying out unpunishable abortions. Catholic counselors and the Church, on whose behalf counselors act in many cases, are thus faced with a situation that conflicts with their basic position on the question of defending life and with the goal of their counseling. Against their intentions they are involved in carrying out

tute the *most* formal cooperation with evil,[12] which would consist in actually sharing the intention of the end (one presumes in charity that a Catholic institution does not share the intention of the end with the malefactor); but it is formal cooperation, because it is direct, essential aid given voluntarily and deliberately to gravely sinful action. For the government to impose this is for it to wage war on Roman Catholic conscience, using coercive means to impose an alien and evil agenda on Roman Catholic institutions. It is morally unconscionable. One can well understand how difficult it is for Roman Catholic bishops to realize that between the historic practice of religious liberty in this country and the abyss of state-mandated persecution, there stands at present only a very fine demilitarized zone of legal argumentation before a court that has manifested very little comprehension of what is at stake. Naturally enough, the desire to persuade oneself that cooperation with the mandate through signing such conscience waivers is not formal but merely material is difficult to avoid. But such cooperation is certainly formal cooperation with evil.

One cannot emphasize enough that the whole force of "direct" and "indirect" is not a mere function of what an agent *proposes*—whether with respect to *operation* or with respect to *co-operation*—but rather *is a function of what the agent chooses to do and does*. If someone *proposes* only to generate heat and light by burning an innocent to death, *this*—presupposing

---

a law that leads to the killing of innocent human beings and offends many people." This was an objectively more difficult case (because counseling truly could move people not to pursue abortion). But the direct and essential role of the certificate could not be ignored. Likewise, the direct and essential role of the putative "conscience" waiver in disseminating funds for vice cannot be ignored. No Catholic institution should consent to or cooperate with such a thing.

12 The objection that there cannot be two formal principles in a moral act is addressed in the introduction to the second edition above, and involves realizing that while the object-species always adds something to the species derived from the end, in the case of *per se* order of object and end that which is added is contained within the species derived from the end as an essential determination of that species. Whereas, in *per accidens* ordering of object to end, the species are formally disjunct. Since it is accidental to health care that one provide those seeking aid for vice with signed forms enabling them to obtain such aid, it cannot be said that signing such a form is in any way ordered to health care. The language of the signed waiver does express a truth—as the one holding up the sign that says "I love Jesus" under coercion as a means to trigger an assassination conveys a truth when that person does love Jesus; but both are wrongful actions.

the knowledge required for voluntariness—does not make the act to be other than *wrongful homicide*, because the object in a morally significant way *includes* (contrary to Professor Lysaught and the intentionalist accounts of moral action upon which she relies), not only the *ratio of appetibility* of the act for the agent, but *the act itself, its integral nature, and its per se effects*. It is not enough to say that the object includes a physical species but that the physical nature exerts no causality that is morally significant. The more material part of the object of the external act clearly can be of moral significance.

For something to be *material* within the object of the external act—which object is *as a whole* formal in the way that essence in material things is formal (that is to say with the formality of essence considered as a whole, which *includes both form and matter*)—is for it to be essential to the object. In choice, our will goes out, not only to the ratio or respect under which we find the chosen action desirable and attractive, but also—*under that ratio* to be sure—*to the action itself*.

To burn an innocent to death for the sake of light and warmth is not justified merely by the fact that one only sought light and warmth, as though the directly effected death of the burned innocent were a "side effect" because, after all, one only *wished* light and warmth. Directly to rip a fetus to pieces for the sake of helping a pregnant woman suffering pulmonary hypertension is not justified merely by the fact that one sought only to help the mother, as though the directly effected death of the fetus were merely a "side effect" because, after all, one only *wished* to help the mother. To sign what is in essence a requisition form *masquerading* as a statement of conscience—a form coercively mandated as the necessary means for attaining government aid in accessing financial aid for immoral "services"—for the sake of being able to function for noble and legitimate ends, is not justified merely by the fact that one seeks to sustain the capacity to serve noble and legitimate ends. The signed requisition form—under the aspect of a "conscience waiver"—that enables persons to gain financial aid for vice is not a mere side effect of institutional integrity.

It is significant that the close examination of what "cooperation" with the HHS mandate concretely specifies confirms this analysis. Professor John Goyette, a Thomistic and Aristotelian scholar, in a document originally shared as a private memorandum among professors, considering what institutional rectitude among Catholic institutions of higher learning requires with respect to the mandate, notes the clear indications in the HHS forms themselves revealing what is at stake in the case of his own institution.[13] Although the legal topography may to some degree alter among institutions—as either self-insured or not—the pertinent element is invariant, namely, that the "certification" commanded by the federal government is essential and necessary to implementing the wrongful distribution of funds for vice. The legal distinction between self-insured and not self-insured notwithstanding, morally there is none that is significant. In each case the institution is commanded to provide certification conveying the command to distribute funds for vice. *In the case of those not self-insured, the insurance company is to be notified by the institution that objects to the so-called "service" that it has a duty pursuant to its contract with the institution to disseminate monies for vice. The institution does not wish to do it, but is commanded to tell others to do it.*

EBSA Form 700 (the "self-certification" form) makes clear even in the case of those institutions that are not self-insured that "the organization or its plan using this form must provide a copy of this certification to the plan's health insurance issuer (for insured health plans) or a third party administrator (for self-insured health plans) in order for the plan to be accommodated with respect to the contraceptive coverage requirement."[14] Professor Goyette observes (again, chiefly regarding his own institution):

> Turning to our present case, we need to be clear about what exactly the self-certification form says, what purpose it serves, and what role we play by signing and submitting it. If one examines the wording on page two of EBSA Form 700, it becomes clear that it is meant to do two things: (1) to give notice to our TPA that we will not act as the plan administrator with

---

[13] Professor Goyette, who teaches at Thomas Aquinas College, shared this memo with me on March 13, 2015, in the context of discussions about the nature of cooperation with the mandate that he pursued simultaneously with several friends, myself among them. It seems likely that in some form his reflections may be published. In their full form they include a consideration of the case of pro-life counseling in Germany where the counselors were required to sign certificates that were legally necessary for women to acquire an abortion. Because of the role of these certificates in the process, Pope John Paul II directed the German Bishops to end official Catholic participation in the signing of such certificates (see note 11 above).

[14] EBSA Form 700 (revised August 2014), 2.

respect to claims for contraceptive services, and (2) it gives notice to the TPS that it is now their responsibility to authorize and administer payments for contraceptive services under IRS regulation 26 CFR 54.9815-2713A. In other words, the form itself makes clear that we are not simply registering our moral objections; we are *notifying* or *instructing* our TPA that it is their responsibility to provide the objectionable coverage. We thereby play a central role in the process by directing someone else to do what we think is intrinsically evil (the TPA might be a willing participant, but that does not excuse our role in the process). If instead of Form EBSA 700, we opt to send a notice to the Secretary of Health and Human Services, we are similarly involved or implicated in the process that arranges for the objectionable coverage since it requires not only that we give notice that we object to providing contraceptive and abortifacient drugs, but it also requires us to provide the name and contact information of the TPS so that the Secretary can designate the TPS as the plan administrator for contraceptive services. So either way, we are participating in the arrangement of financial assistance for intrinsically evil acts.

Further evidence that signing EBSA Form 700—or sending written notice to the Secretary of Health and Human Services—plays an essential role in providing the objectionable services is found in a statement at the bottom of Form 700: "This form or a notice to the Secretary is an instrument under which the plan is operated." There is no ambiguity here. The form, or a notice to the Secretary, is the *means* by which the objectionable coverage is initiated.

One might ask why signing and submitting Form 700 is "the instrument under which the plan is operated"? Why is our signature needed to initiate the objectionable coverage? Because our third party administrator is not a health insurance company, and therefore does not fall directly under the provisions of the Affordable Care Act. Indeed, our third party administrator is contractually obliged to administer only those services that we direct it to administer. Our signature on the bottom of EBSA Form 700, or our written notice to the Secretary, is needed to authorize the TPS to include the objectionable services that fall under the HHS mandate. Without our signature, the TPS cannot provide the objectionable coverage. This is why the self-certification form "is an instrument under which the plan is operated." By signing and submitting Form 700 we are simultaneously registering our moral objections to the contraceptive services, and *authorizing* that very coverage.

A final example: someone opposed to joining a firing squad for a friend is "accommodated" by requiring him instead to shout to the firing line (in the words of a language he does not understand). He is instructed that what the words given to him to shout mean is "I object." But what these words actually mean is "Ready, aim, fire."

The view that cooperation with the HHS mandate is merely material cooperation with evil seems to presuppose an intentionalist analysis of operation. But it is far from obvious that such accounts are easily reconcilable with the Roman Catholic doctrinal tradition. And so, at a moment of great crisis for the Church in North America, the bishops of North America are unfortunately very poorly served by advocates of intentionalism. Such advocates are estimable but erroneous minds for whom the tradition—and the place in it of St. Thomas Aquinas and St. Alphonsus Liguori—is secondary to admittedly "new" logicist or transcendentalist perspectives on the tradition. Of course, by the time that this work is published, this question may be less acute should the Supreme Court in the interim act so as to defend the just claims of Catholic institutions not to be coerced to act contrary to their moral duty. But in any case, it must be hoped that the magnitude of the governmental threat to Roman Catholic integrity in the United States may prove to be a graced occasion for the Church to find its voice in the choir of the tradition—and if need be, in the choir of the martyrs—rather than to lose it in rationalistic quibbles regarding mere material cooperation and double effect.

II. Whether Married Couples Should Abstain from Marital Relations while Using Contraceptives to Regulate the Woman's Cycle

It is commonly understood that a married woman may licitly use a contraceptive pill to regulate her cycle, since such use requires no choice or intention of a venereal act and so cannot be considered essentially contraceptive (thus there is no achieving of the good effect of the regulation of the cycle through a means that is essentially contraceptive, inasmuch as this regulation does not require any conjugal act). However, the questions arise (1) whether it is obligatory for the couple to abstain from conjugal relations during such therapy, to avoid the abortifacient dangers of the high doseage contraceptive pill that is used to regulate the cycle, and (2) whether, if not obligatory, it still may nonetheless be *better* for the couple to abstain in this way.

These questions are more complicated than might at first be apparent. First, and prior to the moral analysis proper, an account that can be followed across all vagaries of scientific judgment on the matter of the causality of the contraceptives with respect to their abortifacient properties is itself a work in process. The biological account of the contraceptive causality vis-à-vis abortion and the frequency of such an effect seems neither to be uncontroverted nor absolutely certain.

But secondly, morally speaking it must be determined whether the circumstance of the evil occurring is such as to be so causally and directly necessitated as *to constitute an added object; or is such as to be a principal condition of the object; or by contrast with both of the preceeding, whether it is such as to be simply a side effect* (to which the consideration of proportionality will thus further need to apply). The complexity of the matter begins to reveal itself. If the abortifacient effect is such as to be directly, essentially causally implicated, this would seem to constitute a new object (and so relations would be ruled out *tout court*); likewise, if the effect is indirect but still knowably highly probable, this too could introduce a new object, or it could constitute the principal condition of the object, and, if so, this would render it wrongful to have relations at such a time. At this point, it is perhaps helpful to observe that the judgment required to address this matter is not simply prudential, because when and insofar as a circumstance introduces a new object or is a principal condition of an object, this clearly *has formal pertinence with respect to the nature of the object itself*. And it must be determined whether any formal issue of this sort obtains. On the other hand, insofar as abortion is merely an improbable side effect of a necessary medical therapy—a point which needs to be determined—and insofar as grave circumstance or the lack thereof could alter the proportionality between the good of therapy and the evil but unlikely effect of abortion, just so far, the consideration requires evaluation of circumstance.

High probability of abortion as an effect of the contraceptive use seems not to obtain (in part because the use of the contraceptive itself renders conception essentially far less likely). Moreover, if the abortive effect is improbable even though there is direct and essential causality—in other words, if abortion is unlikely to occur in the overwhelmingly vast majority of cases precisely because of the contraceptive casuality of the drug, *even though there is something present that would cause abortion, were conception to occur*—then the abortifacient effect would appear to be a side effect. Indeed, inasmuch as the contraceptive character of the drug is itself in this instance a mere side effect of a physical therapy, it might be thought that as a "side effect of a side effect" there could be no real moral question posed by such further causality with respect to abortion. Yet, even if the abortifacient effect is such a side effect, it *could* still be wrong to pursue relations because of disproportion between the good sought through therapy and the (howsoever slight) risk of gravest harm to any conceived person.

To repeat, insofar as circumstance might as principal condition of the object go to the formal aspect of the act, in such a case one might deem it wrong not to abstain. However, the analysis does not seem to support the abortifacient effect as being in this instance the principal condition of the object, inasmuch as, even if it is a secondary effect of the contraceptive, it is a less likely effect, and indeed in this case a "side effect of a side effect." There must yet be proportionality between the evil risked and the good sought. But though the harm risked to the fetus is great, the probability of that harm is small. Because arguably there may be, in varying circumstances, different degrees of proportionate reason for running such risk, it must be considered that many instances of such risk would seem likely to be reasonable.

In short, if we judge the abortifacient effect a side effect, and one that is unlikely, then the judgment of proportionality between the gravity of the possible evil and the good of the therapy remains. Since it must be born in mind that both addressing the medical need of the woman and marital relations are important goods, the test of proportionality between actual serious harm to the married couple and possible harm to a possible fetal person (should one be conceived) is not *necessarily* failed. For instance, a patient whose ordinary life has been humiliatingly destabilized, and who suffers from depression, is not seeking to serve a trivial but a central good.

Thus, if the judgment is correct that the abortifacient effect is a side effect of the medical therapy, and insofar as it is true that the medicine used to regulate the cycle would only very infrequently lead to abortion in the case of marital relations between fertile spouses, it is not certain that the proportionality test indicates the simple impermissibility of marital relations. *This, however, does not alter the fact that there would appear to be very good reason for spouses not to wish to take any such risk without grave reason. If* a life were howsoever improbably to be conceived, *then* it would likely be at risk for the gravest of harm by virtue of the (howsoever calibrated or howsoever infrequent) abortifacient effect of the therapy, causing the fertilized ovum not to implant in the uterus.

And so we return to the simplicity of the original question: Ought spouses to abstain while using this therapy? Nature itself poses threat of miscarriage. Medical therapy is an augmentation of nature, for purposes of healing, and side effects occur here, too. The ordinary good of marital relations, as well as the medical need for therapy, is to be considered. *However, there does seem to be reason for a couple to abstain during such a therapy to avoid possible harm to any newly conceived life, while nonetheless it is unclear that this "preferability" of abstinence could correctly be said to be morally obligatory in each and every case.* If proportionality obtains between good sought and evil risked, then conjugal relations would be permitted. Yet, one might observe that it seems a small sacrifice, always or for the most part, for a married couple to abstain for a time, in order to avoid possible grave harm to any newly conceived life. *This is not a deontological formula. But it forwards the claim that always or for the most part it may be better for the couple to abstain during such therapy, for this reason: it is for the most part better to attain an important objective without risking innocent life rather than by risking it, if this is feasible.*

This is not a deontological mandate, because—pertinent to the consideration of proportionality—there may be particularly pressing issues. For example, take a married woman suffering extreme depression after ten years of constant embarrassment and humiliation, rendering ordinary life, social involvement, the capacity to work, and familial life difficult, all owing to a cycle that is disastrously unpredictable. Perhaps the wife in question suffers other complicating medical difficulties not hard to imagine, possibly serious ones; and perhaps because of all of this, she and her husband are frayed to the point of exhaustion and at times at odds, consoled largely through the encouragement of the marital embrace. Further, add the manifest consideration that the odds are overwhelmingly against any new life being conceived under such a regimen of therapy, and that the causality with respect to abortifacience is controverted. Is it manifest in this case that the test of proportionality is failed? Is it clear that this couple would be committing a *malum in se* in coming together? That would be a difficult judgment to make.

However, because of the piety due the marital act, and the disproportionate harm should conception occur and the abortifacient causality be triggered, couples not in so extreme a position (most couples, perhaps) would do *better*, one might think, to abstain.

This response to the question is such as to *refrain* from analyzing the matter in purely deontological mode or with a digital or logical knife yielding only pure alternatives and thus excluding the manifest obscurities of matter, of the particular, of moral difficulty, and of pathos. Given the degree of likelihood of the evil effect in question and the causality of the chosen action, contemporary moralists are liable to be correct that in the preponderant number of cases conjugal union during the therapy would not be a mortal sin. *Yet, it is hard not to think that temporary abstinence is a more virtuous posture in most cases even though it may not be absolutely required by moral law. To repeat the reason for this judgment: all things being equal, achieving an important good without even minor risk of grave harm to innocent life is always or for the most part better than achieving it with a merely minor risk of grave harm to life.*

If this is so, then why would it not be obligatory for each and all? It is not simply and universally obligatory, because all minor risk of grave harm to innocent life is not in every case avoidable *pari passu* with due regard for more directly implicated proximate goods. Take the example of someone rushing a gunshot victim, who will be dead in minutes unless one arrives swiftly, to a hospital, and therefore darting in and through traffic more than would normally be the case (not in an utterly erratic way likely to end in accident, but rather in a systematically more aggressive mode of driving that is still marginally more risky), knowing that this involves minor but real increased risk of grave injury to oneself and others.

Or, in the case at hand, take the example offered above: namely, that of the woman driven downward toward near-suicidal depression, suffering medical complications (stress, high blood pressure, hypertension with increased risk of stroke, panic attacks, and consequent further hormonal imbalances), and banished from professional and ordinary social life, by the irregularity of a cycle that randomly humiliates and destroys, therefore living in a frayed marital relation held together significantly by the consolation of conjugal relations.

A realist must find such a case more knotty than either a deontologist or a logicist or transcendentalist—more difficult than do most of our contemporaries—because prudence must enter in constitutively in such a matter, which is not simply determined at the level of universal analysis. Thus, one might counsel that for most it will be better to achieve the medical effect sought without imposing the least risk of grave harm to any conceived innocent life. But this would not cause the harder cases— adding weight in the analysis of proportionality—to be transgressions of moral law. Nor is it the point of the extremity of the example to suggest that only such an example could suffice; rather, the extremity of the example is to show that the dignity of proximate goods may legitimately warrant risk of improbable side effects. This is not proportionalism but simple prudence. For the proportionalist, there is no universal norm and no constant virtue. But both apply here—if they did not, outright contraception, and outright abortion, would be permissible. If this treatment has not erred in its understanding of the nature of the contraceptives in question, what is in question is the consideration of possible but unlikely grave side effects. The contraceptive side effect in itself is a pure accident of medical therapy; the possible but unlikely abortifacient effect is a side effect of a side effect, but it still must not be disproportionate to the medical good sought. Given the unlikelihood of abortion—if this medical judgment is correct—it would seem that there could be good proximate reason for not abandoning marital relations during the therapy.

However, the conclusion remains that, for the most part, moving toward the end without risk of harm to an innocent is the better course. Thus—*insofar* as more proximate and less unlikely goods are not unduly harmed by such abstinence (because no person is likely to be conceived, the very existence of such a being is unlikely)—abstinence seems the better course of action. Where there is undue harm to more proximate goods that certainly exist, it would not be the part of moral realism to be blind to this. And *undue harm* pertains not merely to medical matters but to the marital good as such, which is proximate and real.

One helpful development, were it possible, would be for drugs to be developed that do not prevent implantation of the fertilized ovum but that still have the regulatory effect on the female cycle. Inasmuch as contraceptive drugs have, in fact, been designed and manufactured largely for the precise (wrongful) purpose of effecting redundant "safeguards" against the good of conception, are such effects not possibly pharmacologically separable? A pill that lacks such redundant "safeguards" but that regulates the cycle would remove the howsoever unlikely but real grave threat to any conceived fetal person. Such a drug would simply *remove* the side effect of possible grave harm (death) in the unlikely but possible event that the contraceptive did not prevent conception of new human life.

Of course, it would be good to find medicine to regularize the female cycle that does not have a contraceptive side effect either, precisely because this side effect, too, is unfortunate. After all, chemotherapy and radiation therapy for cancer may have similar effects, but no one would confuse these with chosen modes of contraception. The same is true with respect to the side effect of contraception in the use of the high doseage pill. But it would be better were an effective therapy devisable that proceeded without harmful contraceptive effect.

Thus, the conclusion that seems reasonable is that, for as long as there is faint but real possibility of grave harm to a conceived person, it is better for the most part for the couple to abstain from relations. But because this prospect of faint but real harm is being taken as a side effect and also as unlikely, and because there are other important goods at stake, it does not seem that in every case the test of proportionality is necessarily failed. Possible grave harm to a fetal person who may but is unlikely to be conceived should (all things being equal) be avoided—but all things may not be equal. So, while it is better for the most part *to avoid* achieving something *in a manner that runs even slight risk of terrible harm to a person* (since there is risk of grave harm *only* if conception occurs and the improbability of that conception is precisely why the risk is *slight*), nonetheless, a couple may have proportionate reason to suffer such risks.

A last word might be said. If the physical science pertinent to this question comes into greater focus, aspects of the present analysis may cease to pertain. There may, in fact, be scientific judgments available even now of which I am not aware, although papers asserting and denying the abortifacient effect and differing regarding the causality of contraceptives are not unfamiliar to me. Further, the point here is not scrupulosity, but simply what one's habitual judgment might best be with respect to achieving an important good in relation to the slight risk of very grave harm to a possibly conceived innocent, even though this be a side effect, and even an extremely unlikely one.

It would, after all, be very odd if the principle of double effect in all its Cajetanian splendor—in my view ill founded on an erroneous reading of *Summa theologiae* II–II, q. 64, art. 7, but still helpful with respect to a certain array of moral analyses[15]—should have the unintended effect of causing us to abandon obvious truths, such as that it is, on the whole, all things being equal, better to achieve a good *without* slight risk of grave harm to an innocent, than *with* slight risk of grave harm to an innocent. And this principle, of course, implies its complement: that where all things are not equal, it may be reasonable to undertake such a risk when the risk applies to what is only a remote, merely possible, or extremely improbable side effect.

---

[15] The Cajetanian principle of double effect is "helpful" provided that we already understand what is necessary to place acts in their species.

Afterword

THE THOUGHT required to cope with the most difficult cases is indeed striking. But it is perhaps especially at this point that one might recommend a return to the concluding chapter in the body of the text above. For it is these principles which we must keep in mind in coping with the objective demands not alone of the cases of extraordinary difficulty, but also and primarily with respect to ordinary understanding of the object and species of the moral act.

Index